EUROPEAN HISTORICAL DICTIONARIES
Edited by Jon Woronoff

1. *Portugal,* by Douglas L. Wheeler. 1993
2. *Turkey,* by Metin Heper. 1994
3. *Poland,* by George Sanford and Adriana Gozdecka-Sanford. 1994
4. *Germany,* by Wayne C. Thompson, Susan L. Thompson, and Juliet S. Thompson. 1994
5. *Greece,* by Thanos M. Veremis and Mark Dragoumis. 1995
6. *Cyprus,* by Stavros Panteli. 1995
7. *Sweden,* by Irene Scobbie. 1995

HISTORICAL DICTIONARY OF GREECE

by
THANOS M. VEREMIS
and
MARK DRAGOUMIS

European Historical Dictionaries, No. 5

The Scarecrow Press, Inc.
Metuchen, N.J., & London
1995

British Library Cataloguing-in-Publication data available

Library of Congress Cataloging-in-Publication Data

Veremēs, Thanos.
    Historical dictionary of Greece / by Thanos M. Veremis and Mark
Dragoumis.
        p. cm.— (European historical dictionaries ; no. 5)
    Includes bibliographical references.
    ISBN 0-8108-2888-X (acid-free paper)
    1. Greece—History—1821– —Dictionaries. I. Dragoumēs,
Markos, 1926– . II. Title. III. Series.
DF802.V47   1995
949.5—dc20   94-14447

CONTENTS

EDITOR'S FOREWORD, by Jon Woronoff   iv

ABBREVIATIONS AND ACRONYMS   v

CHRONOLOGY   ix

INTRODUCTION: HISTORICAL CONTINUITIES   1

THE DICTIONARY   19

INTRODUCTION TO THE BIBLIOGRAPHY   183

CONTENTS OF BIBLIOGRAPHY   185

Appendix A: Kings of Greece   244

Appendix B: Presidents of Greece   245

Appendix C: Prime Ministers of Greece   246

Appendix D: Basic Data on Greece   252

ABOUT THE AUTHORS   257

EDITOR'S FOREWORD

Greece, the source of much of European civilization, was long cut off from the mainstream, not only by foreign domination before independence but by its own problems and concerns thereafter. Over recent decades, however, it has moved ever closer to the center and is trying to make up for lost time. Today's Greece is a significant member of NATO and the European Community, an increasingly active participant in regional affairs and an attractive destination not only for tourists but businesspeople as well. Thus, what happens in Greece is of interest not only to the Greeks.

Yet, what is happening in Greece, and what has happened there during the period since independence, is still far from well known in the rest of Europe, let alone the rest of the world. This book is an important contribution to general knowledge since it covers the nineteenth and twentieth centuries more closely, while taking an occasional look backward to earlier periods, and informs the reader about crucial persons, places, institutions and events. In addition to history, politics and economics, it deals with language, religion, culture and ecology. It also contains a comprehensive bibliography and several useful appendices, including lists of kings, presidents, prime ministers, and basic data.

The two authors of the *Historical Dictionary of Greece* are both extremely well versed in the subjects under discussion. And both are Greeks who have considerable experience in explaining Greece to outsiders. Thanos M. Veremis is the Director of the Hellenic Foundation for European and Foreign Policy, a professor of political science at Athens University and co-editor of the multi-volume *History of the Hellenic World*. Mark Dragoumis is a writer and government official. He published a book on liberalism and wrote numerous articles on politics and economics before and while working for the Press and Information Service, where he was in charge of press offices around the world.

Jon Woronoff
Series Editor

ABBREVIATIONS AND ACRONYMS

ASEAN	Association of Southeast Asia Nations
BIS	Bank for International Settlements
CERN	European Organization for Nuclear Research
CFE	Coventional Armed Forces Europe
CIS	Commonwealth of Independent States
COCOM	Coordinating Committee
CSBM	Confidence and Security Building Measures
CSCE	Conference on Security and Cooperation in Europe
DECA	Defense and Economic Cooperation Agreement
DEI	Dimosia Epichirisi Ilectrismou (Public Power Corporation)
DIANA	Dimokratiki Ananeossi (Party of Democratic Renewal)
EAM	Ethniko Apelephterotiko Metopo (National Liberation Front)
EBRD	European Bank for Reconstruction and Development

EC	European Community
ECE	Economic Commission for Europe
EDA	Eniaia Dimocratiki Aristera (United Democratic Left) (see Communist Party of Greece)
EDIK	Enosi Dimokratikou Kentrou (Union of Democratic Center)
EFTA	European Free Trade Association
EIB	European Investment Bank
EK	Enosi Kentrou (Center Union Party)
ELAS	Ethnikos Laikos Apelephterotikos Stratos (People's National Liberation Army)
ELIAMEP	Elliniko Idryma Evropaikis kai Exoterikis Politikis, i.e. Hellenic Foundation for European and Foreign Policy
EPC	European Political Cooperation
ERE	Elliniki Rizospastiki Enosi (National Radical Union)
FAO	Food and Agriculture Organization
FYROM	Former Yugoslav Republic of Macedonia
GATT	General Agreement on Tariffs and Trade
GDP	Gross Domestic Product
IAEA	International Atomic Energy Agency
IBRD	International Bank for Reconstruction and Development
ICAO	International Civil Aviation Organization

IDA	International Development Agency
IEA	International Energy Agency
IFAD	International Fund for Agricultural Development
IFC	International Finance Corporation
ILO	International Labour Office
IMF	International Monetary Fund
IMO	International Maritime Organization
INTELSAT	International Telecommunications Satellite Organization
INTERPOL	International Police
IOC	International Olympic Committee
ITU	International Telecommunications Union
KKE	Kommunistiko Komma Elladas, i.e. Communist Party of Greece
KODESO	Komma Demokratikou Sosialismou (Party of Democratic Socialism)
MAD	Mutually Assured Destruction
NACC	North Atlantic Cooperation Council
NATO	North Atlantic Treaty Organization
N.D.	New Democracy (Party)
NEA	Nuclear Energy Agency
NGO	Non-Governmental Organization

OAS	Organization of American States
OECD	Organization for Economic Cooperation and Development
OTE	Organismos Tilepikinonion Ellados, i.e. Greek Corporation of Telecommunications
PAK	Panellinio Antistasiako Kinima (Panhellenic Resistance Movement)
PASOK	Panellinio Sosialistiko Kinima (Panhellenic Socialist Movement)
UN	United Nations
UNCTAD	United Nations Conference on Trade and Development
UNESCO	United Nations Educational, Scientific and Cultural Organization
UNHCR	UN High Commissioner for Refugees
UNIDO	UN Industrial Development Organization
UNRRA	United Nations Relief and Rehabilitation Administration
UPU	Universal Postal Union
WEU	Western European Union
WHO	World Health Organization
WIPO	World Intellectual Property Organization
WMO	World Meteorological Organization
WTO	World Tourism Organization

CHRONOLOGY

1821	Outbreak of the Greek War of Independence against Ottoman rule. Execution of Ecumenical Patriach Grigorios V by the Ottomans.
1822	The first constitution of independent Greece.
1827	Destruction of the joint Ottoman–Egyptian fleet at Navarino Bay.
1828	Count Ioannis Capodistrias comes to Greece as its first President.
1830	Under the London Protocol of 3 February 1830, France, Britain, and Russia recognize the independence of Greece.
1831	Assassination of Capodistrias by members of a powerful clan of Mani.
1833	Arrival of Otto Wittelsbach of Bavaria as the first King of Greece. The Church of the Greek state declared "autocephalous" (independent from the authority of the Constantinople Patriarchate).
1843	Troops of the Athens garrison and crowds demonstrating in front of the royal palace force King Otto to grant a constitution.
1844	New constitution defines regime as Constitutional Monarchy.

1854   Occupation of Piraeus by French and British troops to impose neutrality on Greece during the Crimean war.

1862   King Otto forced to leave the throne after uprisings against his rule occurred in Nafplion and Athens.

1863   Prince George Glucksburg of Denmark becomes ''King of the Hellenes.''

1864   The Ionian islands become part of Greece. The new constitution defines the Greek regime as a Crowned Democracy.

1866–69   Uprising of Crete against Ottoman rule fails to free the island.

1871   The government of Alexandros Koumoundouros grants legal title deeds to unlegitimized peasant landholders.

1875   King George accepts the principle that the leader of any party enjoying the support of the majority in parliament would be called upon to form a government.

1881   The Province of Thessaly and the Arta region are incorporated in the Greek state.

1883–93   The heyday of the two-party system. Harilaos Trikoupis and Theodoros Diliyannis alternate in power. Trikoupis puts reforms into effect.

1895   Trikoupis defeated in elections. Dies the following year.

1896   Cretan rebellion from Ottoman rule leads to Greek involvement.

1897   Greek forces defeated by the Ottoman army in the Thessaly campaign.

1898   Prince George (second son of King George) appointed governor of Crete after the island was granted autonomy.

1903   Founding of the Macedonian Committee by Greek officers to counter Bulgarian claims in Macedonia.

1908   Formation of the Sociological Society supporting the collective organization of workers.

1909   A display of force by the Military League in Athens in August obliges the government to draft reforms in parliament. The Cretan politician Eleftherios Venizelos is invited by the officers of the League to come to Athens as their adviser.

1910   Eleftherios Venizelos wins overwhelming electoral mandate and launches his reforms.

1912   The Liberal Party under Venizelos wins elections. Greece enters the victorious alliance of the first Balkan war on the side of Bulgaria, Serbia and Montenegro against the Ottoman empire.

1913   The Second Balkan war is fought between former allies—Bulgaria against Greece and Serbia. King George is assassinated in Thessaloniki. Treaty of London (30 May) and Peace of Bucharest (10 August) grant Greece significant territorial gains. (Crete, Macedonia, Jannina and islands of the Aegean).

1915   Clash between Venizelos and King Constantine over Greek foreign policy during the First World War. Venizelos proposes Greek alliance with the Triple Entente, while the King prefers neutrality. Venizelos resigns twice.

1916   Greece divided between the revolutionary government of Thessaloniki under Venizelos, General

Danglis and Admiral Koundouriotes and the official Athenian government supported by the King.

1917   Constantine is obliged to abdicate. His second son Alexander becomes King and Venizelos reestablishes his government in Athens.

1918   Ten Greek divisions fight on the Macedonian front in the autumn campaign which broke German and Bulgarian defenses.

1919   Greece among the victors of the First World War enlarges its territory in the Paris Peace Conference.

1920   According to the Treaty of Sevres (10 August), Greece acquires Western and Eastern Thrace, the Aegean islands and is given mandate to the larger Smyrna area.

    King Alexander dies from monkey bite. Venizelos is defeated in elections. The royalists return to power and restore Constantine to the throne.

1922   Greek forces defeated in Asia Minor and Greek population flees to Greece. Constantine abdicates in favor of his eldest son George and leaves the country.

1923   The Treaty of Lausanne determines the boundaries between Greece and Turkey and imposes an exchange of populations. Close to one-and-a-half million destitute refugees arrive in a country of barely five million inhabitants.

1924   Greece becomes a republic following plebiscite.

1924–26   Period of military interventions in politics.

1926–28   Government consisting of all major parties.

1928–32   Venizelos's final term in power.

1933   Tsaldaris wins elections and Liberals fear restoration of monarchy.

1935   Anti-royalist preemptive coup fails and speeds up the process of King George's restoration.

1936   Death of Venizelos, Tsaldaris, Kondylis and Papanastasiou. The King agrees to a violation of the constitution that permits caretaker Prime Minister Ioannis Metaxas to assume dictatorial powers.

1940   Greece resists Fascist attack from Albania and wins first Allied victories of the War.

1941   German armored divisions overcome Greek defenses and establish occupation of the country. Greek and British forces face airborne German onslaught in Crete. Greek government in exile established in London and Greek forces regroup in Egypt.

1941–44   Greece occupied by German, Italian and Bulgarian forces. Thrace and eastern Macedonia annexed by Bulgaria. Greek resistance impedes transportation of German material to the Middle East. Internal strife between left- and right-wing resistance groups.

1944   Liberation of Athens. First clashes of the Civil War.

1946–49   Civil War between Communist-controlled Democratic Army in northern Greece and government forces representing a coalition of Liberals and Royalists.

1947   In accordance with the Treaty of Paris (10 February 1947) Greece acquires the Dodecanese islands. Truman Doctrine results in massive aid to Greece.

1952   Greece becomes a member of NATO. Elections won by Greek Rally led by the commander of the victorious government forces in the war, Marshal Alexandros Papagos. Reconstruction of a war-ravaged Greece is put into effort.

1955   In September a mob in Istanbul demanding the annexation of Cyprus by Turkey wreaks havoc in the sections of the city inhabited by Greeks.

1956   Elections won by the renamed Greek Rally–the National Radical Union (ERE)–under Constantine Karamanlis.

1957   Archbishop Makarios of Cyprus deported to the Seychelles by the British authorities of the island. Cypriot struggle for union with Greece reaches its climax.

1958   In May elections, ERE under Karamanlis maintains its majority with 40 percent of the popular vote.

1959   Greek application to the European Community for associate membership. Greek and Turkish Cypriot leaders sign London agreement on independence of Cyprus.

1960   Cyprus becomes an independent republic with Archbishop Makarios as President and Dr. Fazil Kutchuk as Vice-President.

1961   ERE wins 51 percent of popular vote and faces accusations of electoral fraud.

1963   Karamanlis loses elections to Georgios Papandreou leading the Center Union. Outbreak of violence in Cyprus between Greek and Turkish Cypriot communities.

1964   The Center Union improves its position in February elections. Wins 52.7 percent of the vote.

1965   Clash between King Constantine II and Prime Minister George Papandreou, who hands in his resignation.

1966   December agreement between leaders of the major parties to desist from attacks on the monarchy.

1967   A group of Colonels launch a coup d'etat in April and establish a military dictatorship. The King flees the country after a belated abortive effort in December to oust the military regime.

1968   Close to a thousand civil servants dismissed by the junta.

1973   Abortive coup in the navy against the regime. Attempt against Makarios's life by Greek junta forces in Cyprus.

1974   Turkish invasion of the island. Collapse of military regime and restoration of democracy in Greece. Karamanlis returns from Paris to assume leadership of civilian government and wins overwhelming mandate in November elections. Greece becomes a republic following the December referendum.

1975   New constitution replaces that of 1952, briefly restored after the juntas' 1973 constitution was abrogated. Proclamation of a Turkish Federated State of Cyprus recognized only by Turkey. Influx in immigrants from mainland Turkey to northern Cyprus.

1976   New crisis in Greek–Turkish relations when Turkish survey ship begins to carry out exploration for oil in waters between the islands of Mytilini and Lemnos, claimed by Greece as part of her continental shelf.

1977   Karamanlis's New Democracy wins comfortable majority in November elections.

1979   Karamanlis signs treaty of accession to the European Community with the nine EC members (28 May).

1980   Karamanlis becomes President of the Republic and George Rallis Prime Minister. Karamanlis visits Moscow.

1981   Greece enters the EC. The Panhellenic Socialist Movement (PASOK) under Andreas Papandreou wins October elections.

1982   Papandreou visits Cyprus–the first visit of a Greek Prime Minister to the island.

1983   Turkish Cypriot assembly unilaterally declares an independent Turkish Republic of Northern Cyprus recognized only by Turkey.

            Defense and Economic Cooperation Agreement (DECA) signed which replaces the 1953 US-Greek Defense Agreement and other bilateral security arrangements.

1984   Constantinos Mitsotakis becomes leader of the New Democracy party.

            Greece declares the presence of its forces on the island of Lemnos in the Defense Planning Questionnare (DPQ) and asks that they be placed under NATO command but fails to override Turkey's veto.

1985   Resignation of Karamanlis and election of Christos Sartzetakis as President. PASOK wins 45.82 percent of the popular vote in June elections.

            Greece and Albania formally put an end to the state of war which had technically existed since 1940.

1987   Crisis between Greece and Turkey due to Turkish intention to explore for oil in disputed Aegean waters.

1988   Prime Ministers Papandreou and Turgut Ozal meet in Davos, Switzerland, to defuse problems between their two countries.

1989   A deadlocked June election leads to government under New Democracy deputy Tzannis Tzannetakis of "limited duration" with the support of Communist Party. New elections in November 1989 also inconclusive. Formation of all-party government under Xenophon Zolotas.

1990   New Democracy under Mitsotakis wins elections—Karamanlis becomes President of the Republic once more.

1991   On October 16–17, the European Political Cooperation meeting of the 12 EC Foreign Ministers decides that before granting recognition to FYROM it should "adopt constitutional and political guarantees ensuring that it has no territorial claims towards a neighboring Community state."

        Greek and Turkish Prime Ministers meet in Davos.

1992   Government imposes austerity program. Balkan imbroglio preoccupies Greek foreign policy. Influx of economic refugees from former Soviet Union, Albania and Bulgaria.

1993   Former Foreign Minister Andonis Samaras leaves New Democracy and in September instigates the defection of two deputies which causes the government's fall.

        In the elections of 10 October PASOK wins 47 percent of the vote with New Democracy party in second place with 39.5 percent.

INTRODUCTION:
HISTORICAL CONTINUITIES

Greece, like all emerging Balkan states in the nineteenth century, rose out of a disintegrating Ottoman empire. Unification of its territories did not grow out of a swift series of victories, as was the case with Germany, but from a long, spasmodic process of irredentist rebellions from within the Ottoman realm. The irredentist aims of Greece, Bulgaria, and Serbia often clashed, and after their successful joint assault on the Ottomans in 1912, these countries became entangled in internecine warfare among themselves.

The wars in the Balkans and World War I, which ran from 1912 to 1922, found Greece, Bulgaria and Turkey rotating in different alliances—two of them always pitted against the third. During the First World War, Greece fought on the side of the British, the French and the Americans. The Treaty of Lausanne, signed in 1923 after the expulsion of the Greek forces in Asia Minor, concluded the era of irredentism and heralded a period during which Greece sought to maintain the status quo in its relations with its neighbors. In 1930, the Greek statesman Eleftherios Venizelos (q.v.) and Kemal Ataturk (founder of modern Turkey) signed an accord settling all outstanding matters between their two countries, thus establishing a relationship which outlasted any other treaty concluded in the Balkan region.

Bulgaria, discontented with its failure to achieve its irredentist goals and isolated in the interwar period from Balkan bilateral and multilateral treaties, became a source of irritation for Greece. Whereas Turkey had ceased since 1930 to pose a security problem, a series of hostile incidents with a disgruntled Bulgaria led Greece to fortify its northern borders in the late 1930s. At the heart of Greek-Bulgarian differences was the ethnic makeup of the part of Macedonia annexed by Greece in 1913. Although the issue

1

GREECE
International boundary
National capital
Railroad
Road
International airport

of sizable minorities in this area was largely resolved with the population exchanges following World War I and the settlement of about 700,000 Greek refugees from Turkey, Bulgaria continued to press claims concerning the slavophones of Greece. Furthermore, the Comintern, in its Sixth Balkan Communist Conference in 1924, endorsed the Bulgarian Communist Party's plea for a united and independent Macedonia and Thrace. This policy, which would have amounted to ceding Greek Macedonia to an independent state under Bulgarian tutelage, was naturally abhorrent even to left-wing Greeks. The Greek Communist Party, badly split over the issue, was forced by its unswerving loyalty to the Comintern to underwrite the decision and suffer constant embarrassment until 1935, when the slogan was repudiated. The right-wing regime of Bulgaria and its outlawed Communist Party were both, although from different angles, laying claims on a territory that had been incorporated into Greece.

Greece's attachment to Great Britain, a leading power in the eastern Mediterranean since the mid-nineteenth century, reflected a need to align with an important naval force in the region. Similarly, Greek entry into both world wars on the side of the major sea powers was largely determined by geopolitical vulnerabilities. Yet, on both these occasions the price of wartime commitment was extremely high. During World War I, the decision to enter on the side of the Triple Entente was carried out after an internal schism had damaged national unity. Although Greece's response to the unprovoked fascist attack of World War II was a striking military victory against the invading forces of Mussolini from Albania in the winter of 1940, the subsequent hardships of German occupation culminated in a civil war of unprecedented violence. Communist and other members of the left-wing resistance clashed with nationalists, right-wingers and, between 1946–49, with the regular forces of the official Greek government. No doubt this second and bloodier national schism also reflected the contours of global politics. By the end of this process the Americans had replaced the British as the major foreign influence in Greece, and the country became the first battleground for the Cold War.

The nature of the divisions which culminated in civil conflict is difficult to describe but it is possible to point to some of its causes: the role of the prewar dictatorship (under the throne's tutelage) in diminishing the prestige of parlimentary politics; the emergence of the Communist Party during the occupation as a major force of the resistance; the relative ineffectiveness and apathy of most prominent politicians during the same period; and, finally, the complete destruction of the economy by the occupation forces and extreme privations suffered by large sectors of the population which served to radicalize the masses. If resistance fighters seeking to establish social justice constituted the rank and file of the leftist camp, narrow-minded devotees of Stalinist orthodoxy were its leaders. The nationalist camp included smaller resistance groups, a number of credible liberal politicians of the prewar period and a multitude of conservatives who rallied around the King. It was the Soviet threat, however, which inadvertently nurtured cohesion and resolution in the nationalist camp. Stalin, who had honored his agreement with Churchill to allow Britain a free hand in Greece in 1944, demanded a withdrawal of foreign troops in 1947 and insisted on the demilitarization of the Dodecanese islands ceded to Greece by Italy that year. Finally, the existence of a communist Yugoslavia and Bulgaria with claims on Greek territory, provided the nationalists with their overriding cause.

The urgency of Civil War-related problems and the inability of a divided and paralyzed government to handle the domestic situation effectively led Greek politicians to allow the United States a presence in Greek internal affairs. The Truman Doctrine, officially announced on 12 March 1947, inaugurated an era of U.S. involvement in Europe and an overt American role in Greek affairs. The Marshall Plan was proclaimed in June 1947. Greece's total share of the Plan was $1.7 billion in economic aid (loans and grants) and $1.3 billion in military aid between 1947 and the 1960s.

The fratricidal struggle that raged for four years aggravated the conditions in the already ravaged country. To the 550,000 (8 percent of Greece's population) who died during 1940–44 were added another 158,000 dead between 1946–49. Caught in the middle of a war between the government army and the communist-leftist forces, Greek peasants and townspeople paid the highest price of this civil strife.

Greece's accession to NATO was initially obstructed by Britain's own concept of Western defense and the opposition of certain Scandinavian countries to an overextension and therefore dilution of NATO's primary aims. When Greece and Turkey dispatched combat forces to South Korea in 1950, they were acting as members of the United Nations but their motive was in fact to override objections to their entry into NATO. As far as the United States was concerned, Greek and Turkish participation was planned to provide the missing link between its allies in NATO, the Central Treaty Organization (CENTO), the Southeast Asian Treaty Organization (SEATO), and the security treaty of Australia, New Zealand and the United States (ANZUS). For Greek politicians of the liberal coalition government which pressed for Greek membership, NATO not only provided an additional guarantee against Balkan communism, it also constituted a door to a community of democratic European states and a partial emancipation from exclusive American influence. In September 1951, NATO foreign ministers in Ottawa approved Greek and Turkish entry. Two years later, American military presence in Greece was consolidated by the signing of a bilateral base agreement which provided the United States with the right to establish and supply its bases and to use Greek airspace. It also set out the legal status of U.S. forces in Greece.

Relations between Greece and the communist Balkan states remained troubled throughout the 1950s and 1960s. During the German occupation, Bulgaria incorporated the eastern part of Macedonia and most of western Thrace and subjected its Greek inhabitants to a regime of terror. Bulgaria's subsequent supervised transformation into a communist state initially implied that its position in the community of Socialist Republics could not match that of a self-liberated Yugoslavia with its partisan resistance record. The Yugoslav policy of an autonomous Macedonia which would include Skopje as well as the Greek and Bulgarian Macedonias, provoked a strong general reaction but initially failed to stir the Bulgarians. Since Yugoslavia had more influence with the Soviets, the Bulgarians had to wait until Tito's break with Stalin before they could exercise their own foreign policy over Macedonia. After Tito broke with the Cominform in 1948, the Bulgarians repudiated the existence of a separate Macedonian nation proclaiming instead their own historical mission in the area.

The fluctuations in Yugoslav-Soviet-Bulgarian relations usually had an impact on Greece. The clash between Tito and Stalin terminated Yugoslav support for the Greek communist forces and contributed to their defeat. In 1953 Greece, Turkey and Yugoslavia signed a treaty of friendship and cooperation followed by a formal alliance. The pact might have served as an indirect link between Yugoslavia and NATO had it not been for the former's rapprochement with Moscow in 1955 which effectively ended the treaty. Since the end of World War II, Greece has sought to secure the status quo in Macedonia making it clear that Greece has no claims against its neighbors and will tolerate none in return.

From its emergence in the 1950s, the Cyprus issue has become the main problem in Greece's relations with Turkey. Occupied by Britain in 1878 and a British colony after 1925, Cyprus was no exception to the rule of anti-colonial struggles that rocked the

British empire after the war. Greek Cypriots, who represented 80 percent of the island's population, repeatedly appealed to Greek governments for support and hoped for unification (*enosis*) with Greece. Although Greek liberal politicians discouraged such pleas it was the conservative government of Alexandros Papagos that, in 1954, embraced the cause of the Greek Cypriots. When Archbishop Makarios, political and spiritual leader of the Greek Cypriot community, introduced the issue to the forum of the United Nations, Britain responded by bringing the previously neutral Turkish Cypriots and Turkey into the conflict. The foundations of future intercommunal conflict were thus laid and what began as a struggle for independence gradually deteriorated into a confrontation between Greeks and Turks.

External factors have had an important role in shaping Greek security perceptions. The processes of Greek nationalism and irredentism have been heavily affected by Western influence in the region. The unification of Greek-inhabited territories under Ottoman rule created an ideological link between the citizens of a dependent and impoverished kingdom involved in the difficult task of state building. Dependence on Britain largely determined Greece's foreign and irredentist policies, and Greece's alliance with the Triple Entente, as well as its Asia Minor campaign, must be examined in the context of European alignments and strategic objectives in the eastern Mediterranean and the Near East. The two recurring security considerations of Greece have been Bulgaria and Turkey, and although relations with the latter improved during the interwar period (acquiring an institutional base after entry of both countries into NATO), Bulgaria, throughout the same period, remained a source of problems for Greece. War, occupation, civil conflict and subsequent dependence on the United States, are the dominant features in the public perception of Greece's postwar affiliation with the West.

DOMESTIC DEVELOPMENTS

The Greek Civil War, like others of its kind, had the effect of polarizing politics, ideology and institutions in a way that affected the whole of society. This situation did not arise from dictatorial rule but in a state which, in spite of various constitutional irregularities and extraordinary measures, observed the essential rules of parliamentary democracy. The Communist Party, that abstained from the 1946 elections and called upon its followers to defy the outcome, was outlawed with the outbreak of hostilities, but most of the Greek parties continued to operate, undeterred by the Civil War and equally unresponsive to the new political and social challenges confronting postwar Europe. Consequently, Greece completely missed out on the constructive dialogue between liberal and socialist principles which was occurring elsewhere at this time.

The term of Constantinos Karamanlis (q.v.) (1955–63) in power was associated with the reconstruction of the war-ravaged economy and the state. From 1940 to 1970 the population increased by 19 percent while the number of civil servants increased by 140 percent. Government planning, which consisted of currency controls, price and exchange rate regulation, investment and the extension of credit to the private sector, further enhanced the state's importance in propelling economic growth.

Throughout the war years, the future of the Crown remained an outstanding issue of contention between the Greeks and their allies, and the royal family returned to Greece in 1946 only after a plebiscite had decided the monarchy's fate. King George's death in 1947 brought his brother Paul to the throne. The interventions of his dynamic wife, Queen Frederika, in the affairs of state became a permanent feature of his reign. Both she, and later her son Constantine (who succeeded his father in 1964), failed to understand that the power invested in the throne after the Civil War was an anachronism. Although the monarchy initially secured the unity of the victorious camp, in time it became a cause of dispute even among its former allies. Frederika's rivalry with Marshal Alexandros Papagos (q.v.), head of the government forces during the Civil War, split the officer corps into two camps. The Queen's fear that the prestigious general would wield an influence in the army rivaling that of the King, was confirmed. Long after Papagos's death, some of his military admirers harbored hostility against the throne until they removed its power in 1967 and abolished it altogether in 1973.

Since socialist parties in the 1960s were isolated from central political discourse (albeit not from Parliament), the only political force that could instill vitality into the ossified system, intent on growth but not modernization, was the Center Union Party (EK) under George Papandreou (q.v.). The general objectives of the forces of the center were to end political polarization, reform the educational system, defend civil liberties and further the democratization of the political process. The Center Union Party, which won a resounding electoral victory in 1964, resulted from a merger of forces ranging from moderate right to socialist, and found support in the growing urban areas where the anonymity of large populations weakened the power of patronage while collective grievances were freely and loudly expressed. Communists and socialists formed the United Democratic Left (EDA) which became the second party in Parliament (with over 25 percent of the vote) in the elections in 1958, nurturing discontent against Constantine Karamanlis's ruling National Radical Union (ERE).

Determined to challenge the crown's influence in the armed forces, Papandreou came into conflict with Constantine II soon after taking power. In the summer of 1965 the Prime Minister was forced to resign. At the same time, 40 deputies defected from his party and became supporters of a government formed by the King and designed to prevent the holding of elections that would bring the Center Union Party back to power. The clash between the heads of state and government caused a major political crisis and a power gap which the military filled nearly two years later.

The 1967 coup was to a large extent the reaction of "praetorian" officers against the impact of detente at home. Refusing to accept the end of the Civil War polarization and to give up their role as guardians of a repressive state ideology, the officers invented a threat to internal order—a possible communist uprising—to justify their armed intervention. The takeover succeeded in preventing George Papandreou from winning the upcoming elections. Moreover, it freed a certain military clique from the restraints of a conservative political camp which had failed to remain in power. Many of these officers, in fact, supported the coup knowing that their chances for promotion would increase given the numerous dismissals that would inevitably follow.

In January 1967, King Constantine finally made his move against the rebellious Colonels but his countercoup failed and he had to flee the country with his family. In 1973, following another abortive coup against its authority, the ruling junta formally deposed the exiled monarch and presented the people with a republican constitution, approved by a fraudulent referendum. Although brutal and unprofessional in administering the state, the regime had the good fortune to ride the crest of a sustained economic boom and thus secured the prolonged acquiescence of the populace.

MAJOR INSTITUTIONAL REFORMS AFTER THE RETURN TO PARLIAMENTARY DEMOCRACY

With the Turkish invasion of Cyprus the Greek military regime disintegrated. On 23 July 1974 members of the junta handed over power to politicians who summoned Constantinos Karamanlis (q.v.) from Paris to assume the leadership of a civilian government. This surrender of power, without a struggle that would perhaps clear the field from the legacy of the past, had its negative aspects. Although the transfer was unconditional, the new democratic regime initially operated within a state apparatus permeated by appointments of the junta. Besides matters of the utmost urgency in the field of foreign affairs, Karamanlis was also faced with the task of gradually replacing higher officials with men of his own choice. His government was often criticized for not stepping up the process of "de-juntification" and when his provisional cabinet fixed the election date for 17 November 1974, the opposition claimed that state agencies and local authorities infested by junta agents would affect the electoral results. Although such a criticism was not unfounded, the elections were conducted in an exemplary manner. In spite of the short notice, political parties organized their campaigns and joined the contest with great enthusiasm. The system of "reinforced" proportional representation which had determined most of the postwar elections in Greece was put to use once more.

The conservative electoral outcome signified to a large extent an endorsement of Karamanlis's effort to secure an orderly change of guard without provoking the stunned but still dangerous forces of reaction. The outcome of the referendum to decide the future of the monarchy in Greece was perhaps more in keeping with the public mood for change. Although Karamanlis maintained a neutral stance vis-à-vis the issue in question, his silence was widely interpreted as a condemnation of the institution which had destabilized Greek politics on several crucial occasions. The referendum of December 1974, which was the sixth to be held on the issue of the Crown in the twentieth century (1920, 1924, 1935, 1946, 1973), sealed the fate of the monarchy with 69 percent of the vote against the institution.

The drafting of a new constitution incorporating changes that emerged since the return to democracy as well as the reformist visions of the Prime Minister, began in earnest after the referendum. With more than a two-thirds majority, Karamanlis introduced a draft constitution for discussion in Parliament at the end of December. The draft constitution provided for a strong presidential executive after the Gaullist paradigm and was heavily criticized by the supporters of the powers of Parliament.

The constitution of 1975 replaced that of 1952 (which had been put into temporary force in the summer of 1974) and was the outcome of a compromise between Karamanlis's bid for a Presidential regime and those who upheld the rights of Parliament. The new constitution enhanced the role of the executive over that of the legislature and endowed the President of the Republic with powers that other parliamentary republics did not possess. The President is elected by Parliament for a five year term with the power to declare war and conclude treaties. He also has the right to veto legislation, although a three-fifths majority in Parliament can override his veto. The President is obliged to invite the leader of the majority party in Parliament to form a government, but has the power to dismiss him following consultations within the Council of the Republic. This body is composed of former Presidents, the Prime Minister, the head of the largest opposition party in Parliament and Prime Ministers who have secured votes of confidence in Parliament. The President is also empowered to dissolve Parliament if he thinks it does not reflect the popular will or has proved itself to be incapable of ensuring stable government.

Constantinos Tsatsos (q.v.), a well-known intellectual and a close associate of Karamanlis, became the latter's choice for the presidency instead of the more obvious candidature of Panayotis Kanellopoulos (q.v.)—an eminent statesman who had been widely associated with opposition against the junta. On 19 June 1975 Tsatsos was elected by Parliament and stayed for his entire

term in office. Karamanlis was elected President of the Republic
in 1980.

POLITICAL CHANGE AND THE PARTIES

The proverbial individualism of the Greek ''character'' as well
as certain tenaciously conservative social traits can be partly
explained by the absence of a fully developed civil society in
Greece. Social fragmentation, widespread poverty until the early
1950s and the insecurity compounded by wars and civil strife
allowed the persistence of confusion between private and public
interest and sustained the division between the official world of
the state and an informal order based on networks of patronage,
kinship and personal relations. Political institutions and political
practices therefore often evolved along divergent paths and the
average Greek was left to his own devices for survival.

The rapid urbanization of the 1950s and the 1960s undermined
the traditional structures of rural life and contributed to the
integration of peasants into the mass society of the urban centers.
Horizontal organization based on class interests are gradually
replacing the vertical patron-client networks and the power of
kinship. Furthermore, the economic boom of the 1960s and 1970s
not only relieved the country from underdevelopment but altered
the entire perception and life style of its population.

Concerning the nature of her growth it has been argued that
Greece fits neither the description of underdevelopment, nor that
of a peripheral economy. An average growth rate of 6.6 percent
per year was achieved between 1962–74 in spite of the economic
turbulence during the same period. Others point out that economic
growth was import-based, constantly inflating the foreign trade
deficit. This deficit was covered by emigrant and merchant marine
remittances, tourism and foreign loans.

The Greek socioeconomic system did not cease to emulate its
western pluralistic prototypes even during the junta period. Social
and political emancipation therefore became significant options
of the 1970s, once the old specter of the Civil War faded. The
rising expectations of the Greek public, stifled by the military
regime on the political front, surfaced after its collapse. Initial

fears of a militaristic relapse had a moderating effect on the 1974 elections but demand for change gained momentum during the subsequent elections of 1977 and especially those of 1981. In the meantime, the unprecedented political freedoms enjoyed by the Greeks since 1974 relieved party politics from the rancor and fanaticism of the pre-junta years.

The elections of 18 October 1981 gave a socialist party an absolute majority of seats in Parliament for the first time in Greek history. The Panhellenic Socialist Movement (PASOK) under the leadership of Andreas Papandreou (q.v.) made big strides, winning 13.5 percent of the vote in 1974, 25.3 percent in 1977 and 48.1 percent (with 172 deputies in Parliament) in 1981.

POLITICAL DEVELOPMENTS SINCE 1984

The June 1984 elections for the Greek representatives to the European Parliament proved a turning point in the content, if not the form, of PASOK's policy. The outcome proved a disappointment to the big parties and marked the beginning of an easing of political tension and a gradual turn of PASOK to a moderate course both on the domestic and foreign policy front.

The New Democracy party, faced with an acute identity crisis after its founder Karamanlis opted for the Presidency of the Republic in 1980, changed leadership twice before the position was offered to the forceful Constantinos Mitsotakis (q.v.) at the end of August 1984. A one-time Center Union party deputy who had clashed with its leader in 1965, Mitsotakis was faced with the double task of consolidating his leadership in New Democracy as well as dodging the attacks of PASOK deputies who sought to divert public interest from current problems to past political conflicts.

The election of June 1985 gave PASOK a comfortable margin (45.82 percent and 172 deputies in Parliament) and hence it continued to pursue its program unhindered by leftist or rightist opposition. Papandreou's success was reinforced by Communist losses and consequently his decision not to back Karamanlis for a renewal of his presidential term for fear of alienating left-wing voters was unexpectedly vindicated. PASOK's wage-price index-

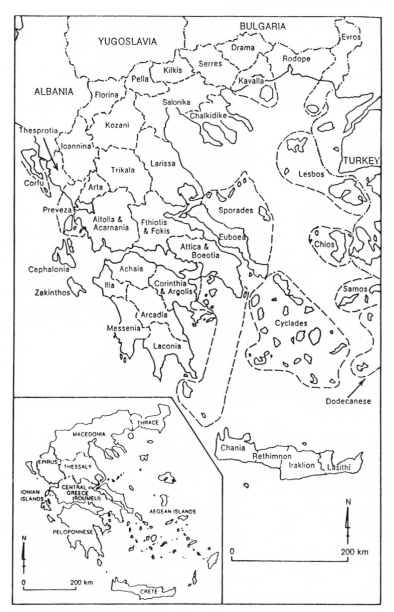

Administrative Divisions.
Source: David H. Close, *The Greek Civil War, 1943–50,* London, Routledge, 1993.

ation permitted people of low and medium income to beat the rate of inflation. Price controls and the protection of workers from being layed off had a negative effect on business but won the support of a larger section of the population. There was therefore a clearer correlation of income level and electoral behavior in 1985 than in 1981. Businesspeople, managers and certain professional groups as well as the legal and medical associations opted for New Democracy. New Democracy, with 40.84 percent (126 deputies) of the vote, added 4.98 percent to its 1981 percentage while the Communist Party (KKE) with 9.89 percent (12 deputies) lost 1.4 percent. Finally the Eurocommunists with 1.84 percent managed to elect one deputy.

The elections were dominated by the verbal exchanges between Papandreou and Mitsotakis but the concerns of all party platforms revolved around the economy and its uncertain future. New Democracy adopted a liberal prescription promising to decrease the role of the state and provide incentives for a revival of the private sector. Mitsotakis's constant references to the country's ever-increasing dependence on foreign loans in order to finance a cumbersome and expensive state underlined the most sensitive issue of the contest. PASOK's own platform focusing on decentralization and redistribution of income made fewer promises of handouts and post electoral bliss and stressed the need for improvement in productivity.

Greece's economy, which has always been sensitive to international developments, became even more dependent on foreign capital. Papandreou's initial opposition to Greek accession to the European Community, and his subsequent promise to hold a referendum to decide the issue, were quietly dropped after 1982, when about $800 million a year of EC funds were directed to Greece's rural areas.

The most significant deviation of PASOK's policy towards Turkey was introduced by the Davos meeting between the Greek and Turkish Prime Ministers in February 1988. Almost a year before, a crisis caused by Turkey's decision to send a research vessel escorted by warships to explore for oil in the disputed continental shelf around Lesbos, Lemnos and Samothrace, brought the two states close to an armed clash. The crisis was defused, but it became clear that perhaps a future confrontation could not be averted given the delicate state of relations in the

Aegean. At the same time, Papandreou began to realize that repeated emergency appeals to the Greek population would eventually blunt sensitivities over Greek-Turkish disputes. Furthermore, the burden of enormous defense spending on the ailing Greek balance of payments and the long military service which detracted from the government's populist image, convinced the Greek Prime Minister that he should take the initiative to raise the threshold of war between Greece and Turkey.

In the spring of 1988, Turkey's Foreign Affairs Minister Mesut Yilmaz raised the question of the "Turkish" minority in Greek Thrace and dismissed any possibility of a Turkish military withdrawal from Cyprus before the two communities came to an agreement and solution. The Greek side soon realized that Cyprus was not considered by the Turks as part of the Davos package while the Moslems of Thrace were being forcefully brought into the picture. Although some progress was made in accident prevention in international territories of the Aegean, the Davos spirit quietly expired in 1989.

Seven years of PASOK in power precipitated certain social and economic changes in Greece. The public sector predictably became more cumbersome than before and the private sector refrained from new investments for lack of confidence in a government which (in spite of occasional retractions) widely publicized its hostility against big business. Modernization followed the path of legal reform. Civil marriages were allowed, divorces were simplified and the institution of the dowry was abolished. The spirit of defiance in foreign policy may have purged the Greeks of feelings of past subservience but ran out of steam as the economy increasingly required foreign loans to fill the financial gaps caused by overconsumption and low productivity.

An important element in the post-1974 developments is that Greece's European vocation was reinforced by the upgrading of her democratic institutions and her full membership in the European Community. PASOK's Third World affiliations notwithstanding, Greece is now more entrenched in the western camp than before 1974. There was nevertheless a strong element of anachronism in PASOK's overall concept of world politics. Since much of the movement's appeal was based on redressing the grievances of the vanquished in the Greek Civil War, Papandreou sought to reconstitute—at least verbally—the fear of the Cold War climate. His constant references to the conservatives as an authoritarian right-wing stratum that could easily revert to the oppressive tactics of the 1950s, his unyielding opposition to American influence and his initial Third World orientation, prevented his followers from coming to grips with a changing world. His belated decision to fall into line with the other members of NATO and the EC did not come in time to eliminate his reputation as the maverick of the western world.

The turning point in PASOK's fortunes was the illness of Papandreou and his absence from the administration of power during the summer of 1988. An influential member of the cabinet, Agamemnon Koutsogiorgas, who replaced the ailing Prime Minister in the actual running of the state, proved an embarrassment for PASOK. The various scandals that erupted in the winter of 1988–89 implicated Koutsogiorgas along with certain PASOK ministers, and reached the doorstep of the convalescent Prime Minister. Although the elections of June 1989 took a toll on the party whose electoral percentage fell to 38 percent, New Democracy with 43 percent was unable to form a government and entered a coalition of limited mandate with the Communists. The electoral system, a variety of proportional representation, was engineered by PASOK in such a way as to prevent the formation of a one-party government. The elections of November 1989 gave New Democracy 46 percent of the vote but still produced no government.

Since the Communists were reluctant to cooperate with Papandreou before a "catharsis" of the scandals was effected, all three parties in Parliament entered a National Union government under the octogenarian former banker, Xenophon Zolotas, as a way out of the impasse. Several months later the declining economy caused the resignation of Zolotas and new elections in April 1990.

New Democracy finally managed to attain the narrow margin required for the formation of a government (with the aid of a deputy from the diminutive D.I.A.N.A. party). PASOK won 39 percent of the vote and the Alliance of Left Wing forces declined to 11 percent.

The Mitsotakis government was faced with the dire prospects of balancing the budget, liquidating problematic firms under state responsibility and trimming the public sector. Although the summer of 1990 was marked by a rash of strikes, New Democracy managed to elect the mayors of Athens and Thessaloniki in the municipal elections of October 1990.

Since that time the Mitsotakis government has been caught in a crossfire between internal and external developments. The permanent name of the Former Yugoslav Republic of Macedonia (FYROM) preoccupied Greek foreign policy much of the time between 1991 and 1994.

Although the contentuous issue prevented international recognition of the new state, Greece's services as the only interlocutor between the Serbian leadership and the EC, kept communication open and allowed for the April 1993 meeting in Athens between the waring parties of Yugoslavia and the Vance-Owen commission.

Situated in the turbulent Balkan neighborhood and open to economic refugees and illegal immigrants from north and east, Greece occupies the most precarious geographic position among European Community members.

A steadfast ally of the West throughout the Cold War period and now a haven of stability, democracy, prosperity, and cohesion in the Balkans, Greece wonders whether it will be the western country to pay the highest price for the collapse of communism.

The elections of 10 October 1993 brought PASOK back to power and obliged Constantine Mitsotakis (q.v.) to resign from his position as head of the New Democracy party. His place was taken by Miltiades Evert.

THE DICTIONARY

ACROPOLIS. A steep rock 156 meters high, 320 meters long and 140 meters wide dominating Athens, was used from early times as a sanctuary and a refuge for the inhabitants of the surrounding Attica plain. Because of its uninterrupted habitation since Neolithic times the site itself is a valuable source of information. The oldest remains, dating back to the fourteenth century B.C., are of a Mycenaean palace which somehow survived the still unexplained holocaust of all Mycenaean citadels in the eleventh century B.C. As of the eighth century B.C., increasing Athenian wealth made monuments and sculptures appear on the Acropolis. The first temple dedicated to the virgin (*parthenos* in Greek) goddess of wisdom Athena, was built by the tyrant Peisistratos in early sixth century. This temple was later sacked by the Persians, but in 480 B.C. after their victory at Salamis the Athenians recaptured their city and rebuilt the temples in a magnificent way. Pericles summoned the artistic talents of Ictinos, Killicrates, Mnesicles and above all Pheidias to construct a perfect marble Parthenon as a homage to Athena. The project lasted 30 years from 448 onwards.

In 149 B.C., when Athens fell to the Romans, they spared the Acropolis from their usual looting, as they fell in awe before its monuments. Likewise, in Byzantine times the Acropolis remained mostly unscathed. When the Ottoman sultan Mohammed III conquered Athens, he too fell under the Acopolis' spell. In 1687 during the Turco-Venetian war the Venetian admiral Francesco Morosini bombarded the Acropolis systematically. One bomb landed on the Turkish arsenal. In the terrible explosion that followed the Parthenon was severely damaged. In 1830 the Greeks, once again masters in their own house, restored the Acropolis, as best they could, to its original state.

Modern Greeks are sparing no efforts to save the Acropolis from air pollution (carbon and sulfur dioxide) as well as from the feet of millions of tourists. They are aware that when two-and-a-half millenia ago ''a conscious stone to beauty grew'' it became the monument of the civilized world and that they must preserve it as best they can.

ADMINISTRATION. The administrative unit in Greece is the *nomos* (prefecture) headed by a *nomarch* (prefect), who is a civil servant appointed by the government accountable to the Minister of the Interior and responsible for implementing government policy in all fields. The *nomarchs* runs the civil service, the police force, and supervises local authorities in their area. The judiciary and military authorities are outside his or her purview.

In the performance of their duties the *nomarchs* are assisted by an elected advisory council.

AEGEAN ISLANDS. The Aegean Sea, bounded by Macedonia and Thrace, mainland Greece, Turkey and Crete is littered with 8,079 islands including islets and rock islands. Of these, 101 are inhabited, the largest being Lesbos (1,630 square kilometers). The total population of the Aegean islands is 495,763.

The islands are peaks of a submerged plateau and therefore mostly mountainous. The climate is warm and their economy is based mainly on tourism (q.v.) and the sea. In the center, the Cyclades forming a rough circle (*kyklos* in Greek) have been the cradle of an archaic civilization spanning 24 centuries (from 3500 to 1100 B.C.). During classical times they were mostly in the hands of the Athenians. Clustering like a chaplet around the rocky island of Delos—the great shrine of Apollo in the ancient world—the beautiful but barren Cyclades fell later to Macedon and Rome. Constantinople left them often undefended against the Goths, the Saracens and the Slavs. In 1204, they were given by the Crusaders to Venice which handed them over to various adventurers. Most of these local dynasties were suppressed by the Ottomans after the fall of Constantinople. The Aegean islands were gradually incorporated into the state of Greece. Due to the long exposure of the islanders to western rule most of the Greek Catholics are to be found amongst the Aegean population.

The latest Aegean islands to join in 1948 the Greek kingdom—as it then was—were the Dodecanese (a word meaning "the twelve islands"). Like the large islands of the north Aegean, the Dodecanese always had great strategic and trading importance because of their accessibility in the Mediterranean and their closeness to the coast of Anatolian Turkey. The large island of Rhodes is only 11 miles from the Turkish coast.

Chiefly Greek in population, the Dedecanese had been taken by the Italians from the Turks during the Itala-Turkish War in 1912. The islands continued to be held by Italy despite the expressed desire of an island congress for union with Greece. When the end of the Second World War (q.v.) forced Italy to give up all its colonial possessions, the Dodecanese, including Rhodes, was made part of Greece, although not until 1948 were the formalities completed.

AGRICULTURE. Only 30 percent of the total land is cultivated in this mountainous country called Greece, about 40 percent is rough pasture land, some 20 percent is forest and the remainder is either unsuitable for cultivation or is unexploited.

Out of 3,950,000 hectares of cultivated land (of which 33.9 percent is irrigated) 67 percent are used for growing crops (field and industrial), 25 percent for arboriculture, 5 percent as vineyards and 3 percent as gardens. Tillage crops are in order of importance sugar, beets, wheat (soft and hard), corn, tomatoes, hay and potatoes. The main industrial crops are cotton and tobacco. Orchards and olive trees have been since antiquity Greece's most typical trees while the country's vineyards produce wines of quality, table grapes and currants. The main agricultural exports are fresh as well as prepared fruit and vegetables, tobacco, olives and olive oil. Greece is also an exporter of grains, including durum wheat, rice and maize.

Greek agriculture underwent significant changes after the Second World War (q.v.). Between 1950–90 the average consumption of N-fertilizers increased from 4.4 to 100 kg/ha. while P- and K-fertilizers also increased but at a slower rate. In the 1970s the gross farm produce more than covered (103 percent) the basic needs of the country. Fruit, tobacco, olives, and raisins are in surplus while meat, fish, and wood products are in deficit.

A limiting factor in the modernization of Greek agriculture is the fact that, due to inheritance laws, farms are continuously being fragmented into smaller and smaller separate lots, a fact which makes their management difficult and costly. The government implements a number of schemes to promote consolidation with varying degrees of success. The problem is becoming less acute as farmers' numbers continue to decline. The percentage of the active population employed in the rural sector (agriculture, stock farming, forestry and fisheries) fell from 46 percent in 1970 to 30 percent in 1980 and 26.6 percent in 1990 while by the year 2000 it is expected to reach the level of 18.7 percent. This is in line with developments in other European countries where the increase of agricultural output has been the result of increased productivity not manpower, which has in fact been steadily dwindling.

AHRWEILER-GLYKATZI, HELEN (1926–   ). Byzantinologist and educationalist of international reputation. Born in Athens (q.v.), she studied philosophy and literature at Athens University and Byzantine history at the University of Paris. She became Professor at the Sorbonne in 1967 and Director of the Center for History and Civilization. In 1976, she was the first woman to occupy the position of Rector of Paris University. In 1982, she became Rector of the French Academy and is currently President of the George Pompidou National Center of Arts and Culture.

Her most important works are *Byzantium and the Sea* (1966), *Essays on Administration and Society in Byzantium* (1971), *Political Ideology of the Byzantine Empire* (1975), and *Byzantium, the Country and the Territory* (1976).

ANASTENARIA (Fire Dancing). Dancing on incandescent coal is an age-old rite performed in Eastern Macedonia (q.v.). The ceremony of *anastenaria,* as it is called, takes place every year in the village of Aghia Eleni near the city of Serres and forms part of the 21st of May festival of Saints Constantine and Helen. The performers belong to both sexes, they are called *anastenarides* in Greek, and dance for lengthy periods of time on a specially prepared surface of hot burning coals. They are in a state of trance and claim to be possessed by the spirit of the saints themselves. The soles of their feet having often been thoroughly examined by qualified medical doctors have never shown signs of damage. The origins of the rite are somewhat obscure but there is some evidence linking *anastenaria* to Dianysian worship in ancient Greece.

Official Orthodoxy (q.v.) frowns upon such practices which include also the frantic worship of the Virgin and its reputedly miracle-working (*thavmatourgos*) icon on the island of Tinos. When the dancers among the red-hot coals clutch the icons of St. Constantine and St. Helen to their breasts to protect their feet from burns, one is usually reminded of the Byzantine iconoclast's outrage at such "festivals" which proved—as they said—that creeping idolatry was a real danger to an icon-venerating Orthodox Church (q.v.).

ANCIENT GREECE. Even before the incursion of Hellenic migrations from the north began to occur between 2000–1100 B.C., the Aegean basin was inhabited by people who had developed advanced cultures. The Achaeans, the Ionians, the Aeolians and the Dorians, who descended into the Greek mainland and the Aegean islands (q.v.), assimilated the existing cultures and marked the beginning of Greek history. Inscriptions in Linear B (deciphered by Michael Ventris) were found to have been written in Greek around 1500 B.C. The authors of the script, the Achaeans, under the leadership of King Agamemnon of Mycenas, set out around 1350 B.C. to conquer Troy, an important commercial city of Asia Minor. This famous expedition which drew in many

Greek states and their kings, was immortalized by Homer in his *Iliad*.

The Ionians occupied the coastal parts of Greece and established footholds in the Aegean islands and in the coast of Asia Minor, while the Dorians around 1100 B.C. overran Macedonia, Thessaly, and the Peloponnese (qq.v.). The Dorians, the last wave of Greeks, mixed with the Achaeans and to a lesser extent with the Ionians and retained the military qualities displayed by Dorian states in the two extremities of Greece, Macedonia in the north and Sparta in the south. The city-state of Athens exemplified the cultural and scholarly disposition of the Ionian merchants who looked at their uncouth Dorian compatriots with some disdain.

The founding of the Olympic games in 776 B.C. infused a sense of cultural unity in the Greeks, but it was the Asian threat of the fifth century which obliged city-states of common language and religious tradition to join forces. The battles between Greeks and Persians: Marathon (492 B.C.), Salamis (480 B.C.), and Plataea (479 B.C.), as well as the defeat of the Persian forces in Cyprus and the Carthaginians in the Greek colony of Sicily (480 B.C.), cleared the commercial routes of the eastern Mediterranean for Greece's eastward expansion.

The Peloponnesian war (431–403 B.C.) between the protagonists of the victory against Persia, Athens and Sparta, allowed the Kingdom of Macedonia to rise as a major power in northern Greece. Under Philip (350–336 B.C.), the Macedonian forces defeated Athenian power. His son, Alexander, a pupil of the philosopher Aristotle, united the Greeks in a campaign against Persia, which began in 336 B.C. and ended 11 years later with the conqueror's death at the age of 33. Alexander the Great in his short life conquered the entire Persian empire, Egypt, Afghanistan and parts of India. The Near East was thereafter known as the "Hellenistic World," with a Greek cultural presence open to all willing participants.

Greece's power ended with the Roman conquest between 215–146 B.C. but its civilization lived on for centuries after its political demise.

ANCIENT GREECE

Crete: 3000–1100 B.C.
Mycenae: 1900–1050 B.C.
Dark Age: 1085–750 B.C.
Classical Age: 750–338 B.C.
Power of Macedonia: 359–323 B.C.
Hellenistic Age: 323–30 B.C.

Map of Greece

Macedonia

ASIA MINOR

Aegean Sea

Thermopylae

Chaeronea Delphi Thebes

Plataea Marathon

Leuctra

Mycenae Athens

Salamis

Corinth

The Peloponnese Sparta

Thera

Mediterranean Sea

Rhodes

Knossos Mallia

CRETE

Phaistos

ANDRONIKOS, MANOLIS (1919–1992). Greek scholar and archaeologist who discovered at the Macedonian village of Verghina (q.v.) treasure-filled tombs of ancient Macedonian royalty as well as gravestones of Macedonian commoners. He produced convincing evidence that ancient Macedonia was populated by Greek tribes.

Andronikos was born in Bursa, Turkey. He was three years old when his family fled to Thessaloniki following the 1922 defeat of the Greek army. As a student he took part in excavations conducted in the late 1930s in Verghina and felt, right from the start, that the place was more important than was generally thought at the time. He graduated in 1940, obtained his doctorate in 1952 and pursued further studies in Oxford under John Beazley. In 1957, he became a Lecturer and, in 1964, a full Professor at the University of Thessaloniki. Although he excavated many sites in Macedonia between 1952 and 1961, he never forgot Verghina which he identified—on solid historical evidence—with the ancient city of Aigae, the early capital of the Macedonian kingdom.

In November 1977, Andronikos stunned his audience in the University of Thessaloniki by announcing that he had found the grave of Philip II, father of Alexander the Great. "I found his very bones in a golden casket," he said. The casket bore the 16-point star of Verghina and the bones were shrouded in a purple and gold cloth topped with a golden wreath.

Since then, Andronikos discovered more than ten royal tombs as well as, in 1982, the theater where Philip was assassinated in 336 B.C.

One of his latest finds was a headless marble statue with an inscription in Greek dedicating it to the goddess Eucleia on behalf of Philip's mother Eurydice. A few days before his death Andronikos was awarded by Constantinos Karamanlis (q.v.) the country's highest distinction, the grand cross of the Order of Phoenix.

ARMED FORCES. Greece's military expenditure in terms of GNP percentage has been the highest among European NATO (q.v.) members for the last ten years. Since the military budget steadily exceeds the sum allocated for public investment, the burden of such spending on the economy (q.v.) is heavy for a small country. Greece established its own arms industries to secure partial independence of armaments and a source of income from the export of weapons. The national arms industry includes a rifle assembly plant, ammunition factories, facilities to upgrade older tanks and the production of communications systems. The Hellenic Aerospace Industry can overhaul, repair, and modify military and commercial aircraft, engines and electronics. The Hellenic Shipyard has been building patrol boats and the Steyer-Hellas Company is assembling heavy-duty military trucks.

The armed forces are divided into three military regions, two of which are located in northern (Thessaloniki) and northeastern Greece. The headquarters, in Athens (q.v.), control forces in the rest of Greece (continent and islands). At present the total military personnel amounts to 214,000, distributed as follows: army—170,500, navy—19,500, marine corps—20,000, and air force—24,000. There is also a paramilitary force of 29,000.

ART. The post-Byzantine tradition of religious art that prevailed before independence was challenged by a western influence that came to Greece with the Bavarians in 1833. The development of Greek art after the creation of the Hellenic state was determined by the administrators and technocrats who accompanied King Otto (q.v.) to Greece.

Most of the important Greek artists of the nineteenth century studied or supplemented their education in Munich. The most prominent of these, Nikolaos Ghysis (1842–1901) became Professor at the Munich Academy and gained fame abroad. Others, such as Constantinos Volanakis (1837–1907), Nikiforos Lytras (1832–1904), and George Iakovidis (1852–1932) returned to Greece to resume posts at the School of Fine Arts in Athens.

The "Munich" period of Greek painting betrays some of the extraordinary talent of its masters only indirectly through their sketches and studies. Their finished works are often stilted and unimaginative as were most of the products of academia in Munich, Rome or Paris. The only Greek element in their work was the occasional folklore in the subject matter. The study of native light and colors would come later with the "Parisian" influence in the twentieth century.

A more indigenous, although less influential, tradition emanated from the Italianesque school of the Ionian islands (q.v.) which became part of Greece in 1862.

The Greek artistic diaspora discovered the Parisian avant-garde with some delay. Impressionism never took roots in Greece but the Post-Impressionists influenced the works of Constantinos Parthenis (1878–1967), Constantinos Maleas (1879–1928), and Spyros Papaloukas (1893–1957). Parthenis became the most influential exponent of modern trends, and the artistic generation that followed his courses at the School of Fine Arts combined modernity with a vivid interest in the Greek light and colors. A parallel, although opposite influence, came from Photis Kondoglou (1896–1965), a refugee from Asia Minor who sought to revive Byzantine art. Kondoglou rejected western incursions into Greek tradition and taught his students to seek out what had roots in Greek culture. The cross-fertilization of Parthenis and Kondoglou produced an extraordinary generation of postwar artists with a deep understanding of Greek art: Yannis Tsarouchis, Nikos Hatzikyriakos Ghikas, Yannis Moralis, and Spyros Vassiliou are some of the more prominent.

Since the 1960s, Greek art has submitted to a cosmopolitan influence which has ceased to explore the native tradition. Takis (q.v.), Chryssa, Samaras and Kounelis are celebrated figures of the diaspora but even such natives as Costas Tsoklis, Dimitris Mytaras and Elias Dekoulakos, belong to a western European mainstream. Alekos Fassianos, with his references to an ancient Mediterranean depiction of figures, is a partial exception to this rule.

ATHENS. The largest city and capital of Greece sprawling in all directions across the Attica plain, 22 kilometers by 10 kilometers, is divided into 27 separate municipalities. Greater Athens dominates the country with a population in excess of 3 million, out of a total population (q.v.) in excess of ten-and-a-quarter million. It hosts 50 percent of industry and two-thirds of the country's wealth. As many as 60 percent of present-day Athenians have been born elsewhere. Athens has a long history as a city, but a relatively short one as the capital of an independent state.

The slopes of the rocky formation which later became the Acropolis (q.v.) have been occupied since Neolithic times. Athens itself became a town as early as the ninth century B.C. Classical Athens developed around the Acropolis, the place where the goddess Athena was worshipped. The city was treated with respect by Alexander the Great and received special privileges from the Romans. Under Byzantine (q.v.) rule, it dwindled to an unimportant small town. It was sacked by the Slavs in 580 A.D., seized by the Crusaders in 1206 after they had conquered Constantinople and fell to the Turks in 1456. It was chosen as the capital of the new state of Greece in 1834.

Although Nauplion, Patras, and Corinth had at least equal commercial advantages with Athens, so that Nauplion was chosen as the first capital of the new Greece in 1827, the historic claims of Athens were so great that six years later it became the capital. But Athens had been bitterly ravaged by invasions, occupations, neglect and time. What had been left at the beginning of the nineteenth century of the low houses fronting many of the narrow, crooked streets had been burned down during the fight for independence so that only a few of the houses clustered on the northern and eastern slopes of the Acropolis remained when the capital was transferred there. Fortunately, the fighting of the War of Independence (q.v.) had done little damage to the Parthenon; it remained as it had been when the irreparable catastrophe of 1687 had struck it. In that year, the Parthenon, used as an Ottoman powder magazine, had its center blown out under the impact of a shell shot during the Venetian bombardment of the city.

Modern Athens was shaped in the nineteenth century by King Otto's Bavarian architects and planners around what was then a mere village north of the Acropolis named Plaka. To this day the Plaka district still displays its village character. In recent years a number of nineteenth-century neoclassical buildings have been beautifully restored. See also ACROPOLIS.

-B-

BALKAN WARS (1912–1913). The first Balkan War began when the smallest partner of a strange alliance, Montenegro, declared war against the Ottoman Empire. Greece, Serbia, and Bulgaria followed on 18 October 1912. Greece's navy played a vital role by blocking the supply of the Turkish forces by sea and the Greek fleet, headed by the heavy cruiser *Averov,* won a series of naval engagements preventing the Turkish ships from leaving the straits.

The Balkan allies made rapid progress. The Greeks advanced into Macedonia (q.v.) and captured its largest city, the port of Thessaloniki on November 1912 and, in January 1913, the capital of Epirus, Jannina. The navy liberated the islands of Chios, Mytilini, and Samos.

The Ottoman government sued for peace and was obliged to accept the territorial gains of the Balkan allies by the London Treaty of May 1913.

Soon, however, hostilities broke out between the allies over the division of Macedonian territories. The second Balkan war was initially fought between Bulgaria and the allied forces of Greece and Serbia, but the Bulgars were soon faced with attacks by Turkey and Romania and were obliged to negotiate. By the Treaty of Bucharest of August 1913, Bulgaria ceded much of her gains in Macedonia to Greece and Serbia.

BANKING. The Bank of Greece is the country's central bank, i.e., the bank of issue and the bank of government (accepting state deposits and extending advances to implement the budget). It supervises all banking operations, ensures conformity with the laws and good practice, regulates liquidity of commercial banks, and finances specialized state credit institutions such as investment and mortgage banks, the Agricultural Bank— which helps farmers with grants and soft loans—and the Postal Savings Bank. The Bank of Greece implements the government's monetary and credit policy as set out annually in Parliament when the budget is debated.

Of the 37 commercial banks operating in Greece, the two largest control between them 80 percent of the assets and 90 percent of lending. They were up until 1992 effectively state-controlled because, by law, the Minister of Finance held the proxy of the shares owned by the church charities, trusts and pension funds. Private sector banks, which have been given a relatively free rein since Greece joined the European Community (EC) (q.v.) in 1981, have consistently outperformed the state-controlled ones in quality and range of services as well as profitability ratios.

Deregulation, a policy implemented by the center-right government of New Democracy (q.v.) since April 1990 when it took office, has been at its most effective in the banking sector renowned for its rigid foreign exchange controls and state interference. Legislation which came into force on 2 January 1992 incorporates most of the EC's first and second banking directives into Greek law, a major step forward. Law 2076 goes beyond the second banking directive in that it stipulates that banks must stop accruing national interest on loans which have not been serviced for 12 months. It also liberalizes consumer credit, allows Greeks to open foreign exchange accounts in Greek banks and—most importantly— provides for a phased abolition of the bank's obligation to finance that fiscal deficit.

Historically, the Greek state has always financed its deficits through the banking system. Commercial banks were required to set aside up to 40 percent of all new deposits and were obliged to purchase government bills and bonds. Since 1985, however, at least part of the deficit has been financed by the sale of government debt to the public at large through monthly sales of Treasury bills and bonds. These bonds yield higher interest rates than anything else on the financial markets and are made even more attractive by the fact that the income they generate is tax free. In order to finance its deficits the state has thus been siphoning off considerable amounts of the public's savings. The system is still in place but at least the government is now less able to fuel inflation by covering its deficits on the cheap and go on flooding the market with money printed by a docile central bank.

BIODIVERSITY. The sum total of life in a given area, i.e., all species and organisms, large and small, terrestrial and aquatic, are what is commonly meant by the term "biodiversity." In spite of an ongoing scientific discussion of the concept itself, the international community now accepts that biodiversity should not be reduced because of human action. Greece is trying its best to implement the environmental policies shaped by the various international conventions to which it is a signatory.

In accordance with EC Directive 79/409 on the protection of wild birds, the Ramsar Convention imposing on its signatories the task of designating at least one wetland of international importance, Presidential Decree 67/1981 on the protection of endemic wildlife, the 1993 Bern Convention of the Council of Europe protecting wildlife and biotapes, the Bonn Convention on the protection of migratory species, the Washington Agreement (CITES) regulating the international trade in endangered species, the Greek framework law 1650 of 1986, and the very important law 69269/1990 introducing the need of prior Environmental Impact Assessment for all important projects, the protected species in Greece include some 800 plants and some 200 rare and endangered species of birds, mammals, reptiles, and amphibians. The protected areas already established include ten National Parks (of which Mount Olympus is one), 19 areas of woods with aesthetic value, 51 areas of natural monuments, including the biotape of the Mediterranean Monk seal (*Monachus-monachus*) in the northern Sporades and of the sea turtle (*Caretta-caretta*), in the island of Zakynthos, as well as 550 controlled hunting areas hosting rare species, 11 important wetlands of the RAMSAR convention (of which one, i.e., the Evros delta, hosts, 272 species of birds) and a further 16 areas of high ecological importance, according to EC standards. For the first time the extraordinary biodiversity in Greece due to the country's geography (q.v.) and climate (q.v.), is formally, officially and—one hopes—effectively protected, not because this is just the people's concern but also because it has become the government's business. See also FAUNA; FLORA.

BYZANTINE GREECE (330–1453 A.D.). The symbiosis between the Greek and Roman traditions, especially in the

Hellenistic world, marked the beginning of a new civilization accompanied by the rise of Christianity.

In 330 A.D. the Roman emperor Constantine established his capital in the Greek city of Byzantium on the Bosporus, which was renamed Constantinople. The Eastern Roman Empire gradually drifted away from its western half and whereas the last western Roman emperor was deposed by the Goths in 476, Byzantium survived until the fifteenth century.

Justinian (527–565) arranged for the translation of the body of Roman law into Greek to make it intelligible to his subjects. In 537, this great emperor inaugurated the church of the Holy Wisdom (Hagia Sophia), the most striking monument ever created in Constantinople. The effort of Justinian to reconquer the western empire from the Goths gave the Byzantines a foothold in Ravenna until the eighth century and at Bari till the eleventh. The western campaigns, however, weakened Byzantine defenses in the north and east and the empire was besieged by Asiatic tribes and the Persians. A siege of Constantinople by the Persians was raised by emperor Herakleios (610–641), who routed this enemy in 627. A formidable new threat came from the Arabs in 636 when they captured Jerusalem.

In the ninth and tenth centuries, Syria, the Holy Land, Crete and Cyprus, were recovered from Arab rule by the emperors of the ''Macedonian dynasty.'' In the Balkans, the Bulgarian challenge was finally and brutally suppressed by emperor Basil II in 1014.

In 1054, the theological breach between western Catholics and Eastern Orthodox (q.v.) reached the final point of separation of the two churches. The great schism (q.v.) that affected political as well as religious relations between Rome and Constantinople was mainly based on a difference concerning the origin of the Holy Ghost in the article of faith (Credo) which was otherwise identical in both churches.

In 1071, the Seljuk Turks defeated emperor Romanos Diogenis and established their state in Asia Minor. Although the Comneni dynasty restored some of Byzantium's old glory, the crusades brought the seafaring antagonists of Byzantine trade, the Venetians and the Genoese, into the eastern Mediterranean. In 1204 Latin armies with Venetian ships took Constantinople and occupied most of the Byzantine provinces. The Greeks created the peripheral kingdoms of Epirus and Moreas and the empires of Trebizond and Nicaea. It was the latter, under the Paleologi dynasty, that liberated Constantinople in 1261 from the Franks. The empire, however, had been reduced to a shadow of its old glory. In 1453 the Ottoman Turks stormed Constantinople and, in 1461, they took Trebizond and Moreas. Thus the history of the hellenized Eastern Empire came to an end.

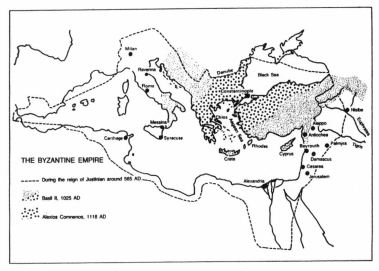

Evolution of the Byzantine Empire

-C-

CALLAS, MARIA (1923–1977). Maria Cecilia Sophia Anna Kalogeropoulou, to call her by her full name, is the Greek soprano who became internationally known as Maria Callas, acclaimed in the 1950s and 1960s as the "prima donna assoluta." She left the United States in 1937 to study at the Athens Conservatory and returned in 1945 to start a dazzling career as an extraordinary singer endowed with unusual acting ability.

According to her biographer, Arianna Stasinopoulos, there were in Maria Callas two women rolled into one: La Callas the singer and Maria the woman. From 1937 to 1957 she became the singer. From 1957 she started being a woman. In fact, her life is nearly summarized in her rendering of Tosca—a role with which she started at the age of 17, in 1940, in Athens and finished, in 1965, in London. When Tosca sings: "Vissi d' arte, vissi d' amore" ("I lived on art, I lived on love"), Callas might have been singing about herself.

As an opera singer she was a perfectionist. Her struggle for identity and excellence led her, in 1954, to achieve a savage and successful weight loss which transformed her from a traditionally ample soprano into a svelte fashion leader of magnetic charm even though her voice was for a time unsettled by this drastic emaciation. She brought the same steely dedication to her acting and singing. The fire that drove her was the fire to succeed. "Only when I was singing did I feel loved," she used to say. She revived the bel canto opera, bringing into it a technical proficiency few conceived possible. She diffused a kind of rapturous pleasure and her changes of register never failed to jolt the audience. Her Norma, her noble, forlorn, "mad" Lucia de Lammermoor, her Violetta, and Tosca remain unsurpassed to this day. Callas was deeply convinced of the inherent beauty of these roles and paid attention to every one of her heroine's gestures, to the music's every nuance.

She had an extraordinary ability to control the tone quality of each single note. She was able to connect the notes to one another exactly as was needed to realize her unique expressive vision. While other gifted singers commanded the art of musical phrases, she commanded the entire melodic trajectory, the entire role itself.

Her stagecraft helped to maintain her magnificently while her voice lost its vitality. In fact, she ruined her voice by overtaxing it. The pressure she put on her top notes and her dark penetrating chest voice with a stabbing timber deployed to lethal effect in such "tigress" roles as Tosca and Lady Macbeth which tore a "hole" in the middle of her voice.

While other sopranos lasted for 30 odd years, her career spanned no more than ten (1948–1958). In 1958, though past her prime, she insisted on giving 26 performances of seven operas in six places around the world. In 1969 she appeared as a non-singing Medea in Pasolini's film "Medea" and, in 1973, she directed a production of Verdi's "I Vesperi Siciliani" in Turin. Without her voice, however, La Callas had no real resource.

She graduated early on from the world of opera to the world of soap opera where you are not immortalized by your successes but by your distresses. Her off-stage agonies, her notorious rows with her mother, her husband Battista Meneghini (30 years her senior, whom she had married for security at the age of 24), her walkouts from performances at the last minute, her turbulent affair with Aristotle Onassis (q.v.), her unsatisfied longing for a child—which made especially tramatic the abortion Onassis forced upon her in 1966—turned her into an anguished, deeply insecure, frustrated woman. Her retirement years were lonely. Onassis left her to marry Jacqueline Kennedy in 1969. After their breakup, she spent her time in her Paris flat listening to pirate tapes of her opera house performances supplied by devotees from all over the world. She died at the age of 53, having lived for many years on her reputation alone. Her career was short: a candle burning too fast. While it burned, though, it shed a light that has not been equalled since.

CAPODISTRIAS, IOANNIS (1776–1831). The first President of Greece and a statesman of high caliber. Born in Corfu, he served as Foreign Minister of the Russian Czar Alexander I. He was elected the first President of Greece for a seven-year term and assumed office in 1828. From the outset, he abolished the third national assembly and replaced it with a council under his direct control. A believer in enlightened despotism, Capodistrias insisted that the war-shattered state required firm administration. If his concept of a unitary state of the Western type was to survive at all, he was obliged to enforce a series of measures that diminished the power-basis of local warlords, notables, and irregular bands. During his term of office he accomplished miracles. He established legal, economic, and military institutions that helped the new state acquire its infrastructure and secured its boundaries through able diplomacy. In 1831, Capodistrias was assassinated by members of the Mavromichalis clan of Mani whose patriarch he had imprisoned.

CAVAFY, KONSTANTINOS (1862–1933). An outstanding poet, Cavafy was the son of a wealthy importer-exporter, born in Alexandria where he lived most of his life. He grew up when one tide of poetry, the Romantic, was beginning to wane while its successor, the Modernist, would not come in until he was 50. After his father's death, when he was only 13, he spent his early adolescence in England and lived briefly in his mother's native Constantinople. He was for most of his adult life an employee in the Egyptian Ministry of Irrigation. His first volume of 14 poems appeared in 1904. In 1910, he published an expanded version (21 poems). Thereafter he circulated his work amongst friends and acquaintances in the form of broadsheets. His collected poems appeared two years after his death.

The impression Cavafy gave as a person was not always endearing. A bit of a dandy for whom only the passing moment counted, a gossip, a miser, a self-satisfied aesthete proud to proclaim his decadent sophistication, a man obsessed by his homosexuality, whose bored, ironic, blasé tone of voice changed only when he described the manifold beauties of the male body, he made few real friends. Cavafy the poet projects a different image: a quiet sceptic who reduces heroes to size, a great recorder of remembered bliss, a coiner of witty epigrams, a master of the understatement, a penetrating observer of human nature, he was able to achieve maximum effect with his low pitched voice free from hysteria and even enthusiasm. He used his poetical means with extraordinary economy.

Cavafy described himself not as a Greek but as a "Hellene." A Greek by culture he drew his inspiration from a variety of sources. Greece for him was not so much a country as an idea. It existed out of space-time; its problems, its agonies, its wars, were never his own. His poetical world was populated with distant Greeks: rulers—often obscure—

and intellectuals—mostly little known—from the Hellenistic world of Antioch, Beirut, Seleuceia, and, of course, his native Alexandria which is a composite of an idealized historical city and a contemporary rather shoddy place where, however, the past can relive and homoerotic love blossom passionately if furtively. He can thus practice "two-plane writing" as James Joyce called it. He defines himself as a historical poet. In one of his rare utterances about himself he says that "a hundred and twenty five voices within me cry that I might have been a historian." His poems are all carefully researched.

In a poignant specimen of the "poetry of departure"—popular during his rootless *fin de siècle*—he describes in his by now famous *The City* (*I Poli*) the sheer pointlessness of seeking a new life elsewhere. "You will always end up in this city," he says in a mood of lucid resignation, ". . . there is no ship for you, there is no road." He is conscious of the ravages of age but finds solace in his task: to capture beauty and fix it forever in his poems. This, then, is the only compensation for the loss of a life of pleasure, folly and sybaritic elegance.

The City in question is, of course, Alexandria—not the dull, philistine, modern place full of the hustle and bustle of confused tongues and mixed races but the older one resplendent with the sights and sounds of lost pagan rites, and the Ptolemaic sense of the exquisite. Out of this reconstructed Alexandria, Cavafy built his personal myth to give shape, form, structure, and coherence not just to his own but to the human condition in general. By making the past contemporary, he helps readers partake in a world where the refined hedonism, the ironic wit, the amused scepticism as well as the search for the exotic, the abnormal, the feminine feeling for beauty and tenderness are no longer a nostalgic "remembrance of things past" but become accessible as a way of life to all sensitive people, readers of his poetry. The world of Cavafy offers no hope of redemption, outside art, *his* art. Alexandria, he explains, is doomed. The Romans, strong, manly, efficient, ruthless are banging at its doors while local rulers, the epitomy of little men in office, vain, impotent, troublesome, never stop quarreling.

Critics never cease to be amazed by the use he makes of his poetical means. His language is prosaic, never emotive, almost flat, his tone didactic but modest so that his work becomes a brilliant specimen of antirhetorical discourse. He is, himself, mostly absent from his poetry. His lyricism is therefore "objective." He does not show emotion, he provokes it in the reader. His use of irony is consummate as he depicts his anti-heroes deluding themselves. He spares no one, not even himself as he portrays the lustful, remorseful creature that he is.

He is, in essence, a man of many cultures. The pace and reflective temper of his mind were of the orient. His education was accidental. His self-restraint was English. He discovered poetry in a coffee shop, in a backyard, in an office. Even his clerking at the ministry was absorbed into his style. A perfectionist, he believed with Paul Valéry that "a poem is never finished, only abandoned." Celebrating ordinariness, the excitement of sexual chase, the wonders of the human body, he pokes fun at the holders of office and revels in the decadent environment of his choice. Through his poems, totally devoid of metaphor, he conveys a sense of rise and decay of all cultures not just that of his beloved Hellenistic period. The voice is dry, the idiom precise, the music subdued. His is a masterful poetry of the laconic. His work translates beautifully into English.

CENTER-UNION—NEW FORCES. The party was reconstituted in 1974 by deputies who had supported Georgios Papandreou (q.v.) in his 1965 clash with the Crown and a coalition of social democrats and resistance fighters against the junta. The Center-Union—New Forces combination entered the campaign of 1974 with the reputation of possessing candidates of the highest caliber, but the overwhelming presence of Constantinos Karamanlis (q.v.) limited its percentage to 20.42 percent of the vote. The elections of 1977 dealt a heavy blow to the party which secured only 11.6 percent of the vote. Badly split even before the elections, members of the New Forces formed an independent grouping and others left EDIK (the name of the party since 1976) after the original leader George Mavros was replaced by John Zigdis. The

New Democracy, with its opening towards the Center attracted some wayward deputies, other joined John Pesmazoglu's Social Democratic party (KODESO) which aspired to create a modernized alternative to the expiring Center. The elections of October 1981, with their polarizing effect, eradicated the splinter parties of the Center from Parliament. (Pesmazoglu won a seat in the European Parliament elections held simultaneously with the national elections). The most significant segment of the Center's traditional constituency opted for PASOK (q.v.).

CENTRAL GREECE. The administrative area including the island of Euboea and the departments of Aitoloakarnania, Attica (with the exception of the greater Athens [q.v.] area), Boeotia, Evrytania, Phokis, and Phthiotis is called Central Greece (*Sterea Ellas*). It is the only part of continental Greece to have been incorporated in the nascent Greek state in 1830. Its present population is estimated at 1,123,000. The largest town is Agrinion (pop. 48,116), the highest mountain is Ghiona (2,510 meters), and the second highest Mount Parnassus (2,457 meters), the site of important deposits of bauxite. The largest river is the Acheloos (220 kilometers). Between the mouth of the Acheloos and the historic town of Missolonghi, where Lord Byron died during the War of Independence (q.v.), lies the largest lagoon in Greece, also one of the most important wetlands in the country.

The Euripos Strait between the mainland and the island of Euboea displays a hitherto unexplained phenomenon: alternating water currents change direction sometimes as often as 14 times a day. It is said that Aristotle in his desperation to solve the problem flung himself into the waters. The most historic archaeological site in Central Greece is Delphi (q.v.).

CINEMA. The seventh art has, to a considerable extent, remained local to Greece or at least confined to Greek-speaking audiences. It started with documentaries in the beginning of the twentieth century and moved on to folkloric stories of passion and death. Amongst the pioneers were the Gaziadis brothers, Dimos Vratsanos and Orestis Laskos. In 1939, the very gifted Filopimin Finos produced the first "talkie" and created Finos Films, a company with fully equipped studios and facilities. In the 1950s, Greek films made their debut in the international market with the work of the gifted director Michael Cacoyannis. In the 1960s, Nicos Coundouros became known mainly in film festivals with his polished work. In the 1970s the new names of directors whose films crossed with some success the borders of their country are Pantelis Voulgaris, and Theo Angelopoulos, who specialized in political films ("Travelling Players," "Days of '36," etc). The latter collected numerous prizes at film festivals, but none of his films was ever a box-office success anywhere in the world. So called "films of quality" are supported or even entirely financed by the Hellenic Cinema Center as they are never popular with audiences. Most new directors make themselves known at the Thessaloniki Film Festival which started in 1960 and is held at the same time as the traditional Trade Fair every September in that city.

CLIMATE. Greece belongs as a whole, in spite of important local variations, to the Mediterranean climatic zone characterized generally by moderate precipitation (700 mm annual average), hot and dry summers, and mild winters. The Mediterranean area constitutes a single "climatic region," marked by winter rains and long summer droughts, by light soils and dry farming for the most part, in contrast to the irrigation farming on which so much of the ancient Near Eastern economy was based. It is a region of relatively easy habitation and much outdoor living. Greece is located between the annual isotherms of 14.5 C and 19.5 C. Annual sunshine ranges from 2,300 to 3,100 hours with the monthly maximum in July (375 hours on average) and the minimum in January (114 hours on average).

When it comes to the climate of Greece, people in the West often tend to take advertisements at their face value. Greece, however, is not just a pretty place, a sun-drenched Mediterranean country of blue skies and purple seas.

It is not true that Greece only comes to life in the spring and the summer for the enjoyment of tourists offering a jasmine-scented dream of white-washed cottages and crystal clear water as the travel posters promise. Greece is not, and has never been, a one-mood country. Alongside Aegean gentility and *joie de vivre*—so vividly portrayed in Odysseus Elytis (q.v.) poetry—there are the ten-foot snowdrifts on the Albanian border in winter, and heavy rainfalls in Macedonia (q.v.), the harsh aspect of a country which is both Central European and Mediterranean.

The climate does indeed belong, as a whole, to the Mediterranean climatic zone, but the country's proximity to the sea and its complex geology give rise to a number of differing regional climates. This goes some way to explain the richness and diversity of Greek wildlife. Mountainous masses of the northern and northwestern parts of the country make for a very uneven distribution of rainfall. The relatively isolated land basins and the numerous dispersed watersheds help to create not just regional but even local climates of some variety. As is well known, what matters in the formation of climate is not just the distance of a given area from the equator but also the distance from sea level. Where, as is the case in Greece, mountains literally rise from the sea and change direction abruptly, rainfall is strongly affected. The humid western winds cause a significantly higher precipitation in the western parts of the country. The overall characteristics of Mediterranean climates, i.e., moderate precipitation, hot and dry summers, and mild winters, are thus diversified as one moves from eastern Greece, which is more typically Mediterranean, towards the northwestern part of the country, which is more like central Europe.

COLONELS' COUP AND REGIME (1967–1974) The Colonels' coup of 21 April 1967 was brought about by various factors:

1) International detente reduced the significance of the army as a guarantor of internal order and diminished the likelihood of an external communist threat. The furious efforts of the conspirators to justify the overthrow of parliamentary democracy were based on allegations of a communist conspiracy.

2) The conflict over the control of the armed forces, which was at the center of the confrontation between Georgios Papandreou (q.v.) and King Constantine (q.v.), resulted in

the gradual emancipation of certain officers from political and royal influence.

3) Professional grievances caused by reduced promotional opportunities also drove officers to the side of the junta. The dictatorship of 21 April 1967 created vacancies in the forces through mass dismissals and retirements, which were predictably filled with friends of the regime. Following a belated attempt to overthrow the military regime in December, King Constantine fled the country.

Colonel Georgios Papadopoulos, an intelligence officer, became the military regime's strongman. His 1968 constitution reflected the insecurity of the Colonels and their ignorance in administering power. By 1973, Papadopoulos decided to seek a way out of his isolation by civilianizing the regime. On 1 June he declared the Monarch deposed following an abortive naval coup, and proclaimed the birth of a "presidential parliamentary republic" ratified by a referendum. Papadopoulos assumed the Presidential office which was vested with wide legislative and executive authority that diminished the power granted to the armed forces by the 1968 constitution. The coup of Brigadier Dimitrios Ioannides (a gray eminence of the regime), that overthrew Papadopoulos in 1973, represented those officers who were reluctant to give up their influence on public affairs.

The attempt of Ioannides against President Makarios's life in Cyprus (q.v.) that triggered the Turkish invasion in 1974, and gave the military regime its death blow. Constantinos Karamanlis (q.v.) was summoned from self-exile in Paris to assume the task of restoring democracy in Greece after seven years of dictatorship.

COMMUNIST PARTY OF GREECE. The Communist Party of Greece, or KKE (Kommunistiko Komma Elladas) by its Greek acronym, is the oldest political party in the country. Its forerunner was created in November 1918, in the wake of the Russian revolution, under the name of Socialist Labor Party of Greece, with the goal to establish a socialist republic in Greece. In 1920, the party jointed the Communist International and, in 1924, it changed its name to "Communist." Its proclaimed political aim was to bring down the "bourgeois fascist republic" of Greece and to "impose by arms a government of peasants, workers and refugees."

The party's appeal to uprooted refugees who in 1922—fleeing the Turks from Asia Minor—had landed in mainland Greece in the hundreds of thousands was not negligible. To this day the deeply felt "anomie" created then by the shock of a gigantic military and diplomatic humiliation, the shattering of a national myth, and a challenge which came close to overwhelming the very structure of the state is pushing ordinary people to extremes and is generating radical attitudes of rejection of any established authority.

In 1926, the KKE obtained 4.38 percent of the votes in a general election and elected ten MPs. In 1931, Nikos Zachariadis, himself coming from a refugee family, became the charismatic leader of the party and retained his post or at least his grip on it; on and off, until 1956 when he was first demoted, then expelled. During the turbulent 1920s and 1930s when Greece experienced 19 changes of government, three changes of regimen, seven military coups and innumerable acts of sedition, the KKE kept an uneasy balance between parliamentary and revolutionary aspirations fuelled by trade union militancy, strikes and street fighting.

The Communist Party was not able to feed upon national discontent and establish a firm foothold in Greek society and politics for two main reasons. The first one has to do with the normal Greek rejection of collective discipline and blind obedience to directives issued from above. The second was the party's proposal—under Soviet insistence—that Greece's Macedonian territories, newly acquired after the Balkan wars, be surrendered again in the interest of a separate Macedonian nation. Such ideas were utterly rejected by the Greeks and even at the nadir of the Greek slump in 1935 the party was never able to muster more than 50,000 votes in a national election. Its fortunes were changed when the Comintern allowed the KKE to change its attitude to Macedonia (q.v.), while the return of King George II (q.v.) from exile in 1935 rekindled radical republican attitudes and helped KKE's fortunes. On the other hand the introduction of proportional representation allowed the Communists to elect in January 1936 enough MPs to allow them to hold the balance of power in parliament with disastrous results which led to General Metaxas (q.v.) dissolving parliament. Under the Metaxas dictatorship, established in 1936, the KKE almost disappeared as an organized force with its leaders in jail and its underground cells heavily and effectively infiltrated by Metaxas's secret police.

KKE's hour came when Greece was occupied by the Axis forces. In the absence of other leaders Communist militants organized the National Liberation Front or Ethniko Apelephterotiko Metopo (EAM), which in due course attracted a large number of non-communists and a number of "agrarian," "democratic," and "socialist" parties. The Front equipped itself with a military wing, the Ethnikos Laikos Apelephterotikos Strator (ELAS), and virtually annihilated all rival resistance organizations while the Communists who controlled it prepared themselves to take over power once the occupation forces had left the country. Their plans were thwarted by the British forces in Athens (q.v.) during the uprising of "bloody December" in 1944, which ended in the total defeat of the Communists. The party, licking its wounds, refused to take part in the elections of March 1946 and, much against the advice of the Italian Communist leader Palmiro Togliatti, started military operations against the state. The KKE was banned in September 1947 and waged a ruinous Civil War which ended in August 1949 with the total defeat of its so called "Democratic Army." The "revolutionary road" having led it to disaster, the KKE played the parliamentary game through its front political organization called United Democratic Left or Euiaia Dimocratiki Aristera (EDA) whose leadership, however, sometimes clashed with the exiled or underground Communists in charge of the KKE party organizations. The Colonels (q.v.) who took over the country in April 1967 banned EDA together with all the other political parties.

In 1968, a serious split between the Moscow-oriented orthodox communists and the Eurocommunists weakened the KKE further. After the fall of the junta in 1974 the Communist Party was legalized for the first time after 27 years. Having opted for the "parlimentary road to socialism'' the Communists tried to win influence and gain votes. In a series of tactical alliances and splits, and amidst much internal dissension, the KKE kept shrinking. In the elections of 1990 it took part in a Coalition of the broad left which polled 10.3 percent of the vote and elected 19 MPs. However, the KKE decided to leave the ''revisionist'' Coalition in June 1991, not without losing to it hundreds of its own activists as well as MPs. Opinion polls showed the KKE's strength in 1993 to be less than the 4.38 percent with which it started its checkered career in the elections of 1926.

CONSTANTINE I, KING (1868–1922). Born in Attica, the first child of King George (q.v.) and Queen Olga, Constantine studied at the Greek Military Academy and the Academy of War in Berlin. In 1889, he married Princess Sophie, sister of the German Kaiser Wilhelm II.

As the commander-in-chief of the Greek armed forces in the disastrous campaign of 1897 against the Ottomans, he was held responsible for the ignominious defeat. He was, however, exonerated during the Balkan Wars (q.v.) after leading the Greek forces to a series of victories. He became King in 1913, after George I was assassinated, and continued to interfere in the shaping of Greek foreign policy. During the First World War (q.v.) he clashed with his liberal Prime Minister, Eleftherios Venizelos (q.v.), who was made to resign on two occasions. A choice between entering the war on the side of the Triple Entente and remaining neutral became the issue that divided the Prime Minister and the King and caused the ''national schism'' among their followers. Constantine was forced to abdicate in favor of his second son Alexander in 1917, but was reinstated in 1920 by a plebiscite. He lost his throne in 1922 following the collapse of the Greek campaign in Asia Minor and died in Palermo, not long after.

CONSTANTINE II, KING (1940–   ). Born in Attica, the first son of King Paul and Queen Frederika (q.v.), Constantine studied at the Greek Military Academy. He won a gold medal in sailing in the 1960 Olympic Games of Rome. After King Paul's death in 1964, Constantine became King of the Hellenes and married Princess Anna Maria of Denmark.

His rule was short (1964–67), marked by his clash with Prime Minister Georgios Papandreou (q.v.) over the actual extent of his royal authority. His involvement in politics undermined the credibility of the Crown and, in 1967, he failed to oppose the Colonel's coup. His abortive attempt to oust them eight months later obliged him to leave the country with his family. He was dethroned in 1973 by the Colonels and, in 1974, Greece became a republic through a plebiscite that decided the fate of the Crown.

CONSTITUTION. The 1975 constitution, which is currently in force, was drafted after the collapse of the Colonels' regime. The document defines the country's political system as a parliamentary democracy headed by a President of the Republic elected by Parliament every five years and is inspired by:

1) The principle of popular sovereignty exercised through a system of representation.
2) The democratic principle which signifies the linking of freedom with equality.
3) The principle of the division of powers.
4) The principle of the legality of the activities of the executive.

The Government must enjoy the confidence of Parliament. The latter consists of one house and has 300 elected members. Aside from the 12 "State Members" elected by the entire body of voters, MPs are elected by free ballot indirect and universal suffrage. The full duration of each Parliament is four years and the electoral system is one of proportional representation.

CONSTRUCTION. Thanks to the construction boom of the 1960s and 1970s this important industry (q.v.) accounted for 8.5 percent of GDP in 1980. In 1990, this figure fell to 6.9 percent. Construction is still, however, one of the leading sectors of the economy (q.v.) because the hunger for housing is far from satisfied, especially as many households are increasingly able to afford a second home in the countryside. There was nonetheless in 1991 a sharp downturn in construction, especially in the sector of private dwellings. Cement consumption rose, however, suggesting that the bulk of construction work was being done in 1991 on infrastructure projects largely co-financed by the European Community (q.v.).

COURTS OF LAW. In terms of their composition, law courts are classified as ordinary (all judges belong to the judiciary), special (such as court martials composed of officers), and mixed (composed of judges and lay juries). In terms of their competence, courts are classified as civil, criminal, and administrative, the latter dealing with citizens' complaints against state or municipal authorities. The highest administrative court is the Council of State.

Civil courts comprise magistrates' courts, courts of first instance, courts of appeal, and the Supreme Court (Areios Pagos), which is the court of last instance and decides on whether the law was properly interpreted and applied by the lower courts.

There are also fiscal tribunals and, finally, the Supreme Special Court, which acts as a constitutional court and deals mainly with electoral matters. See also JUSTICE.

CRETE. The largest Greek island (8,261 square kilometers) with a population of 536,980, Crete's largest town is Heracleion (117,167 pop.), followed by Chania (50,071). Its mountains are the extension of the mountain ranges of the Peloponnese (q.v.) and mainland Greece. The highest is Ida (2,456 meters). There are no noteworthy plains or rivers in Crete. Its main products are olive oil, sultanas, wine, and citrus fruits. The warm subtropical climate allows the cultivation of lucrative early varieties of fruits and vegetables. Crete is a beautiful island with many devotees all over the world. As Edward Lear wrote: "a sort of pearly silver mist involves all the isle." It attracts every year thousands of tourists who have become in recent years its main source of income.

Historically, in the second millennium B.C., Crete witnessed the efflorescence of the Minoan civilization whose sudden disappearance in 1500 B.C. after the volcanic eruption of Thera is still somewhat of a mystery. Crete attracted many invaders during her long history, such as Romans, Turks and Saracens. Venice bought the island in 1204 from Boniface, Marquis of Montferrat, leader of the Crusaders. A long coveted prize whose praises had been sung since the mist of time, Crete became the jewel of the Venetian possessions. According to Homer, ''amidst the dark blue sea, there lies a land called Crete, a rich and lovely island, washed by the waves on every side, populous beyond compute, and boasting ninety cities.'' Whether the island still had as many cities as all that when Venice bought it in the thirteenth century is doubtful, but at least it was rich and strategically located. It was the fourth largest in the Mediterranean and was located about 100 kilometers south of the Greek mainland, almost equidistant from Europe, Asia and Africa.

Crete developed a prosperous commerce under the Venetians, as did many of the islands and mainland ports under their domination. But Venetian control was too arbitrary for the freedom-loving Cretans who have retained to this day a fierce sense of independence and local pride in their traditions and culture. Cretan uprisings had become frequent during the four centuries of Venetian occupation. In the almost 230 years of Ottoman rule the Cretans rose again and again against the Turks. Crete joined the Greek state only in 1913 after numerous abortive uprisings. The protecting powers regarded Crete as too remote and too rich a prize to be handed over to the new Greek state at the dawn of its independence. They therefore experimented with various forms of local autonomy under the control of England, France, Russia, and Greece with results bordering on the disastrous. Union with Greece in 1913 brought lasting peace to this turbulent island which has given birth to prominent Greek statesman. Sophocles Venizelos (q.v.) was Cretan. So is former Prime Minister Constantinos Mitsotakis (q.v.)

CURRENCY. The drachma, as the local currency is called since antiquity, after having been pegged to the dollar for 25 years, was floated on 8 March 1975 in an effort to pave the economy's way into the European Community (q.v.). It was devalued twice by the PASOK (q.v.) government, once in 1983 by 15 percent and by a similar percentage in 1985. It has since been allowed to slide against various currencies, but not as fast as the differential rates of inflation would dictate (in 1991 inflation was at 19.5 percent compared to the EC 5 percent average). This is the policy of the so-called ''hard drachma'' which in fact keeps the currency overvalued and thus helps efforts to reduce inflation (devaluations increase automatically prices of imported goods and thus fuel domestic inflation).

The drachma is in the European Monetary System (0.8 percent of the ECU) but not in the Exchange Rate Mechanism. This helped Greece to successfully weather the storm in the money markets in September 1992, when the Bank of Greece (q.v.) had to draw on a substantial amount of its reserves to defend the currency. Most of the fleeing drachmas, however, were repatriated within a week or so as soon as speculators, having burned their fingers, became convinced that the anticipated devaluation would not materialize.

CYPRUS. Over 225 kilometers in length, Cyprus is the third largest island in the Mediterranean, after Sicily and Sardinia. Located between Turkey and Syria in the southeastern Mediterranean, i.e., 65 km off Syria, the island has always been prized, in history, for its wealth notably in copper. The very word ''copper'' is derived from the name Cyprus. The island's morphology is dominated by the Kyrenia range, rising to a height of over 915 meters along the northern coast. There is also a massif in the southwest, the highest point of which is Mount Olympus (1954 meters) as well as a central plain, the Messaoria. The climate is hot and dry in the summer while in the winter the mountains are for many weeks covered with snow.

The first Cypriots settled on the island even before the Bronze Age around 4000 B.C. The early mining and working of copper sustained a large population. The island came under Egyptian rule at about 1500 B.C. The first evidence of settlement by the Phoenicians, who turned the island into a trading center, dates from the eighth century B.C. By the next century the Greeks had already thickly colonized the island producing beautiful artifacts as shown in the excavations at the ancient cities of Paphos and Citium. Foreign invaders of

Cyprus succeeded each other, over the centuries, Assyrians, Egyptians (again), Persians, Cyprus came under Alexander the Great in 333 B.C. and Ptolemy I of Egypt upon Alexander's death. In 57 B.C. it was made a Roman province.

After the division of the Roman territories, Cyprus, this most Greek of the Mediterranean islands populated by Greeks, but rarely in its history run by Greeks, came under the jurisdiction of the Eastern Roman Empire or Byzantine Empire. Throughout the Christian era, Cyprus has always been a pawn on the Mediterranean chessboard. It suffered savage raids by the Arabs. In 1191, it was captured from its Byzantine despot by Richard the Lionhearted during the Third Crusade and was sold to the Knights Templar who in turn sold it to Guy de Lusignan, titular king of Jerusalem. Descendants of the de Lusignan family are still to be found in today's Cyprus. After three centuries of vain efforts to Latinize the stubbornly Greek Orthodox (q.v.) Cypriots the island was acquired by the Venetians through marriage ties. In 1571, Cyprus fell to the Turks—after a prolonged siege— and became part of the Ottoman Empire. In 1878, the British took over administrative control, though the island remained nominally part of the Ottoman Empire. When World War I (q.v.) broke out Britain annexed the island, in 1914, and the seizure was officially recognized as valid by Turkey in the Treaty of Lausanne in 1923. Cyprus became a British crown colony in 1925.

During World War II (q.v.), and then again during the Suez Crisis of 1956, Cyprus served as an airbase and a refueling station for Britain. It was in the 1950s, the great era of decolonization, that the Greek Cypriots decided the time had come to fight for their self-determination. The struggle led to a form of controlled independence which gave the Turkish community in the island a right to share power with the Greeks while Turkey, Greece and Britain acted as guarantor powers. Cyprus became a republic in 1960 and a member of the Commonwealth in 1961 while Britain retained sovereignty over two military bases.

Thereafter the power-sharing system broke down. There were clashes between the Greek and Turkish communities and in 1964 a UN peace-keeping force was sent to the island.

The Turkish Cypriots—forming 20 percent of the population—withdrew into isolated enclaves and left the running of the government in the hands of the Greek Cypriots who had no access to the Turkish Cypriot enclaves. Following a coup organized by the Greek junta in Athens, in July 1974, the Cypriot President, Archbishop Makarios III (q.v.) was temporarily overthrown.

Turkey then invaded the island, conquered some 40 percent of its territory, drove most of the Greek population out—thus turning them into refugees in their own country—and established a Turkish Cypriot Administration in the occupied territories which was made into a state, in 1983, recognized only by Turkey. Talks have been led between the two sides on and off ever since, under the auspices of the UN Secretary-General, but Turkish intransigeance rendered pointless all efforts at a settlement.

CYRIL AND METHODIUS. Two Greek brothers, monks from Thessaloniki, who evangelized the Slavs and devised a script for the Slavonic languages based on the Greek alphabet. As the expansion of Orthodoxy (q.v.) was blocked by dissident Christian Churches first to the east and south and then to the west of Constantinople this left the way open only to the north. In 863, St. Cyril (826–869 A.D.) and St. Methodius (815–853 A.D.), two learned Greek monks from Thessaloniki, traveled northward to bring to the Slavs the word of the Lord.

Patriarch Photius, one of the most impressive if controversial Orthodox hierarchs, chose them because Methodius was a brilliant administrator while his brother Constantine, later renamed Cyril, was an accomplished theologian and linguist, proficient in Hebrew, Arabic, and even Samaritan. Most important, though, was the fact that they had both been fluent since childhood in the idiom spoken by Slavs who had settled in the wider area around Thessaloniki. They were given the task to go north and spread the word of the Lord in response to a request sent in 862 to the Emperor by the ruler of Great Moravia (roughly today's Czechia and Slovakia). Before leaving, however, they sat down and translated into Slavonic the Gospels, Acts, Epistles, and all basic liturgical texts. It is thus that Church Slavonic became the vehicle for the Christianization of the Slavs, a development very much in line with the Orthodox policy of preaching to heathen in their vernacular and not exclusively in Greek. Rome was—and still is—insisting on the use of Latin only.

The trouble was, though, that the Slavs did not have a written language. The brothers realized that oral instruction in Slavonic would prove ephemeral. No Orthodox Church could exist without texts. Cyril simply had to invent an alphabet. He came up with what is called the glagolithic script also known as Old Church Slavonic. This was changed later in the ninth century A.D. in Bulgaria and has since been called "Cyrillic" in deference to Cyril, though the change was not his personal work.

The two brothers achieved only limited success in their missionary activity proper. The Khazars, north of the Caucasus region, turned a deaf ear to them because, having already adopted monotheism, they were under strong Jewish influence. Hebrew was the language of their court. Their already entrenched Jewish faith made them impervious to the Christian message. This was nothing new. Monotheists such as Jews and Moslems were—as a rule—not convertible to Christianity. In Moravia and Bulgaria the Greek mission clashed with German missionaries who insisted on using the "filioque" though this was not yet officially endorsed by the Papacy. Cyril and Methodius traveled to Rome where they appealed to the Pope to extend his protection over their mission. Pope Hadrian II gave them full support, approved the translation made, and even laid copies of the Slavonic service books on the altars of the principal churches in Rome.

Cyril died in Rome but Methodius returned to Moravia where, in spite of the Pope's approval, he was persecuted by the Germans and put in prison for more than a year. After his death in 885, the Germans expelled his followers from the country, selling a number of them as slaves. The attempts to found a Slavonic Church in Moravia had ended in failure but the Slavonic liturgy lingered on. In Bulgaria, Serbia, Russia and Romania (a Latin country), the Orthodox Church took firm root.

The outstanding contribution of Cyril and Methodius was not just the access they gave Slavs to a sophisticated system of Christian beliefs but also the creation of a literary language which gave them the indispensable tool to create their own civilization. Byzantine culture and the Orthodox faith even if they were, to begin with, restricted to the local elites, became in time, thanks to the Slavonic garb woven by Cyril and Methodius, an integral part of the daily life of the Slavonic peoples. This gift is recognized by Slavs all over the world. Pope Paul II has repeatedly acknowledged the debt owned by Slav Christianity to "our two Greek brothers."

-D-

DANGLIS, PANAYOTES (1853–1924). Officer of the Greek army and politician during the crucial period of the "national schism" between King Constantine I (q.v.) and Eleftherios Venizelos (q.v.). Danglis graduated from the Military Academy in 1877 and saw action in the war of 1897. Between 1908–09 he directed the Macedonian Committee and the Panhellenic Organization, both assigned with the role of coordinating Greek irredentist activities. A Major General by the First Balkan War (q.v.), he served as Chief of General Staff. In 1914, Danglis resigned with the rank of Lieutenant General and was elected deputy of Jannina in Epirus under the banner of Venizelos's Liberal Party (q.v.). Although a moderate by nature, in 1916 he joined Venizelos and Admiral Coundouriotes as part of the triumvirate heading the secessionist government of Thessaloniki. Throughout the war effort on the side of the Triple Entente, Danglis as Commander-in-Chief of the Greek forces, played a vital role in recruiting and organizing troops for the Balkan Front.

In 1920, after Venizelos's defeat at the polls, and his departure from Greece, Danglis acted as his stand-in as president of a governing body of the Liberal Party.

DELIYORGIS, EPAMINONDAS (1829–1879). An important parliamentarian who made his mark as a young opponent of King Otto Wittelsbach (q.v.). He was elected deputy from Messolonghi in 1859, took an active part in the 1862 expulsion of

King Otto and became Prime Minister several times during his lifetime. He was a champion of Greek-Turkish cooperation and friendship.

DELPHI. Delphi is today a modern village (2,462 pop.) built in 1892 about one kilometer west of the former village of Kastri, which stood on the ruins of ancient Delphi. Since then, the archaeologists' skill has revealed the ancient site in all its awesome beauty.

In antiquity, Delphi was not simply the site of the greatly respected Apollonian oracle. It was an institution whose practitioners embodied and transmitted the common cultural heritage of all Greeks providing a moral code of behavior for rulers and commoners alike and even functioning as a kind of court for settling disputes. It was commonly believed that Delphi was the navel of the world.

Delphi as a place was credited with oracular qualities long before its association with the Apollonian worship. Anyone approaching a specific chasm in the ground was said to be seized with supernatural "frenzy" and would begin prophesying. Legend has it that the locals placed a tripod over the opening in the ground and appointed a woman as a full-time professional prophetess. The importation from Crete of the cult of Apolla Delphinios (an island deity worshipped in the form of a dolphin) gave the place its name: Delphi. Apollo was thus a latecomer to the divination function and used mainly as a supernatural authority to back up the pronouncements of the oracle.

The considerable experience and increasing sophistication of the priesthood in the temple allowed them to act, in exchange for gifts and favors, as prestigious political and economic consultants to the mighty. They could not exact obedience nor enforce their instructions. They could only provide guidance to confused humans. In the words of E.R. Dodds in his famous *The Greeks and the Irrational:* "Greek society could scarcely have endured in the Archaic age . . . without Delphi, without the assurance that behind the seeming chaos there was knowledge and purpose." Delphi is today one of the most popular archaeological sites with visitors from all over the world.

DEMOTIC GREEK. A form of Greek based on the vernacular used by the mostly illiterate Greeks in their speech, poetry and songs during the 400 years of Ottoman occupation. Considered vulgar and inadequate by Greek scholars in the nineteenth century who tried to introduce and impose linguistic forms closer to ancient Greek it nevertheless found supporters among authors and linguists—some of them with extremist views on the subject—who tried to properly codify its morphology and syntax in order to have it officially recognized as the language of the nation. The issue was finally resolved in the mid-1970s by the government of Constantinos Karamanlis (q.v.). See also KATHARE-VOUSA; LANGUAGE.

DIASPORA see GREEK-AMERICANS; GREEKS OF THE DIASPORA

DILIYANNIS, THEODOROS (1824–1905). A political opponent of Harilaos Trikoupis (q.v.) and an exponent of populist direct rule. Born in Tripolis of the Peloponnese (q.v.), he studied law at the University of Athens and initially pursued a career in the civil service. He became Foreign Minister in 1863 and Prime Minister for the first time in 1885. Along with Harilaos Trikoupis, his long standing political opponent, he dominated Greek politics during the last quarter of the nineteenth century.

Diliyannis's personality and political position contrasted those of Trikoupis's in every respect. He was a populist who believed in direct democracy and in a self-sufficient agrarian rather than industrialized Greece. A xenophobe who accused Trikoupis of making Greece dependent on its foreign creditors, Diliyannis was at the same time an ardent exponent of irredentism, thus implicating Greece in Balkan power politics and causing the fiasco of 1897.

-E-

ECONOMY. Greece's age old problem has been the optimal use of the country's scarce resources of fertile land. After the devastating seven-year War of Independence (1821–28) (q.v.). Greeks lived mostly in a natural economy since non-existent road communications prevented any extended exchange. In the 1850's the growth of merchant shipping (q.v.), a rudimentary banking (q.v.) system and the emergence of a basic road infrastructure promoted an embryonic form of a market economy. In the 1880s the economy entered its precapitalism phase with the expansion of the use of machinery, the introduction of income tax by Harilaos Trikoupis (q.v.), the building of roads and railways, and some development of industry and commerce as 36.7 percent of the population became gainfully employed in such activities. Between 1909 and the onset of the Second World War (q.v.) in 1939 the Greek economy became recognizably market-oriented with a stock exchange, a banking system, a large merchant fleet, tolerable communications and expanding foreign trade (q.v.).

The decade 1940–50 was lost for Greece because of the war, the occupation and the ensuing Civil War. A large part of the country's fixed assets (industrial plants, roads, ships) was destroyed during this period. In the 1950s rehabilitation work started forthwith, generating high rates of growth (6 percent on average) and nearly full employment with negligible inflation—thanks to tight fiscal discipline. Average per capita Gross Domestic Product rose from $112 in 1951 to $270 in 1956, reaching $500 in 1960.

The 1961 Association Agreement with the EEC, though rudely interrupted during the seven-year dictatorship by the Colonels from April 1967 to July 1974, did prepare Greece for entry as was its proclaimed goal and, in January 1981, Greece became a full member of the European Community (q.v.).

The high growth rates of the 1960s, however, were impeded by the 1973 oil shock. Still, GDP grew by 6 percent per annum on average during the decade of the 1970s. Growth in the 1980s declined to 1.6 percent and, in 1987, Greece was overtaken by Portugal (until then the poorest member of the EC) although, in the former, more equitable distribution of income has eradicated poverty. The main reason for this decline of growth was the failure of the government to restructure the economy after the second oil price shock when most developed countries moved away from labor-intensive industries (q.v.) to output with higher technological content. These readjustments were followed by unemployment which Greek governments considered socially divisive. Instead of allowing uncompetitive firms to close down, PASOK (q.v.) undertook expensive measures to salvage them and made them the responsibility of the public sector.

Although EC membership revived foreign investment (q.v.) in Greece, the end of protectionism hit local firms hard. High levels of consumer demand have always outstripped domestic supply causing high imports and inflation, but the redistributive income policies of PASOK fueled private demand further and worsened the chronic trade imbalance. Transfers from the European Community cushioned the current account deficit although, at the same time, it encouraged demand and contributed to the trade deficit. The persistent trade imbalance owed much to the high unit labor costs and therefore low productivity. The income policy under the 1985 stabilization program reduced, within two years, unit labor costs below those in the Community, but when the policy was suspended the problems returned. High inflation since 1974 is largely due to cost-push through wage increases unmatched by a corresponding rise in productivity.

The factor which renders formal statistics unreliable in their negative picture of growth, is a vigorous "parallel" economy which defies fiscal control. Remittances from seamen and émigrés constitute another source of untaxable income that cannot therefore be monitored accurately. It is suggested that thanks to a vigorous "parallel" or "paraeconomy," Greece's GDP is actually 29 percent higher than officially recorded.

Remedies for the ailing economy do not differ widely and resemble the measures employed during the successful term of Kostas Simitis as Finance Minister (1986–87). New Democracy's (q.v.) stabilization program strives to lower inflation to single digits, to curtail PSBR (Public Sector Borrowing Requirement) to a level which will reduce aggregate public sector debt as a proportion of GDP and to cut the current account deficit to a level at which it can be sustained by non-debt capital inflows. See also AGRICULTURE; BANKING; CONSTRUCTION; ENERGY; EXPORTS; FISHERIES; FOREIGN TRADE; IMPORTS; INDUSTRY; INVESTMENT; MINERAL WEALTH; SHIPPING; STOCKBREEDING; TOURISM.

ECUMENICAL COUNCILS. The Orthodox Church (q.v.) has always upheld Christian traditions in an active, conscious way. During its long uninterrupted history it tried hard to give shape and consistency to the faith while keeping its flock fully informed of developments through intense theological activity and discussion. That is why the Orthodox Church is sometimes called the "Church of the Seven Councils" through which it gave final form to its doctrine.

1) The first General or Ecumenical Council of the Christian Church was convoked by Constantine himself in Nicaea in 325 A.D. The Emperor presided in person. The main work of this Nicene Council was to condemn a doctrine preached by a priest in Alexandria named Arius who maintained that the Son was inferior to the Father. A superior creature, no doubt, but less than a god. The Nicene Council decreed that this view was wrong and that Christ is "one in essence" (*homoousios*) with the Father, "true God from true God," "begotten not made," as mentioned in the official Nicene Creed which the Council drew up for the Christians to recite.

2) The second Ecumenical Council in 381 A.D. was held in Constantinople—which had in the meantime been built by Emperor Constantine. This Council, summoned by Emperor Theodosius, expanded and adapted the Nicene Creed to include the "right doctrine" (i.e., the Orthodox view) on the Holy Spirit. The Spirit—it was officially decided—is God exactly as the Father and Son are God, and He "proceeds from the Father" and is therefore worshipped and glorified together with Them. The Council also decided that the "Bishop of Constantinople" shall have the prerogatives of honor after the Bishop of Rome, because Constantinople is "New Rome" (Canon III).

This second Council is therefore very important for the Orthodoxy (q.v.) because it consolidates two significant positions which became crucial in the relations between the East and the West; namely: 1) the Spirit proceeds from the Father and 2) the Pope is recognized as "first among equals" but not as an absolute ecclesiastical monarch. This decision duly alarmed Rome which chose to ignore the offending Canon. On the procession of the Spirit, the Council was once again unanimous and unambiguous, drawing on the theological work of the three Cappadocian Fathers, i.e., of the Saints Gregory of Nazianzux (329–390), Basil the Great (330–379), and his younger brother Gregory of Nyssa (who died in 394), who left a vivid description of popular participation in the doctrinal controversies at the time of this second Ecumenical Council.

"The whole city is full of it, the squares, the market places, the crossroads, the alleyways; old-clothes men, money changers, food sellers; they are all busy arguing. If you ask someone to give you change, he philosophizes about the Begotten and the Unbegotten; if you enquire about the price of a loaf, you are told by way of reply that the Father is greater and the Son inferior; if you ask is my bath ready? the attendant answers that the Son was made out of nothing."

While the Nicene Creed had formerly emphasized the unit of God—Father and Son being one in essence (*ousia*) which makes each one *homoousios* to the other—the three Cappadocian Fathers stressed God's threeness: Father, Son, and Holy Spirit are three persons in one essence. The delicate balance between God's oneness and threeness was thus both firmly established and further developed. Arianism quickly ceased to be a living issue after 381 A.D.

3) The third Council, held in Ephesus in 431 A.D., dealt with a new challenge to the Trinitarian doctrine coming this time from a bishop of Constantinople named Nestorius. This hierarch made such a sharp distinction between Christ's humanity and Godhead that he seemed in danger of ending up not with one person but with two persons coexisting in the same human being. He sharpened the conflict by refusing to call the Virgin Mary "Mother of God" (*Theotokos*) arguing that she was to be called "Mother of Man" or at most "Mother of Christ" (*Christotokos*). The Council of Ephesus firmly rejected this view arguing that, if allowed, it might

separate the Incarnate Christ in two. The Virgin Mary did not give birth to a man loosely connected with God it was agreed, but to a single person who is both God and man.

4) The fourth and very important Council of Chalcedon, summoned in 451 A.D. by Emperor Marcian, dealt once more with an important Christological problem. Dioscorus of Alexandria and other theologians in that city maintained that there is in Christ only one nature, one *physis*. This is known as Monophysitism which some scholars hesitate to call a heresy, considering it more of a schism. The Council of Chalcedon rejected the views of the Monophysites and stipulated that Christ is not only *from* two natures (God's and Mary's) but *in* two natures "unconfusedly, unchangeably, indivisibly, inseparably." The peculiar property of each nature is preserved and both combine in one person and in one *hypostasis*. The Monophysites, who had overwhelming support in Egypt and Syria, opposed the Council of Chalcedon for dividing—as they saw it—Christ in two. They formed the non-Chalcedonian Oriental Churches which to this day continue their separate existence. Many Emperors tried to bridge the gap but to no avail.

5) The fifth Ecumenical Council, held in Constantinople in 553 A.D., reinterpreted the decrees of Chalcedon and sought to explain how the two natures of Christ unite to form a single person. The problem now centered on whether there was one or two activities in the incarnate Christ. It was therefore argued at the Council that one might accept the two natures but at the same time assert a single activity (*energia*) a doctrine called monenergism. Monenergists remained, on the whole, good Chalcedonians but attempted to gain Monophysite support by making this verbal allowance to a single energy which could perhaps function as a compromise. It was a good try but it didn't work. Compromise on issues of doctrine was never much appreciated in the Orthodox world.

6) The sixth Ecumenical Council (680–81 A.D.) condemned the "heresy" of the Monothelites whose view that there was only one will in Christ impaired, as the Council decreed, the fullness of Christ's humanity: human nature without a human will would be a mere abstraction. Christ therefore possessed both a divine and a human will. Mono-

thelitism was wrong and that—the Council authoritatively opined—was that.

7) The seventh Ecumenical Council took place in 787 A.D. in Nicaea as the first had done. This was the Council which settled a virulent controversy about the use of icons in the Church known as Iconoclasm (q.v.).

EDUCATION. In ancient Greek the verb *paidevo* meant to educate. In modern Greek it means to torment. It is obvious that teaching a lesson to Greeks over the centuries has generated some linguistic resentment. The noun *paideia* however, has always meant education, culture. For Greeks, education is a serious business especially since its acquisition has meant upward mobility ever since Greece became independent. In a country without an established aristocracy, the learned man has always had the edge.

The Ministry of National Education and Religious Affairs is responsible not just for shaping policy in this field but also for providing educational services to young Greeks. Education is compulsory for nine years (six years of elementary schooling and three years secondary) and free at all levels. About 9 percent of total budget spending goes to education. Secondary schools offer a choice between a technically-oriented course for those planning to pursue higher technical or vocational education and a general academic course intended for those wishing to end their education with a secondary school certificate or those wishing to enter institutions of higher education. Poor teaching, however, in state schools at the secondary level obliges most families to pay for private cramming schools (*frontistiria*) preparing pupils for university.

Families are extremely keen on securing university degrees for their offspring, believing it matters a lot for their economic and social advancement. Until 1964, most universities were concentrated in large cities. The University of Athens was founded in 1837, the National Technical University of Athens (Polytechneion) in 1836, the Aristotelian University of Thessaloniki in 1925, the Piraeus School of Industrial Studies in 1938, the University of Ioannina in 1964 and the University of Patras in 1966. After the fall of the junta in 1974, universities were founded in Crete, Thrace, Thessaly and the Aegean. In spite of this proliferation, the demand for tertiary education remains unsatisfied and annually drives thousands of young people abroad regardless of the great cost involved.

ELYTIS, ODYSSEUS (1911–   ). Contemporary poet born in Crete (q.v.) to a family of soap manufacturers named Alepoudelis who came from the Aegean island of Lesbos. His pen name Odysseus Elytis was adopted in 1935 when he contributed to the magazine *To Nea Grammata* (''New Letters''). It is a compound of the words *Ellas* (Greece), *Eleni* (Helen), *Elpida* (Hope) and *Eleftheria* (Freedom), all dominant in his poetic vocabulary.

Elytis is not a prolific poet. Though he matured in the 1930s, he managed to stay away from the *mal du sicle,* i.e., the angst and the despair which drove two of his contemporary authors—Kostas Kariotakis, a minor poet, and Pericles Yannopoulos, a writer obsessed by the worship of ancient Greece (archaeolatry)—to take their own lives. Elytis is the polar opposite of a suicidal intellectual. He has a passionate love affair with his small world of the Aegean which he consistently depicts as a kind of private Eden full of light, color and happiness.

Elytis studied law at Athens University and, in 1940, when Mussolini attacked Greece, served as an army lieutenant in Albania. His poem entitled ''The Heroic and Mournful Song for the Lieutenant Killed in Albania'' stems from his wartime experiences in the bitter winter of 1940–41. His first collection of poems appeared in 1940 under the title *Prosanatolismoi* (''Orientations'') and showed him to be, right from the start, a bold user of Surrealist technique obsessed with the celebration of the Aegean. His second volume *''Sun the First''* (1943) continues in the same vein. In 1945, he went to Paris where he studied literature for four years at the Sorbonne. He traveled widely and never married.

His main work, published in 1959 after 15 years of silence, is ''Axion Esti'' (translated both as ''Worth It Is'' or ''Praised Be''), a long poem similar in intent to the ''Mythistorima'' (''Myth of History'') by George Seferis (q.v.) or the

"Romiossini" ("Greekness") by Yannis Ritsos (q.v.), in
that Elytis too attempts to identify the vital elements in
Greece's 3000 year old historical, mythical and religious
tradition. In this long ambitious poem which combines the
Biblical account of Creation with an imaginative vision of
Greece's history Elytis shows his predilection for Orthodox
(q.v.) liturgy (not its beliefs), echoes deliberately the language of the New Testament and blends it with his luxuriant
imagery about the sun, the sea, and the birds. In this
poem—which most probably gained him the Nobel prize—
heavy with pagan and Christian symbolism, Elytis projects
himself as a magician, a wordsmith and a prophet. He charts
most faithfully Greek experiences of defeat, humiliation and
struggle only to enthusiastically celebrate the regenerative
powers of living life to the fullest not in the imaginative
future but in the earthly tangible "worth-living-for" present.
The poem closes with a hymn of praise which seeks to sanctify
the simple and eternal features of the Aegean after the poet has
extensively dealt with the essentials: Nature, Love, Death, and
Honor. In his "Six and one Regrets for the Sky," which also
appeared in 1959, he contrasts a world at the mercy of
uncontrollable passions with an ideal of luminous serenity.

The Nobel prize for literature was given to him in 1979
under his real name, Odysseus Alepoudelis, "for his poetry
which, against the background of Greek tradition, depicts
with sensuous strength and intellectual lucidity modern
man's struggle for freedom and creativity." His language
ranges from the Septuagint to demotic ballads, Cretan epics
and the vernacular prose of the self-taught hero of the War of
Independence (q.v.), General Makriyannis. The feeding is
often deep, the structure intricate, the imagery lush but
always extraodinarily precise. He graduated from Surrealism
with a capacity to trace beauty in the concrete, a kind of
Salvator Dali of poetry. His lyricism and his flamboyance,
his exultation in the possibilities of language have found
great favor with French audiences. The exuberance and
allusiveness of Elyti's verse translates well into French.

ENERGY. The country is not self-sufficient in energy. Local
production does not exceed 7 million ton oil equivalent

(TOE) a year, so that it must import annually 17 TOE, mainly in the form of crude oil (of which however some 6 TOE are reexported as petroleum products). The long-term policy is to replace oil with indigenous resources such as lignite and hydroelectricity. Successive governments have ruled out the use of nuclear energy because of seismic activity. Solar and wind power are as yet undeveloped.

Greece has only one oil field of its own named Prinos, 8 kilometers southwest of the island of Thassos in the northern Aegean. Production in 1991 was 6mm barrels. Gas is produced in small amounts in a field south of the city of Kavala in Northern Greece. Output in 1991 was estimated at 91 million cubic meters. Lignite, on the other hand, is plentiful. Proven reserves, mainly in Northern Greece, are estimated at 6.4 billion tons of which 60 percent are exploit-able. Most mines are operated by the state-run Public Power Corporation (DEI by its Greek acronym) in charge of production and distribution of electricity.

About 99 percent of the population use electric power. Annual per capital consumption is 2,909 kwh (as against 75 kwh in 1950), compared to an EC average of 4,559 kwh. Progress, however, has been phenomenal. In 1950 only 823 towns and villages in Greece were supplied with electricity while the Athens (q.v.) area accounted for 84 percent of the country's total consumption. By 1973, some 6,657 villages were receiving electricity while Athens' consumption had fallen to 40 percent. The largest consumer of power today is industry (35 percent) followed by domestic and commercial use (33.1 percent) and the transport sector (29.4 percent). Most of this power is produced by lignite-fired units (61.0 percent). A power station at Megalopolis in the Peloponnese (q.v.) successfully utilizes lignite of very low calorific value and high moisture content. Oil-fired units account for 28 percent hydroelectric units for 10 percent and coal-fired units for 3 percent of production. Some power is imported from neighboring countries.

In the consumption of energy from all sources, petroleum products come first (53 percent), followed by electric power (40 percent), while direct burning of solid fuels is small (7 percent). Consumption of gas is insignificant.

ENVIRONMENTAL PROBLEMS. The long history of human settlement in Greece has left its marks on the country. As early as 2,300 years ago, Artistotle noted in his *Meteorologika* the connection between desertification and big floods. Since then, farming, the mechanization of agriculture (q.v.) and the weight of increasingly numerous active human beings have increased the pressures on the environment. Of special importance during the past 40 years are the growing use of fertilizers and specialization, partly encouraged by the European Community's (q.v.) Common Agricultural Policy. Nor is Greece exempt from the problems created by rapid industrialization.

Meanwhile, environmental issues have become popular in Greece. The media are dealing with them on an almost daily basis. However, after an initial enthusiasm reflected in the view that anything greener must be better the sober language of priorities, of costs and benefits, has had to be learned anew. The most extreme forms of anti-development fervor have not been prevalent in Greece, not even among militant ecologists, perhaps because memories of poverty, famine, and technological backwardness are still vivid in those individuals over fifty years old who practically run the country. Nor is there too much nostalgia for the good old days of simple village life *à la* Zorba the Greek.

In dealing with environmental problems the Greek government has tried to find solutions compatible with economic development. It is also joining in collective efforts through the United Nations and European Community. Among other things, it has raised the costs of being dirty. Polluters have been made to pay stiff fines. Some have cleaned up their act, but there is still much to do. This process requires a lot of state funds and diligent bureaucrats, both in short supply. However, the environmental problems have been identified and measures to address them devised. The most serious problems in order of significance are: air pollution, water pollution, solid waste, land degradation, and noise. See also LAND DEGRADATION; POLLUTION, AIR; POLLUTION, WATER; SOLID WASTE; WATER MANAGEMENT.

EPIRUS. The northwestern part of Greece is called Epirus which means mainland or continent. Although Greece had acquired the town and district of Arta in western Epirus in 1881, it was not until the end of the Balkan Wars (q.v.) in 1913 that the southern and central parts of the province came into Greek hands. It borders with Albania to the north, Macedonia to the east, Thessaly to the south, and the Ionian sea to the west. It occupies an area of 9,203 square kilometers and has a population of 339,210. The largest town is Ioannina. Epirus is almost entirely mountainous, dominated by the Pindus range with the smallest percentage of arable land in the country (11.8 percent). The Epirotes have, therefore, since ancient times, turned to animal farming, i.e., sheep and goat breeding. Principal rivers are the Arachtos, the Kalamas and the Mavropotamos.

In antiquity the most Epirote was Pyrrhus of "pyrrhic" victory fame. The area became a Roman province after the defeat of the Macedonians at Pydna in 168 A.D. In the Middle Ages it achieved fame when a Greek "Despotate of Epirus" was set up there after the capture of Constantinople by the Crusaders in 1204. This was not an accident. Epirus had always been Greek and its inhabitants had staunchly maintained their traditions, language, religion, and home-grown culture (there have been Epirote intellectuals under the Turkish yoke) against all foreigners.

Epirus was incorporated into the Greek state in 1913 and suffered the brunt of the Italian Fascist attack in 1940.

EUROPEAN COMMUNITY, RELATIONS WITH. Greece was the first country to conclude an association agreement with the European Community in 1962. Association however was suspended during the dictatorship resulting from the Colonels' Coup of 21 April 1967. On 24 July 1974 relations were restored and, in June 1975, Greece applied for full membership. Negotiations were concluded on 28 May 1979 with the signing of the Treaty of Accession which became effective as of 1 January 1981.

The PASOK (q.v.) government which came to power in 1981 sought to renegotiate certain aspects of the treaty that according to the socialists overlooked some peculiarities of the Greek case. The "Greek Memorandum," which included these views was presented to the Council of Ministers and the Commission on 19 March 1982. Certain requirements of the Greek Memorandum were met by the Integrated Mediterranean Programs submitted by the Commission to the Council and adopted on 23 July 1985.

Greece has played her part in the process of European Political Cooperation and participated in all its organs: informal meetings of Foreign Ministers, political committee, working groups, coordinating groups within the framework of international organizations, etc.

Andreas Papandreou's (q.v.) initial objections to Greek accession to the European Community were quietly dropped after 1982, when about $800 million a year of EC funds were directed to Greece's rural areas. His position vis-à-vis the EC nevertheless often coincided with that of other mavericks such as Denmark and Britain. At the Milan Summit Conference of June 1985 the three joined forces to oppose a decision of the founding EC states to reduce the right of members to veto majority decisions.

As of the late 1980s Greece has become a strong exponent of the deepening of Community institutions and supporter of rapid progress towards European Union. Greece was therefore one of the first governments to ratify the Maastricht treaty.

EXPORTS. The value of exports in the early 1960s totaled $203 million. They now stand at $5 billion. Fresh and processed foods accounted for 24.4 percent of the dollar value of exports in 1990 while clothing and textiles accounted for 27.2 percent. Manufactured goods accounted for 54.1 percent.

Exports remain subject to some exchange controls which are progressively being removed. Exporters are now allowed to open accounts in foreign exchange with banks in Greece. They may also use the factoring and forfeiting services of foreign credit institutions and pay for them in foreign currency. Greek exporters lobbied the government to relax its policy of the "hard drachma" so that by a devaluation of the currency (q.v.) Greek goods will become cheaper for foreigners and therefore more competitive. The New Democracy (q.v.) government, however, keen to combat inflation, refused to yield to this pressure and urged reduction of costs, rationalization and modernization as healthier means to increase competitiveness of Greek commodities. See also FOREIGN TRADE; IMPORTS.

-F-

FAUNA. Seen from the air, the Greek islands of the Aegean (q.v.) look like mountain peaks surrounded by water. The impression is correct. According to recent geological research, some 25 million years ago the Aegean region was part of the mountain range linking Europe to Asia. Fossils from that remote period, when the Aegean sea was not yet born, indicate the existence of a savannah-type vegetation overrun by herds of giant animals.

At the time when the indefatigable Greek geographer, cum naturalist, cum social historian, cum travel-writer Pausanias wrote his *Description of Greece* (circa 150 A.D.) bears and wild boars roamed the slopes of Mt. Parnes to the north of Athens, while panthers and wolves could be found in the thick forests of Thrace and Macedonia (qq.v.), as well as wild goats, ibex and chamois. The existence of lions has not been proven to everybody's satisfaction, though Aristotle mentions he had encountered them on the banks of the Nestos River.

Birds also abounded, according to the testimony of various authors. Nightingales sang and owls flew silently in Athens, bee-eaters thrived on the banks of the Kifissos River in Attica, hoopoes and storks nested in gardens, while pelicans were frequent visitors to Greece.

These winged creatures have not totally disappeared. Stork colonies still exist in the wetter northern regions, pelicans still nest in the Little Prespa Lake near Arta in Epirus, the owl and the nightingale have been driven out of modern Athens but are still found elsewhere in Greece. The Kifissos River is, of course, history and the splendidly colored bee-eaters have become rare in Attica.

Greek fauna is mainly of the paleolithic period. Estuaries and lakes shelter rare aquatic birds while also providing hibernation grounds for migrants. Mountains are the natural habitat for eagles of which 38 European species have been recorded. Biodiversity (q.v.) is further ensured by the existence of naturally protected areas providing unique habitats for rare or endangered species of which some 200 birds, mammals, reptiles, and amphibians are protected. Among these are the monk seal (*Monachus-monachus*) of the Northern Sporades in the Aegean, the sea turtle (*Caretta-caretta*) of Zakynthos in the Ionian, the wild goat or chamois (*Rupicapra rupicapra*) (*Capra aegagrus cretica*) of Crete, and the brown bear (*Ursus arctos*) of northwestern Macedonia. In addition, several rare endangered species of birds of prey nest in the area of Evros in Thrace, such as the black vulture (*Aegyptius monachus*), the white-tailed eagle (*Haliaetus albicilla*), the lesser-spotted eagle (*Aquilla pomarina*), and the imperial eagle (*Aquilla heliaeca*).

FEREOS, RHIGAS (1757–1798). Poet, visionary, and martyr of Greek independence. Born in Velestino, Thessaly, he traveled widely in the Balkans and in Western Europe. He acted as Secretary of the Phanariot administrators of Wallachia and founded a secret revolutionary society in Vienna in 1796. His most important works were his *Declaration of the Rights of Man, Thourios* (War Hymn) and *the New Political Constitution of the Inhabitants of Rumeli, Asia Minor, the Archipelago, Moldavia and Wallachia.* The latter was influenced by the revolutionary costitutions of 1793 and 1795 in France.

Fereos's views predate nationalism, because his vision of a Balkan Republic included all Balkan people (including the Turks) freed of Ottoman tyranny. He was arrested by the Austrian police in 1797 and was handed over to the Ottoman authorities of Belgrade. He was strangled in 1798 and his body was cast in the river Sava.

FIRST WORLD WAR (1914–1918). Beginning 14 months after the end of the Second Balkan War (q.v.), it placed the head of the Greek government Eleftherios Venizelos (q.v.) at odds with the Head of State, King Constantine I (q.v.). The Prime Minister strove to bring Greece into the war on the side of the Triple Entente, while the King, who believed in Germany's invincibility, preferred neutrality. This conflict of differing foreign policies caused the resignation of Venizelos twice before he decided to support a coup in Thessaloniki favored by the Entente in 1916. In May 1917, France and England deposed Constantine and a united Greece under Venizelos's leadership continued the war against Germany, Austria, Bulgaria, and Turkey. In the Paris Peace Coference of 1919, Greece was granted West and East Thrace and a mandate to occupy Smyrna (1920). The landing of Greek troops in Asia Minor in 1919, the defeat of Venizelos by the royalists in the elections of 1920, and a protracted campaign against the nationalist forces of Kemal Ataturk (the father of modern Turkey) led to defeat and the expulsion of 1,300,000 Greeks from Turkey in 1922. These destitute refugees descended upon a Greece of barely five million and became the foremost consideration of all interwar Greek governments.

FISHERIES. Fishing activities by Greek nationals are carried out throughout Greek waters (internal and territorial), in the high seas and in territorial waters of other countries following agreements concluded with them. The great bulk of fishing is done in the coastal zone (22,000 vessels registered), a smaller amount off-shore in the Mediterranean (860 vessels), while a few vessels (90) sail overseas outside the Mediterranean. There are 70 fishing grounds (30,000 ha) in lagoons and 19 in natural and artificial lakes (58,500 ha). Fishing in rivers is negligible. In recent years there has been an expansion of aquaculture in fresh, brackish, and sea waters where trout, carp, eels, bass, golden beam, and shellfish are cultivated. In spite of this increase, which allowed Greece to consume some 160,400 tons of local produce in 1990, the country must still import annually 60,000 tons of fish for its needs.

FLORA. The geological and climatic features have fostered an extraordinarily rich plant population in Greece which hosts some 6,000 species. Of those some 750 are protected by law because they are endemic, i.e., to be found only in this country. Greece possesses about a third of all the endemic plants of Europe. Many genera such as *Dianthus, Viola Campanula, Centaurea,* and *Colchicum* are represented by hundreds of species. Crete (q.v.) alone has almost as many plant species—more than 2,000—as all the British Isles, though Crete is 35 times smaller. The number of species in Greece by unit of surface is six times that of France.

With its numerous protected biotopes, the mainland mountains which separate it into thousands of isolated valleys, its enormous coastline and innumerable islands, Greece can claim the title of Europe's botanical gardens where plants from Europe, Western Asia, and Northern Africa have taken root since time immemorial. It should be noted that Greece was largely shielded from the effects of the Ice Ages so that much of the pre-glacial flora has not become extinct. Even the long, dry, windy summers have not taken their toll on Greek flora.

Wealth of diversity, however, should not be confused with abundance. Endemicity, in particular, is confined to special areas in Crete, Mt. Athos, Mt. Olympus, and Mt. Taygetos, i.e., habitats with a high degree of isolation. The sturdy, hardy plants on the other hand grow more or less everywhere from coastal areas to alpine slopes and from the Ionian to the Aegean islands (qq.v.). They can survive almost on any soil, in any climate under any conditions and are, therefore, found almost anywhere in the Mediterranean lands. The endemic ones are perforce more delicate, as they have adapted only to special soils and climates, whence their rarity.

The relation of people to the world of the plants is manifest both in Greek mythology and in early Greek science. The word *botane* (from *boskein,* to feed, nourish) meant for Homer "pasturage for cattle." Later it acquired the meaning of "weed, herb, plant." *Botanikos* was an adjective referring to herbs and a *botanologos* was a "gatherer of herbs." The Greeks, it must be remembered, were great, full-time storytellers and their intimate relationship with the plant kingdom is vividly reflected in their colorful mythology. The very name of *chloris,* meaning the totality of plant species in a given area, is the name of the goddess of flowers, the exact equivalent of the Latins' Flora.

FOLKLORE. The term meaning "what the folk knows," as coined by William John Toms in 1846, has been rendered in

Greek as "laographia" by the scholar Nikolaos Politis in 1884 and covers the study of folk customs, rites and beliefs (including superstitions). The subject matter of this discipline acquired some importance during the nineteenth century. Those subscribing to the romantic version of the "nation" believed that the backward, illiterate peasants ensured best, through their own culture, Greek continuity as they had remained mostly immune to foreign influences. They were deemed to be "living monuments," precious gems of the ancient civilization, preserved intact and unspoiled in the countryside. The peasants were considered the unconscious carriers of the ancient cultural inheritance albeit often in an irrational form as "superstitions." This traditionalist view contrasted sharply with the modernists' attitude of considering the "vulgar populace" a hindrance to progress as defined by the values of the Enlightenment, i.e., the primacy of reason and the need for education. The promoters of folklore values may have been ideologically inspired by Romanticism but they nevertheless embarked on a serious study of popular culture. Their philosophical pretensions regarding Greek continuity were soon abandoned; their scholarship remained.

FOREIGN TRADE. There has always been a substantial deficit in the country's trade balance with other countries. This balance deteriorated dramatically in the 1980s—called by some "the lost decade." In 1980, some 41.6 percent of imports (q.v.) were covered by exports (q.v.). In 1990, this rate fell to a mere 35.5 percent.

This structural trade imbalance has produced current account deficits which have historically been covered by strong invisibles. However, shipping slumps, the occasional bad year in tourism (q.v.) and fluctuations in migrant workers' remittances, coupled with spendthrift policies at home, the squandering of currency resources and high inflation, while foreign investment (q.v.) is discouraged by political turbulence and open hostility to it, can and often do exacerbate the current account deficit. In 1990, this deficit rose to a staggering $3 billion or 5.3 percent of GDP. International credit rating agencies relegated Greece to the lowest level of the 12 countries of the EC (q.v.). Under the New Democracy (q.v.) government which came to power in April 1990, the situation improved dramatically. In 1991, imports in dollar terms rose by only 2.1 percent, exports rose by 6.5 percent, while invisibles rose by 24 percent. As a result, the current account deficit fell by 59 percent to under $1 billion or 2 percent of GDP in 1992.

The Ministry of Trade is responsible for policy on imports and exports while the commercial banks deal with the formalities. Usually, the banks grant import approvals automatically. The requisite amount of foreign exchange is thereupon made available to the importer. Settlement is within 60 days of the goods' arrival in the country. See also EXPORTS; IMPORTS.

FORESTS AND FOREST FIRES. In the *Iliad*, Homer speaks on four occasions of raging fires lasting for a whole year because of the winds which kept fanning their flames. Fires have never really stopped, but in modern times this particular scourge of the Greek forest has become more menacing as the construction of roads for easy and fast access to mountainous areas opened formerly inaccessible regions to human activities, human negligence and human destructive or criminal behavior.

Meanwhile, regeneration by natural seeding has been hampered by the voracious herds of sheep and goats which have since ancient times been grazing in lowland areas, hillsides and mountains. Though timber production is today minimal in Greece, while grazing is somewhat controlled, forest protection remains a major concern for the authorities. Reforestation is an urgent national priority.

The main contemporary danger to forests are the 700—on average—fires breaking out every year which destroy 30,000 to 50,000 hectares of forests and forestlands during the hot, dry, windy summer months. As a rule, ten times more forest area is destroyed annually than is replaced. Even though burned stands regenerate naturally after two to five years, the damage is serious. Fires cause soil erosion, destroy summer houses, wheat crops, vineyards, and olive groves. They also destroy fauna (q.v.) and are mainly to blame for the sharp decline in the population of almost all the large herbivorous and carnivorous mammals, for example the deer *Cervus elaphus,* the roe deer *Capreolus capreolus,* the wolf *Canis lupus* and the bear *Ursus arctos.*

Forest fires are attributed (in order of importance) to negligence, arson, burning of rubbish dumps and crop residues, as well as to undetected causes. Efforts to combat forest fires have been increasing steadily over the years but to little avail so far.

FORESTS AND RANGELANDS. The first settlers in Greece found themselves in a land covered with thick primary forests. The fact that civilization started there some thousand years earlier than elsewhere explains the very early changes to the environment (q.v.).

The type of vegetation has not changed significantly since antiquity. About 38 percent of forests are made up of conifers. The Greek Fir (*Abies cephalonica*) covers extensive areas, especially in the higher mountains, and is sometimes accompanied by the Black Pine (*Pirus nigra*), as happens for instance on Mount Olympus. The Aleppo Pine (*Pinus halepensis*), so characteristic of the Mediterranean area in general, grows often singly or in scattered clumps and can be seen forming woods even at a height up to 1,000 meters above sea level.

Deciduous broad leaves form 43 percent of forests in Greece. Of these, Sweet Chestnut (*Castanea sativa*) is the most common and forms woods on the slopes of Mount Pelion, in southern Epirus and elsewhere. Deciduous species of oaks such as Valonia Oak (*Quercus aegilops*) sometimes accompanied by *Quercus languinosa,* are also encountered on hills.

Of special importance to Greece was, and still is, the olive tree (*Olea europea*) of the *Oliaceae* family. The edible fruit is pressed to obtain the precious olive oil which was considered such a valuable source of wealth in Periclean Athens that the city was granted a monopoly in its export. The wood is resistant to decay, the leaves are leathery, lance shaped, green above, silvery on the underside and are paired opposite each other on the twig. The olive tree is the most frequently depicted on ancient vases because it was an integral part of Greek culture. Sophocles's dictum that "It is the gray-leaved olive that feeds our boys" is still valid today up to a point. Until only three decades ago the olive crop was probably the most important single factor in Greece's economic performance. In 1961, a record oil production of nearly 228,000 tons boosted Greece's GNP by 11 percent. In 1962, the lean year which—inevitably—followed, reduced growth to a mere 3 percent. The long-lived drought-resistant olive tree has been a blessing for Greeks. No wonder they believed that it sprouted from the ground on the Acropolis (q.v.) when the spear of Athena hit the sacred spot.

Broad-leaved evergreens form the remaining 19 percent of forestlands of which the evergreen oaks, more often shrubs than proper trees, are the most common. In a mountainous country such as Greece the forest is a source of wood, protects soils and slopes from erosion, regulates mountain stream hydrology, provides a habitat for wild animals, recreation opportunities for people, and forage for grazing animals. Alas, forests in Greece are today in real danger. They cover only 19 percent of the country's total area, the smallest such percentage in Europe.

Although some 60 percent of the total land area—mainly hilly and mountainous—is grazed, the contribution of rangelands to the production of meat, milk and their products is only 45 percent of the country's total needs. This is due to vegetation degradation and to the reduction of soil fertility by soil erosion and compaction. Soil erosion would have devastated the countryside had measures not been taken to avert it. Among those, the most important has been the systematic terracing of the steep hillsides which helped to conserve and even improve the precious soil.

FORMER YUGOSLAV REPUBLIC OF MACEDONIA (FYROM). After the German invasion of Greece, Bulgarian forces annexed Eastern Macedonia and subjected its population to ethnic cleansing. In Greece's Western Macedonia the German occupation authorities gave the Bulgarians a free hand in propaganda and intimidation of the local population. In 1943, at a conference between Yugoslav and Greek left-wing partisans, Tito's representative for the first time used the term "Macedonian nationals" to describe the Slav-speaking natives in the region. In 1944 Tito renamed the Serbian southern province of Vardar into the Federal Republic of Macedonia. By doing so, he absolved all those who had identified with the Bulgarians and had collaborated with the occupation forces and at the same time laid irredentist claims on both Bulgarian (Pirin) and Greek territories. Prior to Tito's break with Stalin in 1948, the Bulgarians had no choice but to accept Yugoslavia's supremacy; the Greeks, who belonged to the western camp, were faced with the hostility of both Communist states. Yugoslav resistance hero, Tempo (Vukmanovich) informed Skopje that it was Yugoslav policy to incorporate Greek Macedonia along with the Bulgarian and Yugoslav parts into a unified republic. As of 1944 (year of birth of the "Macedonian" state) the term ceased to signify geography for the citizens of the Federal (later Socialist) Republic and become the name of a new nation.

The most irritating problem for Greece has been the explicit irredentism of the new state and its nation. The "Macedonians" of the Socialist Republic from the outset laid claim to all territories bearing the name Macedonia. After the recent collapse of Yugoslavia, the Socialist Republic sought recognition as an independent state under the name "Macedonia." Greece initially objected to the appropriation of a Greek name which preceded the Slavic incursion in the Balkans by a thousand years, but later agreed to a mixed name that would signify the geographic location of the new state and would therefore exclude territorial ambitions at the expense of Greece and Bulgaria.

The state was admitted to the United Nations with the temporary denomination Former Yugoslav Republic of Macedonia (FYROM), in April 1993.

FREDERIKA OF GREECE (1917–1981). Frederika Louise of Hannover, Duchess of Brunswick and Queen of the Hellenes, was born in 1917. Her mother was the only daughter of the German Emperor, William II, and her father was the son of the Prince of Hannover (House of Welf). She was married to the heir of the Greek throne, Prince Paul (House of Glucksburg) in 1938.

When Greece was overrun by the German forces in April 1941, she fled with her two children, Sophia and Constantine (q.v.), to Egypt and then South Africa, where she bore her third child, Irene. Throughout the war years the future of the royalty remained an outstanding issue between Greeks. Frederika and her family returned to Greece in October 1946 after a plebiscite had settled the question of the monarchy. King George's premature death on 1 April 1947 brought Paul to the throne and heralded the interventions of his queen in public affairs.

Frederika's loyalty to her family was unquestioned, but her intense pursuit of the throne's interests caused considerable damage to the image of the institution. Her rivalry with Marshal Alexandros Papagos (q.v.)—head of the government forces during the Civil War—constituted one of her most conspicuous interventions in politics.

Constantinos Karamanlis's (q.v.) resignation in 1963 involved a direct clash with Frederika who refused to pay heed to her Prime Minister's objections against a trip to London after having been harassed by demonstrators on a previous visit to that city. Between 1963, when King Paul's illness became apparent, and his death in March of the following year, Frederika in effect reigned in his place. All efforts of Prime Minister Georgios Papandreou (q.v.) to disengage the young King Constantine from his mother's influence came to naught. Although there is no way of assessing her part in his clash with the popular Prime Minister in 1965, it may be assumed that she continued to draw on Constantine's filial devotion.

The military junta of 21 April 1967 subverted royal power in the armed forces and used the King as a figurehead in their regime. When Constantine made his belated attempt to confront the rebellious Colonels (q.v.) in December 1967, he met with defeat and had to leave the country. Frederika followed her son and his family in their flight into exile. She died in 1981 and her body was brought to Greece for burial followed by the controversy that had been her life companion.

-G-

GEOGRAPHY. Greece is situated between the 35th and 41st parallels north of the equator in the temperate zone. It is a stony and mostly mountainous country dotted with villages clinging to rocks, stretching across the tip of the Balkan peninsula from the Ionian Sea to the Aegean and surrounded by 9,841 island formations (including islets and rock islands) in both seas. Its total area is 131,957 square kilometers. The coastline of the mainland is 4,000 kilometers long whereas the coastline created by the islands exceeds 11,000 kilometers. Greece shares borders clockwise from the northwest with Albania, former Yugoslavia, Bulgaria and Turkey.

The Greek mainland, an integral part of the European continent jutting out from the Balkans (a name of Turkish origin meaning mountain range), has been compared to a forearm and hands with fingers reaching out into the Mediterranean. Such is the forbidding shape of this mountainous land that it has given rise to a bitter Greek myth. When the Demiurge created the world he distributed all the available fertile soil through a sieve and, when he had provided every country with enough of it, he tossed the remaining stones over his shoulder—and there was Greece.

The mountains of Greece are a continuation of the Dinaric Alps. Following the general northwest-southeast trend of the mountains of the Balkan Peninsula, the Pindus range sweeps down in a series of rugged, roughly parallel ridges from the Albanian and Yugoslavian frontier. This system was created relatively late in geological time, and earthquakes continue to afflict the region as the mountain structures settle down. The highest point in this region is Smolikas (2,637 meters). The mountain scenery, with jagged granitic peaks, wild gorges and a succession of magnificent views glimpsed from winding roads, is justly famed.

The Pindos chain runs southwards into the Agrafa (south Pindos) range and is then further extended by the mountains of Central Greece (q.v.) which terminate in Attica. The Peloponnese (q.v.) highlands continue the selfsame geological bow which sweeps eastwards to form the mountains of Crete (q.v.). The Aegean islands (q.v.) are in fact protruding tips of these branches of the Pindos chain. Northerners are often enchanted by the vivid clarity of the atmosphere which makes natural colors come to life and allows even distant mountains to become visible in every detail. Greek mountains are never very far from the coastline. In fact they seem to rise out of the sea in palisades. They fragment the inhabited lowland into a thousand-and-one, more or less isolated, land parcels. The highest mountain in Greece is Olympus (2,917 meters)—presumed habitat of the twelve gods in antiquity, the longest river is the Aliakmon (297 kilometers) and the largest lake is Trichonis (97 square kilometers).

The Balkan peninsula, of which Greece forms a part, differs from the Italian and Iberian peninsulas in that it is not separated by a high mountain barrier from the rest of Europe. This is a peninsula with a broad base which is geographically part of Central Europe sharing in its climate and flora (q.v.) while its southern extremity, including most of Greece, is distinctly Mediterranean. The limestone and their often red soil *(terra rosa)* are a well known feature throughout the Balkan peninsula. In the southern part of Greece, the seasonal distribution of rainfall and the absence or rarity of frost, account for the great areas of exposed limestone which is a striking element in the Greek landscape. The soil in these areas is alkaline and rich in mineral salts, though often shallow and subject to much loss from the rainfall, frequently heavy when it occurs.

No country in Europe has more than two-thirds of its surface classified as hilly and mountainous and none is so savagely splintered because of them. Valleys and plains are found only between the elevations or along the coasts. What Homer said about Ithaca applies to Greece in general: ''We have no level runs or meadows, but highland, goat land . . . . Grasses and pasture land are hard to come by.'' Mountains have always been seen in Greece as vaguely threatening to people, often the abode of powerful gods commanding human destinies from high above. Many writers have pointed out that all the elements making up the Greek environment— sea, sky, lowland and mountain—are so intimately contrasted and opposed that they acquire an almost symbolic, theatrical quality as if their purpose was more to humble humans than to support them. ''At times,'' wrote George

Seferis (q.v.), the modern Greek poet and Nobel prize-winner, "you cannot discern whether the mountain opposite is a stone or a gesture."

The Greek landscape is conspicuous not only for its beauty but also for its complexity and its variety. The dominant influence—as noted by Strabo, the great geographer of classical antiquity, and confirmed by a glance at the map—is the sea. An ever-present factor, the sea presses deep into the land in a host of arms and inlets, which are often separated by the rocky spines of peninsulas that thrust back into the sea and are continued in the arcs and clusters of beautiful islands across its surface.

Separation, scission, is thus inherent in Greece's physical geography. The formidable ranges and the difficult passes cut Greeks off from one another. Such physical schism encouraged no doubt the creation of small independent city-states in the past and has often contributed to a sense of deep loyalty to one's local community even—at times—at the expense of a wider and more abstract sense of nationhood. This geography—dividing as it does homeland Greeks—has, however, the added effect of rendering it exceedingly difficult for others to invade their land as Mussolini discovered much to his discomfiture in 1940. Yet, contradictorily, it seems that in prehistoric, historic and modern times significant numbers of people found it relatively easy to enter Greece through the Macedonian "massif." Such infiltrations, however, are not invasions. They are simply the other side of the geomorphological coin. What constitutes an obstacle to an invading army is, at the same time, an opportunity for the intrepid infiltrator.

If mountains have divided them, the seas, on the contrary, have united Greeks both with other Greeks and with the world at large. The sea in Greece is always near, in fact it is never more than 80 odd kilometers from any given point in the country. The mountains hemmed people in, the sea pushed them out. It even brought them in contact with compatriots only a few miles away as some coastal hamlets are more accessible by sea than by land. Almost everywhere the sea penetrates the shores in deep, winding gulfs except on the comparatively smooth and unbroken northern coast of the mainland. The country has therefore a crenellated coastline measuring 15,000 kilometers, the longest in Europe per territorial surface, well endowed with numerous natural harbors which not only made Greeks a nation of seafarers but also provided safe havens for the invaders who coveted the control of the eastern Mediterranean.

Geopolitics have, of course, changed much in the age of technology. Today communications have greatly improved. The country is effectively unified as roads crisscross it in all directions, ports have been modernized and many airports built. Yet, hopping from island to island in the Aegean is still virtually impossible while it is easier for a villager in Thessaly to travel to Ioannina or a peasant farmer in Euboea to visit Athens than for either of them to reach an upcountry community some 30 kilometers away. One can fly from Athens to Thessaloniki in fifty minutes but it takes about a day on mule to visit a village 15 kilometers away in the Pindos range.

The country is subdivided into ten regions: the Athens area, Central Creece, the Aegean islands, Crete, the Peloponnese, the Ionian islands Eprius, Thessaly and, last but not least, Macedonia and Thrace (qq.v.).

GEORGE I, KING (1845–1913). George I was born in Copenhagen in the royal house of Glucksburg, the second son of Danish King Christian IX and Queen Louisa of Essen. He became king of the Hellenes in 1863 after he was selected by the Greek Parliament.

Although on various occasions he took an active part in internal Greek politics, he was in general terms a prudent King who preferred compromise to confrontation. An Anglophile in his foreign policy choices he was assassinated in Thessaloniki in 1913, probably by an Austrian agent.

GEORGE II, KING (1890–1947). The son of King Constantine I (q.v.) and Queen Sophia, he graduated from the Military Academy in 1909 and furthered his military studies in Berlin. George followed his father into exile in 1917 because the Entente forces chose his younger brother Alexander to become King. He returned with his father in 1920 and became King in 1922 after Constantine was exiled once more. In 1923, he was forced to leave Greece upon being accused of complicity in the abortive coup of November of that year. The Republic was officially proclaimed in 1924 and his return was thereafter prohibited. Following the coup of 1935 he was recalled to the throne after a rigged plebiscite of dubious legitimacy. He backed Ioannis Metaxas's (q.v.) dictatorship (1936–41) and followed the Greek government in exile when the Axis forces occupied the country. He returned to his throne in Greece after a plebiscite in 1946.

GONATAS, STYLIANOS (1876–1967). Soldier and politician of the interwar period. Gonatas was born in Patras of middle class parents. He studied at the Military Academy and entered the Infantry Corps. He took part in the war of 1897 and the Balkan Wars (q.v.) (1912–1913). He became Chief of Staff of the First Army Corps in Asia Minor and was promoted to Divisional Commander during the summer of 1922. Although Gonatas was known for his neutralist position during the *"dichasmos"* (national schism), he was called to lead, along with the Venizelist Nikolaos Plastiras (q.v.), the Revolutionary Committee of 1922 which forced King Constantine I (q.v.) to abdicate, and executed six royalist ministers. He became Prime Minister in the military dictatorship of 1922 until 1924 when he left the army. In 1929 he was elected Senator and remained a staunch supporter of Venizelism in politics. His implication in the coup of 1935 was marginal.

GOVERNMENT (CENTRAL). Under the 1975 Constitution (q.v.), as amended in 1986, Greece—no longer a monarchy since 1974—is a Presidential Parliamentary Republic founded on the principles of popular sovereignty, the rule of law, the respect and protection of human rights and the division of powers between the executive, legislative and judiciary.

The President, the titular Head of State without executive powers, is elected by Parliament for a five-year term by a two-thirds majority or on the third ballot by a three-fifths majority. If that proves impossible, an election is held and the

President can be elected by a simple majority of deputies in the new house. The present holder of the post, Constantinos Karamanlis (q.v.), was first elected in this manner in May 1980.

The government is in charge of the executive and responsible for general policy both in foreign and domestic matters. It is headed by the Prime Minister while individual ministers are masters in their own house responsible both for implementing policies and for initiating new legislation where appropriate.

Policy is debated and decided in the Government Council (in essence the inner cabinet composed of principal ministers and chaired by the Prime Minister in person). There are also more specialized policy-making bodies such as the Government Council for Foreign Affairs and National Defense, the Supreme Council for Economic Policy and the Prices and Incomes Board.

Ministers are directly answerable to Parliament and bear legal responsibility for their actions according to article 85 of the Constitution.

GOVERNMENT (LOCAL). Communes and municipalities—in excess of 5,000 in the whole of Greece—are run by elected officials whose duties, rights and functions are written into the Constitution (q.v.). Local authorities are responsible for local parks, children's playgrounds, the collection of garbage, landscape works, sanitation, local irrigation schemes as well as building and maintenance of the local road network. They can also set up hospitals, orphanages, homes for the aged and other welfare or cultural schemes. Local authorities do not levy taxes themselves though they do raise revenue in other ways. They are mainly financed by the central government (q.v.). The state budget devotes 5 percent of its expenditure to local authorities whose activities (both mandatory and discretionary) are supervised by the *"nomarch"* (prefect) who ensures their conformity with the law of the land. Local authorities are run by officials elected by universal suffrage and seats are usually contested by a great variety of electoral lists often reflecting the policies of political parties.

GREEK-AMERICANS. The most important community in a western country (some three million) is to be found in the

United States (q.v.). Migration of Greeks to the US occurred in five stages:

1) Before 1890 there was only a trickle setting out for that faraway land.
2) From 1890 to 1920 there was mass migration in consecutive waves through which some 350,000 Greeks representing one-sixth of the population migrated to the States. In 1921, their remittances reached a peak of over $120 million a year. It was then, however, that the American government introduced a quota system which admitted no more than 100 Greek immigrants a year. This stopped Greek immigration in its tracks.
3) From that date to 1940, Greek-Americans created their own institutions (AHEPA, GAPA). The Greek Orthodox Archdiocese of America was established as early as 1922 and has since been the focus of most of the community's activities.
4) The period from 1940 to 1965 can be considered an ''era of consolidation'' during which Greek-Americans perceived themselves and functioned as an important part of American life in general.
5) The contemporary period since 1965 saw Greek-Americans realizing that they could exercise power within the American political system and influence the policies of the government. Such activism was displayed twice in recent years, once in 1976 at the time Congress imposed an arms embargo on Turkey (q.v.) for her invasion of Cyprus (q.v.), and again in 1992, when Greek-Americans campaigned with extraordinary success to avert the recognition by the US of the breakaway southernmost republic of former Yugoslavia under the—Greek—name of Macedonia (see FORMER YUGOSLAV REPUBLIC OF MACEDONIA).

Early immigrants to the US worked in factories, railway construction, mills and mines. Within several decades they moved on to small businesses, candy stores and restaurants. Later they entered the professions, universities, larger businesses and politics. This process of assimilation linked with pride for their ancestry has not been altogether smooth. Second and third generation, professionals and businessmen, coexist—not without strains—in the same organizations and go to the same Orthodox churches as first generation arrivals. The record of their achievement surpasses that of almost every other ethnic group in the United States. In 1970, second generation Greek-Americans ranked first in educational levels when compared to all other second generation Americans. Greek-American incomes are an incredible 31.6 percent higher than the native white American average.

The largest concentrations of ethnic Greeks are in New York (namely in Astoria, in the Borough of Queens, with 60–70,000), Chicago, Boston, San Francisco, New Orleans, and, generally, in the major urban areas. There are actually 20 regular schools, operated by the Church, of which 14 are in New York. There are also more than 400 evening schools for children who wish to learn Greek. The most famous Greek-American was Dr. Georgios Papanikolaou (q.v.) who saved the lives of thousands of women through the cancer detecting smear test known as the "Pap" test. The most notorious was the poker player Nick the Greek who played for the biggest pot in the history of stud poker ($797,000). The most popular was the baseball superstar Micky Mantle (Mantopoulos). Michael Dukakis and George Stefanopoulos are just two of the prominent Greek-Americans in U.S. politics. See also GREEKS OF THE DIASPORA.

GREEK CHURCH. In the strict sense of the term, the Orthodox Church in Greece is distinguished from the Orthodox Church in Russia or Bulgaria. Confusion arises because the term Greek Orthodox Church is often applied to the Orthodox Churches as a whole to distinguish them from the Latin or Catholic Church of the West. The Church in Greece dates from the first century and it is closely connected with the activities of St. Paul himself. The Epistles to the Corinthians written by St. Paul to the Christian Church at Corinth in about 57 A.D. are important Christian documents dealing with marriage and celibacy, the resurrection of the dead and the Eucharist. In the second epistle, St. Paul, as fluent in Greek as he was in Latin, explains his own apostolic ministry and defends his views against dissidents in the Corinthian Church. Under the Patriarchate of Constantinople, the Orthodox Church whose official language was Greek became a very important Christian center. Orthodox Christianity gradually permeated all aspects of life in the Eastern Roman Empire as the—later named—Byzantine Empire was called by those who belonged to it. With the fall of Constantinople to the Ottoman Turks in 1453 the Patriarchate came to represent all the Christian subjects of the Sultan.

Upon Greece's liberation from the Turkish yoke, and in accordance with a settlement in 1833, the Orthodox Church in Greece was declared to be autocephalous, i.e., independent of the Ecumenical Patriarchate of Constantinople. This move would have probably not even been considered by an Orthodox monarch (King Otto Wittelsbach [q.v.] who dared it was Roman Catholic). The nascent Greek state did not wish its Church to be under the jurisdiction of a Patriarch highly susceptible to pressures by the Sultan. Relations with the Patriarchate resumed only in 1850 when Constantinople was obliged to recognize in essence the 1833 settlement.

It is estimated that 97–98 percent of Greeks are baptized as Christian Orthodox. Non-Orthodox Christians include some 45,000 (in a population of over ten million) Roman Catholics of whom some 2,500 are "Uniates," i.e., Christians following the Eastern rites but pledging allegiance to the Pope. The historical links between Church and State have been progressively weakened. In the 1980s the government introduced civil marriage and legalized abortion against the bitter opposition of the Church authorities.

The Church of Greece is involved in a great number of charities, orphanages, old people's homes, clinics, etc., and various philanthropic activities such as help to the Orthodox in Albania, relief to Serbian children and various other projects. Church attendance has been falling, especially among the young. The low educational standards of many priests—quite adequate for the mostly agricultural Greeks of the nineteenth and early twentieth century—has been deemed responsible for holding back the expansion of the Church's influence over an increasingly sophisticated urban population. However, progress is being made in this field.

The Greek Church today has its own Charter and is governed by a Synod composed of all 78 bishops of the land, meeting once a year. For the rest of the time the Church is administered by a smaller 12 member body called the "Holy Synod" or "Permanent Synod" on which all bishops serve in turn. The thirteenth member of the Holy Synod, is the Archbishop. For historical reasons, State and Church have close links in Greece. The State pays the salaries of priests, approves the enthronement of new bishops, the creation of new parishes or the erection of new church buildings. The penal code punishes blasphemy against sacred symbols. The Constitution (q.v.) guarantees freedom of worship of every known creed but forbids proselytism.

Within the Greek territory there are three orthodox "communities" which are independent of the Greek Church and come under the jurisdiction of the Ecumenical Patriarchate of Constantinople: The Orthodox Church of Crete whose Archbishop has his seat at Heracleion; The Episcopates of the Dodecanese; and The Holy Community of Mount Athos (q.v.). See also ORTHODOX CHURCH; ORTHODOXY.

GREEKNESS. What makes a Greek, Greek, has been preoccupying Greeks since the dawn of their history. When, near the end of the Persian wars, the Spartans rushed a delegation to Athens to stop the Athenians from defecting to the Persians—as was then rumored—Herodotus, the "father of History," had the Athenians utter some reassuring words obviously deemed necessary to dispel any Spartan misgivings. "And then, there is our Hellenism, our being of the same stock and the same speech, our common shrines of the gods and rituals, our similar customs. . . ." Thus, according to Herodotus, the ancient Greeks seemed indeed to satisfy all the modern criteria of a nation: common descent, common language, common religion, common customs and a consciousness of belonging together. Some nagging questions, however, remain unanswered.

Their professed Hellenism may have inhibited Athenians

from allying themselves with Persia but it never stopped them from "enslaving Hellenes, reducing to slavery those who were bravest in fighting with them against the barbarians, that is the Aiginetans, the Potidaeans, and all such others" (Aristotle, *Rhetoric* 1396 a 18). Hellas certainly did have a meaning but this should be considered in a context of a complex society where every Hellene belonged to a multiplicity of groups, of which the "polis" was the most demanding. An Athenian visiting nearby Megara was an alien but not a foreigner much as a contemporary Syrian visiting Cairo, for instance. Only outsiders could be taken as slaves but in the Greek world citizens of the next city were indeed outsiders.

Whatever its internal cohesion—or lack of it—Greece has over the millennia stretched and shrunk over the whole Mediterranean area from its "core territory" or springboard at the southern extremity of the Balkan peninsula. Paradoxically, the very absence of a central political or ecclesiastical authority seems to have helped Greeks stick to their culture, their common identity and, occasionally, together—when Hellenic patriotism was not too much in conflict with overriding demands of a more local nature. In fact, with no "center" from which to flee there was never any destructible structure to bring down. Even when conquered the Greeks continued to speak to each other in the same language (dialects never diverged significantly from the mainstream), cultivate the arts, and retain their Greekness.

The various names by which they collectively called themselves or were called by others, have an interesting history.

The nation state at the southern extremity of the Balkan peninsula is today called Hellas for short or the "Hellenic Republic" to give it its full official name. Its citizens call themselves "Hellenes" or "Ellines" in transliterated Greek. The term stems from a man. No less an authority than Thucydides mentions in the opening pages of his history of the Peloponnesian War the famous Hellen, son of Deucalion, as the eponymous ancestor of all the Hellenes. Before him, the poet Hesiod (ca. 700 B.C.) had also mentioned Hellen, a grandson of Prometheus and great-great-grandson of Heaven and Ocean, as the common progenitor of the race.

The term "Greece" used by the Romans to identify Hellas after they had completed its conquest in the second century B.C. has prevailed ever since in the West. The term has impeccable credentials. Aristotle mentions in his *Meteorologika* (A. 14) that in the territory around Dodona in Epirus and the river Acheloos—believed by some to be the cradle of the nation—"there used to dwell those anciently called Greeks but now Hellenes." Hesiod, an authority on genealogy, mythical or otherwise, mentions a hero by the name of Greek, son of Zeus and Pandora.

Christianity dismissed the term "Hellene" as synonym of pagan. In the Eastern Roman Empire and in its capital Constantinople no distinct nationality could be ascribed to the Emperor's subjects. They thus opted to call themselves Romans or *Romaioi* in Greek and their language *Romaic.*

After Constantinople fell to the Ottomans in 1453 and for the four centuries of their rule, the Turks did not innovate. They called *Rum* all the European Christians of their Empire including Serbs, Bulgarians, Rumanians and Albanians. They called *Rumeli,* i.e., "land of the *Rums*," all their European provinces with the exception of Moldavia and Wallachia, Bosnia, Crete and the Aegean islands (qq.v.). The term *Rumeli* is still used in today's Greece referring mainly to Central Greece (q.v.) and including the prefectures of Attica, Boetia, Phtiotis, Evritania, Phokis and Aitoloakarnania. The surname "Rumeliotis," meaning (q.v.) inhabitant of *Rumeli,* is quite common in the Hellenic Republic today.

Contemporary Greeks still call themselves colloquially *Romioi* when they wish to emphasize their more recent past and especially their struggle against the Ottoman ruler. The values of Greekness in modern times subsumed under the term *Romiossini* are therefore mainly the ones forged in the combat against the Ottoman: courage, endurance, bravery and cunning.

Today's Greeks are those who think of themselves as Greeks (even if they are only the offspring of a mixed marriage of a Greek immigrant in the USA) thus making Greekness a largely subjective, chosen attribute. They live on producing culture and poetry (q.v.), using their language (q.v.), taking care of their heritage, their monuments, their texts, their values, and—since 1830—their country. Their identity is not racial, or religious, but cultural, as illustrated in the ancient dictum of Isocrates: "we call Greeks those who partake of our culture."

GREEKS OF THE DIASPORA. The Greek diaspora is a phenomenon almost as old as Greece itself. It is due to a large extent to the pioneering adventurous spirit developed in a seafaring nation whose homeland is mountainous, stony, and mostly arid. In the classical era, pressure of population and scarcity of land drove people away from the mainland. The ancient emigrants did not have countries to go to. They formed colonies along the coastline all over the Mediterranean. In Hellenistic times, colonists followed the Macedonian troops almost everywhere in the then known world.

After the fall of Constantinople in 1453, many (especially scholars) sought refuge in the Christian West. In the eighteenth and nineteenth centuries they emigrated to Russia, Hungary, and Egypt and some, having become very rich, used their wealth to establish endowments in their mother country. At the end of the nineteenth century the tide of emigration shifted to the United States. Greeks sought economic prosperity not only there but also in Australia, Canada and, more recently, in Germany and other EC countries. Of the once thriving communities in Egypt and the Middle East nothing much remains after President Nasser began, in the mid-1950s, to squeeze all foreigners out of Egypt.

Greeks emigrate hopefully but live to regret it. The sense of exile is pervasive and nostalgia is bitterly felt. The very word *xeniteia,* which means "living in a foreign land," is tinged with a deep sense of loss of the native land. It is not a sense of loss of identity, it is more a feeling of being uprooted. That is why the return to the homeland is always so emotionally charged.

It is difficult to estimate the number of Greeks living abroad. The Foreign Ministry, however, believes that there are all over the world at least five million people who could reasonably be considered ethnic Greeks. Of these, 400,000 speak the language, belong to the Greek-Orthodox rite and live in the Republic of Cyprus (q.v.). Some 700,000 live in Europe, 700,000 in Australia, 130,000 in Africa and 40,000 in Asia. Ethnic Greeks living abroad—other than Greek Cypriots who are virtually indistinguishable from mainland Greeks—maintain ties of varying intensity with the language, religion and mores of their country of origin. See also GREEK AMERICANS.

-H-

HELLAS (GREECE). During the five millennia of their uninterrupted presence in much the same area as the one where they still live today, the Greeks evolved many successive civilizations of which three were prehistoric, i.e., the Cycladic, the Cretan or Minoan, and the Mycenean, and three historic, i.e., the Archaic (8th–6th century B.C.), the much admired Classical (8–4th centuries B.C.), and the Hellenistic (4th-1st centuries B.C.) which covered the greater part of the then known world with the conquests of Alexander the Great.

The loss of Alexander's empire and the withering of the Greek states, however, did not mean that the Greeks disappeared from their homelands. Under Roman rule they continued to philosophize and cultivate the arts. With the emergence of the Eastern Roman Empire, or Byzantium as it was to be renamed in the nineteenth century, which combined Roman law, the Christian religion and the Greek language, the culture of the Greeks became infused with Orthodoxy (q.v.). With the fall of the Empire to the Ottoman Turks in the fifteenth century, Greek culture became more focused, providing the foundation of a modern nation-state which is today called the "Hellenic Republic."

The milestones in this development stretch over the milennia. Up until 338 B.C., there was no single Greek state but numerous city states often at war with one another, sharing the same language, culture and religion. From 338 onwards, and for two centuries, all the territories comprising Hellenes come under the rule of the Macedonian kingdom. As from 142 B.C., and for the following five centuries, the Greek lands were ruled by Rome. From 324 A.D., the Eastern

Roman Empire ensured a kind of Greek continuity mainly through the Greek speaking Orthodox Church (q.v.) which unified within the same "universalist" doctrine a multi-ethnic population. From 1452, when Constantinople fell to the Ottoman Turks, the overwhelming majority of Greeks came under Turkish rule aside from a brief period (1686–1715) of partial Venetian occupation.

In 1832, after a long and bloody struggle, the first Greek nation-state was born comprising initially only Peloponnese and Central Greece (qq.v.). In 1863, Greece acquired the Ionian Islands (q.v.) from Britain; in 1881, Thessaly (q.v.), and part of Epirus (q.v.) from Turkey; in 1913, after the Balkan Wars (q.v.) Crete, the Aegean islands, Thrace, and Macedonia (qq.v.) from Turkey; and in 1948, the Dodecanese from Italy. It always comes as a shock to many Greeks when they realize that prominent compatriots of theirs such as Karamanlis, Seferis, Elytis, Onassis, Andronikos, Solomos, Kalvos and Elephterios Venizelos, to name but a few, were not born in the "Kingdom of Greece."

In fact Hellas, or Greece, can be perceived as a historical nation—in the loosest possible sense of the word—which has occupied much the same core region over the millennia, has changed very gradually its language and radically its religion from paganism to Orthodoxy, does not belong to any wider ethnic or cultural group as is the case for Slavs, Arabs or Anglo-Saxons, but embodies—with Rome—much of the cultural and political heritage of Europe to which it now belongs institutionally. See also GREEKNESS.

HELLENIC FOUNDATION FOR EUROPEAN AND FOREIGN POLICY (ELIAMEP). An independent, non-profit think tank founded in 1988 (originally as Hellenic Foundation for Defense and Foreign Policy) to promote the study and understanding of foreign policy issues. The Foundation holds meetings, seminars and conferences on current questions of international affairs, publishes their proceedings as well as the outcome of specialized research projects and maintains a library and a computerized documentation center. Between 1988 and 1993 the Foundation has published over 50 titles.

Although ELIAMEP welcomes discussions of any important international topic, it places special emphasis on European and Balkan affairs as well as on Greek foreign and security policy. During its six years of life ELIAMEP has organized or co-sponsored 20 international conferences.

As of the summer of 1990, the Foundation holds teaching seminars in the island of Halki (off the coast of Rhodes) for the benefit of young scholars from Southeastern Europe, the Middle East and Western Europe.

HESYCHASM. A form of direct communion with the "energies" of God achieved through a special form of praying.

The practice of certain hermits on Mount Athos (q.v.) to live in holy stillness (*hesychia*) prompted Barlaam, the learned Byzantine theologian and scholar who had put the view of Orthodoxy (q.v.) to the papacy at Abignon in 1339, to attack the "Hesychasts" as guilty of error if not of heresy. The controversy which shook the Orthodox Church (q.v.) in the middle of the fourteenth century involved a point of doctrine relative to God's nature and a point of liturgy related to the methods of prayer. It is of course true that, unlike Roman Catholic ones, the Orthodox monasteries— originating in the late and early fourth centuries and gradually evolving as places of disciplined life, even of voluntary martyrdom, when Christians ceased to be martyred by the Roman authorities—were much more devoted to asceticism and mysticism than to missionary activities, social work, and other worldly activities. Be that as it may, the Hesychasts seemed to Barlaam to have tilted the balance too much in favor of contemplation.

A distinctive feature of Hesychasm is the value of silence. In doctrinal terms this means silence about God Himself as He can only be described negatively by what He is not, never positively. Inexact—of necessity—positive statements can only be made about His creatures, not about the Creator. This is the so-called apophatic approach much appreciated in Orthodox circles even today. The apophatic language is extra-rational: "God is infinite and incomprehensible," wrote John of Damascus, "and all that is comprehensible about Him is His infinity and incomprehensibility . . . God does not belong to the class of existing things: not that He has no existence, but that He is above all existing things, nay even above existence itself.'' However, the Hesychasts maintained divine unknowability does not preclude direct communion with God. What is needed is the right method.

Following the precepts of their leading figure, Gregory Palamas, the Archbishop of Thessaloniki in the fourteenth century, ''Hesychast'' monks claimed that repetition of the Jesus prayer and certain psychosomatic techniques, such as holding one's breath while praying in order to achieve the beatific vision, helped them to experience the divine ''uncreated'' light which had shone round Christ on Mount Tabor. This was a prayer of silence, stripped of images, many words and elaborate thoughts. Their claim sounded preposterous: with the right technique men could know God in their life! Barlaam was outraged. God—he argued—was in essence totally unknowable and any claims to the contrary were deeply suspect if not outright heretical. To pretend that one could reach God directly by constantly repeating the ''Jesus prayer'' (''Lord Jesus Christ, Son of God, have mercy on me, a sinner''), keeping one's head bowed, chin resting on the chest, eyes fixed on the heart while doing the proper breathing exercises in order to help concentration and thus allow the prayer to ''enter the heart,'' was reminiscent of magical practices and superstition. Even more suspect was the fact that the experience seemed to require no hierarchy, no mediator, no institutional guidance. God, asserted the anti-Hesychasts, could only be known indirectly. Claiming to gain access to Him with one's senses was grossly materialistic and plainly wrong.

Barlaam and others who argued along those lines lost their case. Palamas proved conclusively with sound theological arguments that although God was indeed unknowable ''in his essence,'' He was on the other hand knowable ''through his energies.'' ''His energies,'' he said, ''come down to us, His essence is inaccessible.'' By ''energies'' are meant the ways He revealed Himself to us in His three Persons, the ways He interacted with us through His Son and through the Holy Spirit. As the whole person, body and mind, was created in the image of God—argued Palamas—the body can also be trusted as a partner to the soul. Since the Incarnation, flesh too is an inexhaustible source of sanctification. So why all this aggravation about reaching God through bodily techniques as well as by mental striving as the Hesychasts maintain?

These views became official doctrine in 1351 while Palamas (who died in 1359) was officially canonized in the same year. Patriarch Philotheus Coccinus even wrote his encomium. Palamas's theology spread throughout the Slav countries, especially in Russia, and was seen as a reaffirmation of the spiritual experience of deification, the basis and purpose of Christian life in the Orthodox Church (q.v.). Palamas's teachings have a special appeal to the so-called neo-orthodox movement active at present in Athens, Thessaloniki and Mount Athos. Hesychasm is a typical product of Byzantine monastic life, rich in divinely revealed "energies" and considering in fact all creation as a gigantic Burning Bush permeated but never burned by the fire of God's energies which are not a gift but God Himself in His action and revelation to the world.

-I-

ICONOCLASM. A movement which developed in the eighth and ninth century in the Eastern Roman Empire—or Byzantium as it was later named—aiming to ban the use of icons in Christian worship.

Icons play a central part in the Orthodox religion and their painting was and still is subject to strict rules. Shadows do not exist. The images are suffused in a yellow light conveying feelings of eternal bliss or torment as the case may be. The gaunt, elongated figures in stylized poses—which have inspired, among others, the famous Cretan Renaissance painter who lived and worked in Spain, Dominikos Theotokopoulos (1541–1614), better known as El Greco—are portrayed in vivid colors against a gold background representing a heavenly aura. The respect of tradition has been such that icon painting has practically remained unaltered throughout the centuries. It takes today an expert to date the icons. Devout people in the Empire believed that icons were windows through which the inhabitants of heaven revealed themselves. There have been many legends about the miraculous apparition in certain places of icons which were allegedly "not made by hands" (*acheiropoietoi*). The Neo-platonic notion of icons being sacred images of holy archetypes led some people to consider them not just as an object of veneration but of worship, an attitude smacking of idolatry according to iconoclasts.

The opponents of the use of icons pointed out that the early Church avoided figural representation of Christ both because the second commandment (Exodus 20:4) forbade graven images and because the Old Testament stressed the spirituality of worship. In their view, the only true image of Christ was the Eucharist and the only true image of a saint was the reproduction of his virtue. The truth is that, in the sixth and seventh centuries, the use of images took on a strange forms. Icons were believed to perform miracles, were prayed to and believed to possess some of the supernatural powers ascribed to their prototype. An element of magic seemed to be surreptitiously creeping into the faith. In the minds of many devout churchgoers there was no doubt about the Palladian qualities of the icon of St. Demetrius of Thessaloniki or of the Mother of God in the various sieges of Constantinople.

To maintain therefore that the Iconoclasts who wanted to "cleanse" Christianity from such practices were simply under the influence of Jewish or Muslim ideas (i.e., monotheists who forbid any attempt to depict the deity) is to disregard the very strong "puritan" streak in the Orthodox faith. When Emperor Leo III, of North Syrian origin himself, born in Germanicia and reputed to have been under Islamic influence in his youth, first attacked the icons in 726 A.D., he found plenty of support inside the Church. The Iconodules, on the other hand, were at pains to stress that they were not in favor of superstitious practices and disguised magic. They maintained, however, that to repudiate all representations of God was to question the reality of Incarnation, this exclusively Christian version of monotheism distinguishing it from its Jewish and Islamic rivals. They thus drew sharply the line between veneration (*proskynesis*) due to an icon and worship (*latreia*) due to the deity. The icon was warranted, in their view, because when God took on a material body he showed in practice that matter could be redeemed. An icon was not a pagan idol, they said, because it depicted a genuine saint or Jesus and his disciples, not a non-existent demon.

The Seventh and last Council, held in Nicaea in 787 A.D., seemed to have settled the issue. However, the controversy went on under various guises until the use of icons was formally, officially, and finally restored on the first Sunday of Lent in 843 A.D., celebrated ever since as Orthodoxy Sunday. Patriarch Photius, who presided over the liquidation of the last traces of Iconoclasm, loudly proclaimed that all heresies had finally been defeated once and for all. See also ECUMENICAL COUNCILS; ORTHODOX CHURCH; ORTHODOXY.

IMPORTS. The value of imports is about double the value of exports. The largest import item is crude oil, next come foodstuffs where imports have climbed ever since Greece joined the European Community (EC) (q.v.), capital goods (mainly agricultural machinery), motor vehicles as well as manufactured consumer goods (mainly threads and yarns) and raw materials. The main source of imports is the EC (58 percent of the total import bill).

Any improvement in the business climate increases—sometimes dramatically—the import bill and may temporarily affect adversely the balance of payments. Conversely, the indicator showing first the best results during the implementation of an austerity plan or during a recession is the balance of payments which improves dramatically as imports slow down. See also EXPORTS: FOREIGN TRADE.

INDUSTRY (MANUFACTURING). The largest industrial employer is the food processing sector. Next, in order of importance, come shoe making, textiles and metal production. Other branches of lesser importance are paper, furniture, electrical and transport equipment. The shift to industry started in the 1960s and has proceeded apace ever since.

Manufacturing industry accounted for 16.3 percent of GDP in 1990 but contributed 54.1 percent to the dollar value of exports. There are 150,682 industrial and artisanal establishments in Greece. The units are labor-intensive and tiny by European standards. They employ a total of 754,507 people. Of these about a quarter are working proprietors or non-paid family members. Some 36.4 percent of the establishments (and 39.7 percent of the jobs) are in the Athens (q.v.) area.

There is now a tendency towards larger enterprises, investment in new technologies and better use of the capital market. Traditionally, businesses have been family affairs. In the 1980s, securities accounted for less than one percent of private company financing. This is rapidly changing. The Stock Exchange has acquired a new importance, especially after the introduction of the 1988 legislation which provided for traders and underwriters to replace traditional brokers. It also provided for the creation of an unlisted securities market for smaller firms. By the end of 1991, the number of companies listed had risen from 110 to 154 (though 26 were later suspended) and the number of issues had risen from 160 to 241. There are eight companies with 16 issues on the unlisted market. It is expected that throughout the 1990s the capital market in Greece will develop further as manufacturing industry adopts European standards and practices.

INVESTMENT (FOREIGN). Foreign nationals may invest in Greece, acquire control of various enterprises and transfer—as of January 1992—profits abroad in three equal instalments over three years. Ever since 1953, foreign investment enjoys protection, not simply of the law but of the constitution (q.v.) itself, against nationalization and any change in the original conditions. Other legislation governs offshore companies whose business is exclusively outside Greece (Law 89) and offshore shipping companies (Law 378).

Foreign investment is expected to grow in the 1990s as the managed slide of the drachma leads to a depreciation of the currency (q.v.) which is, however, sufficiently slow to allow gains in relative labor cost competitiveness because of the correspondingly slow rate of wage increases.

IONIAN ISLANDS. The first addition of territory and people of Greek background to the young nation-state happened nearly

40 years after its formation when Britain ceded the Ionian islands to Greece, Lying along the western coast of Greece in the Ionian Sea, with a population of 191,003, they are also called "Seven Islands" from the number of principal ones. Corfu (592 square kilometers with a population of 105,043) is the northernmost and most populous of the seven. The islands are peaks of a mountain range running parallel to the ranges of continental Greece. They contain no rivers and no lakes but have enough groundwater to keep them green most of the year. Their main income comes from tourism (q.v.).

The Ionian islands differ somewhat from the rest of Greece in the sense that they developed their own Septinsular culture in close contact with the West having only very briefly been subjected to the Ottoman yoke. They were for four centuries under the occupation of Venice up to its fall in 1797, after which they were passed to the French, then came under Russian control, were given back to the French and were finally captured by Britain in 1809–10. Some 15 years later they were turned into a British protectorate which they remained until pressure from the islanders to unite with their mother country, free at last, convinced the British to give them up in 1864. During the long centuries of Venetian rule an Italianate upper class did emerge but the religion, the mores and the language (with some Italian admixtures) remained Greek. Thanks to the British influence, Corfu acquired a cricket team which is still in existence.

In fact, the Ionian islands—as witnessed by their music, architecture and literature—became an important channel of western influence in an otherwise Orthodox world insulated from Europe, if not hostile to it.

IOANIDES, DIMITRIOS see COLONELS' COUP AND REGIME

-J-

JEWS. Greece's Jewish community consists of the ancient Jews, who resided in Athens and Macedonia (qq.v.) from the time of St. Paul, and the Sephardic Jews, who were compelled to leave Spain in the fifteenth century. During the centuries of Ottoman rule (q.v.) most of the Macedonian Jews were forced to move to Constantinople and their place was taken by the Sephardic refugees.

In the Second World War (q.v.) the Greek Jews shared the fate of their brethren throughout Europe. More than 65,000 of a total of 80,000 perished during the Axis occupation. On the eve of the war, over 70 percent of the Greek Jews lived in Thessaloniki, 3,500 in Athens, 2,200 in Kavala, 2,000 in Corfu, 1,950 in Jannina, and the rest in Drama, Larissa, Kastoria and Volos. By August 1943 about 46,000 from Thessaloniki alone were deported to German concentration camps. Mass deportations had already taken place in the Bulgarian annexed territories of Kavala and Drama that very same year.

After the Italian armistice in September 1943, the Germans took over Athens and tried to round up its Jewish population. A universal refusal to hand them over to occupation authorities and, indeed, organized concealment, saved most of the Athenian Jews. The EAM-ELAS resistance movement, the Archbishop of Athens Damaskinos and the Greek Church (q.v.), the Chief of the Athens Police, Angelos Evert, who was in contact with the English, all conspired to save the Jews from the Nazi liquidation program. On Evert's orders the police issued about 18,500 false identity papers to protect all those hiding from the German authorities.

JUNTA see COLONELS' COUP AND REGIME

JUSTICE, ADMINISTRATION OF. Justice in Greece is administered by law courts (q.v.), most of which are composed of professional judges who enjoy life tenure and total independence in the performance of their duties under the constitution (q.v.). The judicial system deals with disputes between citizens, ensures the protection of their rights, the unhindered pursuit of their lawful activities, and protects the state from criminal acts against its authority. The judiciary acts by issuing decisions "in the name of the Greek people." Justice is usually administered at two levels: the lower courts judge cases in the first instance while recourse is always possible to a higher court by both litigants. Greece has a "civil law" system whereby judges rely not so much (or even not at all) on precedent but on detailed written codes.

Procedure in the courts follows the French mode. An investigating magistrate examines the evidence, interrogates the witnesses and eventually refers the case to the public prosecutor who decides whether or not a charge shall be brought.

-K-

KAFANDARIS, GEORGIOS (1873–1946). Prominent liberal politician of the interwar period. Born in a village of Evrytania, Kafandaris studied law in Athens (q.v.) and practiced in Messolonghi and later in Athens. He was elected deputy in 1905. Although a supporter of political change, he disavowed the pronunciamento of 1909 and abstained from the elections of October 1910. Later, he made peace with Eleftherios Venizelos (q.v.) and held ministerial positions in most of his governments. In 1923 Kafandaris emerged as the politician most likely to replace Venizelos in the Liberal Party (q.v.). He became a minister in January 1924 and Prime Minister after Venizelos's resignation in February 1924. He too resigned due to pressure by the military on 12 March 1924, and formed the Progressive Liberal Party. After the fall of Theodoros Pangalos (q.v.), he played an important part in the "Ikoumeniki" (i.e., all party) government in which he held the Ministry of Finance and stabilized the drachma. Venizelos's return to active politics caused a rift between the two.

KALVOS, ANDREAS (1792–1869). Kalvos was a poet born in the Ionian island (q.v.) of Zakynthos six years before Dionysios Solomos (q.v.), who also started writing in Italian. He married an English headmistress in Lancashire and ran a girls' school at Louth with her. For the last 40 years of his life he wrote not one single verse. He seems to have led a strange and solitary life and never even met Solomos, practically his neighbor in Corfu. The death certificate lists him as a "Professor of Languages and Mathematics."

Kalvos's work consists of two thin collections of poems published at the age of 32 and 34, the first in Geneva, the second in Paris, containing "Odes" of great lyrical beauty—a kind of Pindaric hymn to the Greek War of Independence (q.v.). The "Odes" seems to have aroused little interest among his contemporaries. They became known and appreciated as late as the end of the nineteenth century, after the poet's death, mainly because of the interest shown in them by Kostis Palamas (q.v.).

Kalvos's poetical career is in many ways unique. In 1811 he wrote in Italian an ode entitled "To Napoleon." He also wrote, again in Italian, two worthless tragedies named *Thiramenis* and *The Danaides,* in which he slavishly imitates the style of Hugo Foscolo (1778–1827), a poet and political activist born in Zakynthos who took Kalvos under his wing when the latter became the tutor, in Florence, to a ward of his. In 1815, Foscolo had to flee to Switzerland because of his involvement with the radical movement of the Carbonari who advocated constitutional government in Italy. Kalvos stayed behind for a year but then, in 1816, he also joined his mentor in Switzerland because he also became involved with the Carbonari. They both went to London in the same year where they quarreled and separated for reasons never completely elucidated. Kalvos returned in 1821 to Florence, but had to flee again to Switzerland. The outbreak of the War of Independence (q.v.) that year in Greece, and his contacts with the enthusiastic Swiss philhellenes, prompted him to publish, in 1824, his first ten "Odes" in Greek. A further ten were published in 1826. His poetic genius seems to have burnt itself out after that. His brief but disastrous encounter with the factionalism of mainland Greek leaders is believed to have damaged his poetic impulse. He belonged spiritually to the culture of the French Revolution, combining literary output with radicalism and love of the classics. His tolerance of real Greeks in flesh and blood, warts and all, was minimal, if not nil. He remained attached to the Greek cause . . . but from afar.

The "Odes" are intriguing. The meter is highly original. There is evidence that Kalvos attempted to imitate Sapphic or Alcaic stanzas, yet the basis is the commonplace demotic

15-syllable line cut in two. He uses archaic words, even Homeric imagery. His language is highly personal, a unique blend of the purist and the demotic. It is the language (q.v.) of a sensitive modern poet seduced by a 3,000 years old idiom. His thought is lofty, his voice thunderous but crystalline and the cold passion which he displays in portraying a people in search of freedom and dignity makes his work a classic in modern Greek literature. Some of these "Odes," however, such as the "Altar of the Fatherland," are full of bombast and worthless anti-Turkish propaganda. Such flops are not frequent, however.

Kalvos poetry has always had its devotees, George Seferis (q.v.) being the most prominent among them in recent times.

KANARIS, CONSTANTINOS (1790–1877). Major figure in the naval history of the Greek War of Independence (q.v.). Born in the island of Psara, Kanaris began his naval career in the merchant marine of the Aegean Sea. At the outbreak of the War of Independence he joined the fleet of the insurgents and made his name when he destroyed the Ottoman flagship in Chios on 7 June 1892.

Kanaris served as minister and Prime Minister in several governments of the Greek state and was considered a wise figure who enjoyed high esteem among his contemporaries.

KANELLOPOULOS, PANAYOTIS, (1902–1986). Scholar and statesman. Born in Patras, Peloponnese (q.v.), in 1902, Kanellopoulos studied law and philosophy in Athens and Heidelberg and became the first Professor of Sociology in Athens University at the age of 31. A nephew of Dimitrios Gounaris, he became involved in politics and was interned between 1937 and 1940 by the Metaxas (q.v.) dictatorship for his unyielding opposition to the abolition of parliamentary politics. In October 1940, when Greece was under attack by the Fascist forces, he was granted his plea to fight as a common soldier. After Nazi occupation, he formed his own resistance group and fled to Egypt, in 1942, to join the Greek government-in-exile, first as Minister of Defense and later Deputy Prime Minister.

After liberation, he served briefly as Prime Minister in

1945 and in several ministries of the Populist, the Greek Rally and the National Radical Union governments. Between 1964 and 1967, he took over the opposition party after Constantinos Karamanlis's (q.v.) departure and was heading the caretaker government that would have run the elections of May 1967.

The military, who organized the coup of 21 April 1967, arrested Kanellopoulos and kept him first in detention and then under close surveillance, but this did not deter him from actively opposing the Colonels' regime throughout its seven-year tenure. After the return of democracy, in 1974, he became member of Parliament again and a champion of moderation in politics. He left an important body of philo-sophical works inspired by German idealism and a personal record of service to high principles.

KARAISKAKIS, GEORGIOS (1782–1827). A chieftain from Epirus before the Greek revolution against Ottoman rule, Karaiskakis became commander of the Greek forces during the final year of the War of Independence (q.v.). His extraordinary talent in conducting military operations and his death in the field won him the halo of a hero.

KARAMANLIS, (CONSTANTINOS) KONSTANTINOS (1907–   ). Greece's leading postwar politician. Karaman-lis was born in Serres, Macedonia (q.v.) in 1907. He was first elected deputy in 1936 with the Populist Party and was reelected after the war (1946) under the same banner. He joined the Greek Rally party in 1951 and served as minister on several occasions before he assumed his most successful post as Minister of Public Works. Karamanlis became Prime Minister following the death of Alexandros Papagos (q.v.) in 1955 and founded his own party, the Greek Radical Union, soon after. This party, under his leadership, won the elections of 1956, 1958 and 1961. His long term as head of govern-ment rallied against him in 1963 an assortment of political opponents under Georgios Papandreou (q.v.). The assassina-tion of a left-wing deputy by extreme right-wingers contrib-uted to his electoral defeat in 1963.

After his defeat, Karamanlis established himself in Paris

and made his triumphant return to Greece in 1974 when the seven-year Colonels' regime collapsed. He reconstituted his party under the name New Democracy (q.v.) and ran successfully in 1974 and 1977. He was elected President of the Republic in 1980, but chose not to be a candidate in 1985 following the Socialist party's reluctance to vote for him. He was elected once more as President in 1990.

Karamanlis is the most influential Greek politician of the postwar period. He made his mark as the premier of reconstruction in a war-ravaged country, the statesman who engineered Greece's orderly return to democracy after the fall of the military dictatorship and the architect of Greek entry into the European Community (q.v.). His stature as a wise figure of Greek politics is now well established.

KATHAREVOUSA ("PURIST" GREEK). A somewhat stiff form of language by means of which Greek scholars tried in the nineteenth century to "cleanse" and enrich the "low life" demotic (q.v.) vernacular spoken by mostly illiterate Greeks under Ottoman rule. It became, after the successful end of the War of Independence (q.v.), the language of state institutions and the law, a function "demotic" Greek was allegedly unable to perform because of its lack of abstract terms. This was deeply resented by a number of authors and scholars in favor of the demotic language. They deemed *Katharevousa* to be a socially divisive, artificial fabrication which would stifle the natural development of modern Greek instead of restoring it to its pristin Attic purity as was the professed aim of its champions. See also LANGUAGE.

KAZANTZAKIS, NICOS (1885–1957). Author known to the English-speaking world mainly through his novels. Born in Herakleion, Crete (q.v.), Kazantzakis grew up during a period of violent rebellions in his native island which deeply influenced his work. He studied law in Athens (q.v.) and philosophy in Paris where he came under the spell of Henri Bergson, the irrationalist French philosopher who believed in the existence of a "vital force" apprehended intuitively. The young Cretan wrote, at the age of 23, an essay entitled "Sickness of the Age" in which he maintained that the classical age was the childhood of man in which simplicity and instinct were supreme. This untrammeled joy was destroyed by the "pale Nazarene" who diverted men away from the good things in life promising them a non-existent Heaven. He later came under the spell of the German philosopher Nietzsche.

In Greece Kazantzakis became actively involved in the linguistic war between the "demoticists"—proponents of the spoken popular language (q.v.)—and the "purists" who dreamed of the reintroduction of ancient Greek as a first step towards the restoration of the glory that was Greece. During the decade 1910–20 he became active in politics, educational reform and even business ventures including a financially disastrous attempt at mining with a foreman named George Zorbas. His subsequent disillusion with politics, the educational establishment, business and Greece made him turn against his former nationalist beliefs and display bitterness and scorn against Greek aspirations.

Katzantzakis's writings become, thereafter, replete with metaphysical anguish; he increasingly perceived human existence as tragic. However, he never lost his belief in the possibility of redemption provided man were strong enough to transform his life into spiritual value, a gift not possessed by everyone. His most abstract and least comprehensible work, embodying all these beliefs, is his *Odysseia* (Odyssey), a philosophical epic of 33,333 verses arranged into 24 books.

Katzantzakis's popular novels, such as *Zorba the Greek* (1952), *Christ Recrucified* (1954) and *The Last Temptation of Christ* (1956) have gained him international acclaim and were made into successful films often incurring the wrath of practicing Christians. An enthusiastic traveler, he published books on Britain, Spain, China, and Japan.

KINGS see CONSTANTINE I; CONSTANTINE II; GEORGE I; GEORGE II; FREDERIKA OF GREECE; OTTO WITTELSBACH

KKE. Greek acronym for the words "Kommunistiko Komma Elladas," i.e., Communist Party of Greece. See also COMMUNIST PARTY OF GREECE.

KOLOKOTRONIS, THEODOROS (1770–1843). General of the Greek insurgents in the Peloponnese (q.v.), he was widely known as the "Old Man of Moreas" during the War of Independence (q.v.). A mercenary soldier employed by the British in the Ionian islands (q.v.), he offered his experience and military talent to the cause of the revolution and won many battles against the Ottomans.

KONDYLIS, GEORGIOS (1878–1936). A military activist in politics. Born in Roumeli, Kondylis joined the infantry as a volunteer in 1896, rising through the ranks. In 1897, he was in Crete (q.v.), and between 1904 and 1908 fought as a guerrilla in Macedonia and then in Thrace (qq.v.). He served in the Balkan Wars (q.v.) and in the army that was made up by the National Defense of Thessaloniki in 1916. Kondylis also served in the Ukraine in 1918–19, and in Asia Minor as a Colonel in 1919–20. From November 1920 until September 1922, he joined the antiroyalist cause as a fugitive in Constantinople. In 1923, he was instrumental in putting down the Gargalidis-Leonardopoulos coup. He retired that year and became involved in politics. Kondylis changed political camps in 1931, moving from extreme republicanism to a royalist position. He became Viceroy in 1935 and helped restore the monarchy.

KORAIS, ADAMANTIOS (1748–1833). Leading figure of the Greek Enlightment. Born in Smyrna, the son of a rich merchant from the island of Chios, Korais spent time in Amsterdam attempting to follow the family trade. Between 1782–86 he studied medicine at the University of Montpellier and became a prominent classical scholar. He lived in Paris between 1788–1833 and came to know the great changes that occurred during that period from close quarters. He disliked radicalism and became the exponent of a "middle way" in democratic liberal politics.

Korais believed that the Greeks would never attain true freedom from the backwardness of Ottoman bondage if they did not become versed in the scholarly tradition of their ancient roots. The "Hellenic Library" of ancient Greek authors was his own contribution to the Greek War of Independence (q.v.)

and his influence on the development of the language (q.v.) of the Greek intelligentsia became his lasting testament.

KOUMOUNDOUROS, ALEXANDROS (1815–1883). Important early politician. Born in Mani of the Peloponnese (q.v.), he was elected to Parliament for the first time in 1851 and became Minister of Finance in 1956. Prime Minister in 1865, Koumoundouras assumed that position ten times during his lifetime. He was a political opponent of Harilaos Trikoupis (q.v.) and was credited with the extension of Greece's territory in 1881 to include Thessaly (q.v.) and parts of Epirus (q.v.). He was also responsible for distributing land to landless peasants and title deeds to long standing squatters on public estates.

-L-

LAND DEGRADATION. In Greece, land is degraded and the soil eroded because of deforestation, overgrazing, and the wrong agricultural policy encouraged by the European Community (EC) (q.v.). Salinization is due to improper drainage and the poor quality of scarce irrigation waters. Land degradation in the countryside is also due to livestock units, mainly those established before 1986, i.e., without the prior Environmental Impact Assessment studies which have been required since. Small agricultural units used for packaging and processing tomatoes, fruit, sugar, meat, vegetables, and olives as well as pulp and paper factories are often sources of unpleasant smells and water pollution. Finally, opencast mining as well as the location of industrial units in areas of good agricultural land in conjunction with a lack of anti-pollution measures, have resulted in a number of areas around metal producing factories in the pollution of soil, vegetation and agricultural produce with lead and cadmium. The government is keenly aware of these problems and is trying to confront them with the assistance of the EC.

LANGUAGE. Indo-European in origin and highly inflected, Greek is the most ancient European language in existence, with a history spanning three-and-a-half millennia of continuous use in roughly the same geographical area. While the ancestors of the Greeks entered Greece around 2000 B.C., a language which could be called Greek only emerged in the late Helladic period (c. 1600–1100 B.C.). Since then, the language developed to this day as a vehicle of thought and emotions as a direct descendant of classical Greek and in spite of numerous additions it retains the structure, the phonemes and almost 60 percent of the vocabulary of ancient Greek.

While Latin sprouted many languages from French to Romanian, and died off in medieval Italy, Greek did not branch out but lived on, changing and enriching the vocabulary of every single European language. Since it was chosen to be the language of the Gospels it has also profoundly affected the development of theology in the form of patristic Greek and through Byzantine culture in general. Documents in Greek cover a longer period of time (34 centuries) than those in any other Indo-European language. Until 1952, the oldest written record in Greek was believed to be an alphabetic inscription written on an Attic jug and dated to c. 725 B.C. In that year, however, Michael Ventris, the very gifted young British architect scholar and archaeologist (1922–1956), deciphered the so-called Linear B script and proved conclusively that the language it recorded—however inadequately—was Greek of at least the 13th century B. C.

The development of Greek throughout its long history has been marked by continuous conflict between the proponents of change and the bastions of tradition or even—at times—of regression to the fourth century B.C. form of the language or to one approximating it as closely as possible. There are good reasons for this. Classical Greek is too impressive a language to jettison. Subtle, diaphanous, flexible, delicate, and clear, it made thinking wonderfully attractive as it encourages the formation of general ideas from perceptions and impressions. Greek provided a great variety of how to say things and how to pack a great deal of meaning in elegant, concise formulations. While Latin had only three ways of slipping subordinate clauses into a sentence, Greek had at least ten. Conjunctions and particles signposted a sentence to avoid confusion as to what lay ahead. Its wealth allowed great subtilty in distinctions; its great tonal variety allowed rhetorical brilliance and quite impressive dramatic effects. No one who had mastered it could easily let it go.

It was this tendency to go back to the original "pure" source of Greek which prompted some militant scholars to launch in the first century B.C. a movement called "Atticism" inspired by the notion that to revive the "Golden Age" Greeks should first try to revive its language. The split continued to haunt the Byzantines over the next centuries, though in a different form. They stuck to the *koine* (i.e. common language) of the holy texts, while the real, spoken, vernacular continued to evolve separately. A few tried to atticize after the classical revival of the eleventh-century writing—as S. Runciman puts it "in a language slightly different from their own." The vernacular makes its appearance in writing for the first time in the eleventh century in certain accepted forms of secular verse such as romances and plays.

The controversy persisted throughout the Ottoman rule and became more virulent towards its end. Centuries of Turkish occupation, argued scholars such as Kodrikas, Voulgaris, Doukas, Vamvas and others, had degraded the language so much that a foreign traveler to Greece such as the British W.M. Leake thought it, for instance, natural to mention in the preface of his *Researches in Greece* (1814) that modern Greek was but "a corrupted dialect of an ancient language." What bothered Greek scholars was that nobody could say this for French or Italian, languages which had all been shaped after the tenth century A.D. The conclusion they drew was that a form of Greek was needed which would reestablish the broken link with the ancestors and uplift the nation from its "decadence." Militant activists, however, such as Rigas Fereos disagreed completely for a very simple reason. The Greek people would not rise, they said, unless addressed by an elite who used a language they could readily understand.

A serious attempt at resolving the conflict was made when, in the nineteenth century Adamantios Korais (q.v.) proposed as a compromise a linguistic form resulting from a serious effort to drastically simplify the atticizing form and purify the spoken one while at the same time enriching it with comprehensible neologisms patterned on the learned model. Korais's choice, *Katharevousa* (q.v.) (purist language), was first used as a term in 1798 according to Peter Mackridge (*The Modern Greek Language,* p. 7). By 1850, more and more purification was clamored for while Korais's efforts at a compromise were denigrated as old-fashioned. The "official" language of the Greek kingdom diverged more and more from the spoken vernacular.

The reaction was not slow in coming. It took the form of a struggle for the spoken, "demotic" (q.v.) language or *dimotiki,* a term which according to Peter Mackridge appears first in 1818. The first demoticists were authors who quickly realized that stories, plays and poems, unlike official documents, could not easily be written in the purist language (though there are exceptions such as the excellent short stories of Papadiamantis and the elegant, mordant novels by Roidis, for instance). The roots of demoticism can be traced in the works of Solomos (q.v.) and in the writings of Katartzis, Vilaras and Christopoulos born in the eighteenth century. The demoticist movement became polemical and somewhat strident when Yannis Psycharis, a Greek professor of linguistics at the School of Oriental Studies in Paris, attempted in a book published in 1888 to lay its "scientific" foundations.

The "language question" (*"to glossiko zitima"*) as it became known was, or course, much more than an academic controversy. It touched on matters having to do with religion, national identity and political affiliation. In general (but with notable exceptions) the "purists" tended to be traditionalists and conservatives of the right while the demoticists proclaimed the need for change and for adopting the "language of the people." After the post-Psycharis "purist" backlash in the first decade of the twentieth century, the liberals of Eleftherios Venizelos (q.v.) came out cautiously in favor of the demotic although Venizelos himself never used it in his speeches. The issue continued to stir emotions for more than a generation with the demotic scoring points while both forms influenced each other. A kind of new *koine* called the *kathomiloumeni,* i.e., "everyday spoken tongue," began to appear in the 1920s and 1930s.

Modern Greek, which emerged after the end of the linguistic war, marks the final triumph of the *koine* over the attempts to put it down and is the outcome of centuries long linguistic development. ''The Greek vocabulary records only births not deaths,'' an Athenian lady once told the French de-constructionist philosopher Jaques Derrida, who described it as ''rich with all the alluvia of its history. . . .'' Modern Greek is nowadays one language where hidden layers of meaning can always be uncovered as Konstantinos Cavafy (q.v.) and Odysseus Elytis (q.v.) have proven with their poetical experimentation. New compounds can always be created as Nicos Kazantzakis (q.v.) has done, often abusively. The insatiable greed of the language is constantly assimilating new words, in creating new ones, its reluctance to relinquish anything, its bewildering multiplicity of parallel forms of the same words, even of parallel grammars make life difficult for the lexicographer and the teacher but allow for an almost infinite variety of expression from colloquial speech to erudite writing. The fact is, that this multiformity (*polytypia*), though baffling at times, allows users of Modern Greek to make stylistic choices from a great wealth of alternatives and establish a large set of different registers.

LAUSANNE TREATY (1923). The treaty settled the boundaries of Greece and Turkey. Greece retained all but two of the Aegean islands (q.v.) (Imvros and Tenedos). Turkey was given eastern Thrace, thus reverting to her 1914 European boundaries. British sovereignty over Cyprus (q.v.) was confirmed. A demilitarized zone was established on both the Asian and European shores of the straits and their security and free navigation were guaranteed by the signatories of the Straits Convention and especially by France, Britain, Italy and Japan (the Soviet Union signed but did not ratify). A convention was signed in January 1923 concerning the compulsory exchange of Greek and Moslem minorities.

LIBERAL PARTY. Founded in the summer of 1910, the Liberal Party was inspired by a politician from Crete (q.v.) who had just made his impressive entry into Greek politics, Eleftherios Venizelos (q.v.). The symbol of the party was the anchor, and the intention of its founders was to create an institution firmly based on a set of liberal values comparable to those of its British prototypes.

In his first public speech in Athens (q.v.) on 5 September 1910, Venizelos described his own intentions:

"Recognizing the need for the education of the Greek people and for its emancipation from personal parties, I will work with those with whom . . . my ideas coincide for the organization of a political association branching out throughout the land, which is going to become the organization of the new political party of a generation."

The content of his speech, however, materialized only ten years later in May 1920 when the Liberal League was created to become the party's nationwide mass organization.

Venizelos's long absence from active politics between 1920–28 made the Liberal Party an institution of notables. After his return to power Venizelos attempted to endow his party with a democratic charter but was met with opposition from within. In 1933, a party caucus decided to form a committee for the management of party affairs. This committee also appointed local party organizations in the prefectures. The central office, the Liberals Clubs of Athens and Thessaloniki, a party office in Piraeus and one hundred provincial associations, constituted the organizational nexus of the Liberal Party.

The problem of succession to the party's leadership after Venizelos's 1920–28 absence was partly solved by having General Panayotes Danglis (q.v.) act as a stand-in for the Cretan statesman.

After Venizelos's final departure from Greece in 1935, and resignation from the party, Themistoklis Sophoulis (q.v.) was chosen as the new leader. The party was closed down by the Metaxas (q.v.) dictatorship in 1936. After the war, the Liberal Party operated again under the leadership of Sophoulis and later Sophocles Venizelos (q.v.), son of its first leader.

LITERATURE (MODERN). The origins of modern Greek literature can be traced back to the eleventh century A.D. with the epic of the legendary Byzantine folk hero Dighenis (i.e., the one "born of two races" as his mother was Christian and his father a converted Arab emir) Akritas (frontiersman) who bravely defended the true faith and the borders of the Empire against formidable enemies. His exploits are sung in the "demotic" or spoken language of the time thus providing evidence of a linguistic continuity as well as the literary sophistication of the then natural speakers of Greek. From that time on and until modern Greeks finally acquired their own state in 1830, the demotic literary tradition was continuously enriched by popular songs, ballads, laments, love poems, and tales of bravery composed by unknown authors and polished by constant repetition. Notable exceptions to this rule of impersonal literary creation are the two long poems in rhyming 15-syllable verse by Vincenzo Kornaros in seventeenth century Crete (q.v.), *Abraham's Sacrifice,* and *Erotokritos,* which are still sometimes declaimed today in Cretan villages on festive occasions.

With the emergence of the Greek state in 1830, a number of authors marked the birth of the new Greece with works of major significance. Noteworthy names in this first period are Dionysios Solomos and Andreas Kalvos (qq.v.), the most prominent representatives of the culture of Septinsular Greeks.

Others in this category are Ugo Foscolo (1778–1827), poet and mentor to Kalvos; Antonios Matessis (1794–1875) the gifted playwright; Iacovos Polylas (1826–1896), a serious critic; and Julius Typaldos (1814–1831), a mystic, deeply religious poet. In Athens (q.v.) flourished the romanticism of the Athenian School using mainly the purist form of the language *Katharevousa* (q.v.). Also notable was the work of Emmanuel Roidis (1836–1904), with its corrosive irony directed against official pomposity, grandiloquence, and corruption; the short stories of Alexandros Papadiamantis (1851–1911), dubbed "the secular monk" ("kosmokalogeros") for the purity of his Greek-Orthodox approach to problems of everyday life; the mainly folkloric stories of Dimitris Vikelas (1835–1908), and George Vizyinos (1849–1869). All such literary works as well as essays, historical treatises, and books written by intellectuals both in Greece and abroad, were animated by a common purpose. They reflected the striving of modern Greeks to forge themselves an identity out of a glorious and distant pagan past, a closer Byzantine Christian tradition and their contemporary experience of a national struggle which had not yet ended since most ethnic Greeks were still living outside the new state's borders.

The Romantic school of Athens (q.v.) which held sway during the latter half of the nineteenth century provided poetry which was rather shallow and highly colored but which gave vent to feelings of buoyant patriotism, melodramatic love and passionate views on politics and the "language question." Achilles Paraschos (1838–1895) is considered the most representative of this school which has vanished without trace.

With the eclipse of the Romantic movement in the 1880s Greeks were regaled with the works of a vigorous torrential poet who used and enriched the "demotic" idiom Kostis Palamas (q.v.). At the same time, Konstantinos Cavafy (q.v.) produced his exquisite esoteric poetry of understatement in Alexandria, while Angelos Sikelianos (q.v.) cultivated in his poetry his own idosyncratic vision of a renaissance of ancient Greek values in modern times. Aristotelis Valaoritis (1824–1879)—a lesser poet who followed his Ionian compatriots in the use of the vernacular—used his dynamic eloquent verse patterned on folk songs to extol Greek patriotism, while another Ionian poet from Cephalonia, the maverick Andreas Laskaratos, (1811–1901) used sarcasm in such a vituperative way that he was excommunicated by the Church. In response he offered them his pair of shoes for excommunication as it was then believed that the corpses of those dying outside the Church would never decay in all eternity.

The prose of the same period is on a lower level than poetry. Notable exceptions are the prose writings of Solomos and the memoirs and autobiographies of some of the protagonist, of the War of Independence (q.v.). The most important of these are the *Memoirs* of the revolutionary hero John Makriyannis (1797–1864), a seminal work written in vivid vernacular by a semi-literate fighter of the War of Independence.

Other important writers of twentieth century Greece are Grigorios Xenopoulos (1867–1951), the novelist and playwright of the urban middle classes; Nikos Kazantzakis (q.v.); Kostas Varnalis (1884–1974); Andreas Embirikos (1901–1975), whose books in surrealist verse and erotic prose in purist Greek are a best-seller in Athens today; Stratis Myrivilis (1892–1969), the chronicler of the inhumanity of war and provincial life; Kosmas Politis (1893–1974), whose sensitive novels focused on the anguish of growing up in prewar Greece, and many others. The literary revival in twentieth-century Greece produced two Nobel prize winners, George Seferis and Odysseus Elytis (qq.v.).

An issue often raised by Greeks and non-Greeks alike refers to foreign influences on the shaping of modern Greek literature. It is true that Solomos and Kalvos were Italianate in culture and might even have never escaped from it had they not been goaded by the War of Independence and European philhelenism to exploit the riches of their native tongue. Palamas had consumed almost all the works of Goethe, Hugo, Leconte de Lisle, the Symbolists, Verhaeren, Tolstoy, D'Annunzio, Pascoli, Unamuno and William James. Seferis's "tone of voice" was mainly shaped by T.S. Eliot while Cavafy was completely conversant with the poetic fashion in Europe. All this is natural and happens all the time. The only reason it has fueled controversies is the obsession of some Greeks with their "Greek fueled identity" even when they slavishly imitate foreign modes. Cross-cultural influences are a common phenomenon in the history of literature. Chaucer looked to France, Yeats to England, Joyce to Norway and the Parisian avant-garde while Samuel Beckett was a bilingual writer in French and English.

The Greek writers, turned both outward to Western Europe and backward to their own past, often seeing it through western eyes. In each case they blended in a unique way modernism with history, the foreign with the indigenous, and the sophisticated with the popular. See also POETRY.

-M-

MAASTRICHT CONFERENCE (December 1991). The Maastricht Summit of the Intergovernmental Conference on Economic and Monetary Union and Political Union resulted in the adoption of the Treaty on European Union. This treaty was greeted with enthusiasm in Greece and was ratified by Parliament with the support of all parties (except for the Communists). Greece's accession to the Western European Union (WEU) by the end of 1992 was also decided at Maastricht. It was through European Community (q.v.) pressure, however, that article 5 of the Modified Treaty of Brussels (providing for military help to a member subject to aggression) was nullified between member states of NATO and the WEU. The treaty was thus deprived of an important security guarantee for Greece.

MACEDONIA (MODERN). Part of Greece since 1912, and covering an area of 34,177 square kilometers, Macedonia is one of the two northernmost provinces of Greece. The other one is Thrace (q.v.). With a population of 2,263,099 Macedonia has borders on the north with Albania, the "Former Yugoslav Republic of Macedonia" (q.v.) and Bulgaria, on the east with Thrace, on the south with Thessaly (q.v.) and the Aegean Sea (q.v.), and on the west with Epirus (q.v.). The largest city is Thessaloniki (pop. 239,998), the capital of northern Greece, also sometimes called the "co-capital."

Three large rivers (Axios, Strymon, Nestos) flow through Macedonia from the north separating the province into three parts. Macedonia's economy is buoyant. Its industries are thriving, its substantial mineral wealth (lignite, iron, chromite) is well exploited, the Thessaloniki Trade Fair every September is an event of international, not just Balkan, importance while the magnificent finds of the royal tombs in Verghina (q.v.) are attracting more visitors by the year.

The population of Macedonia became so mixed during the Middle Ages that the territory has provided in French a synonym for fruit salad. Bulgarians, Serbs, and Turks dominated the inland area while the coast from Aliakmon to the Strymon Rivers including the Halhkidiki trident was mainly Greek. Under the clauses of the Treaty of Lausanne (1923) (q.v.) some 348,000 Moslems living in Macedonia were exchanged for 548,000 Greeks from Asia Minor. After the

Second World War (q.v.) and the Civil War (1946–49) the Slav population withdrew across the frontiers. The few families left in western Macedonia who speak a Slavonic idiom opted to consider themselves Greek so that there is actually no Slavomacedonian minority in Greece.

MAKARIOS III (1913–1977). Archbishop (1950–77) and President of the Republic of Cyprus (1960–77) (q.v.). Makarios was born Mikhail Mouskos in Paphos. Following theological studies at the universities of Athens and Boston, he was elected Metropolitan of Kitium in 1948. In 1950, he organized a plebiscite among Greek Cypriots which resulted in an overwhelming vote in favor of *enosis* or union of the island, then under British rule, with Greece. As Archbishop of Cyprus he championed the *enosis* cause and convinced the government of Greece to raise the question at the United Nations. In 1956, the British authorities banished him to the Seychelles. In 1958, Makarios declared himself for independence rather than *enosis* and opened the way for the Zurich and London agreement in 1959. As the first President of Cyprus (with a Turkish Cypriot Vice-President) Makarios called in 1963 for amendment of the unworkable constitution. Armed clashes between the Greek (80 percent) and Turkish Cypriots (18 percent) threatened to bring in Turkey (q.v.). The Turkish invasion occurred in 1974 after a coup engineered by the Greek dictatorship obliged Makarios to flee the island. The coup prompted the occupation of 40 percent of the territory of Cyprus by Turkish forces which have not left since. Although Makarios returned to his position in the same year, he never recovered from the disaster that befell Cyprus.

MARSHALL PLAN. A plan to prevent a war-ravaged Europe from sliding into economic disaster and ultimately into Soviet influence. The plan was proclaimed by American Secretary of State George Marshall in his famous Harvard speech on 5 June 1947.

The Marshall Plan was administered by the Economic Cooperation Administration on a vast scale. It included within its scope the United Nations Relief and Rehabilitation

Administration (q.v.) beneficiaries—Austria, Greece, and Italy—but extended its protection to the entire group of Western states—Britain, France, Benelux, etc. The primary objective of this aid was to supply the working capital to get international trade moving in Western Europe after the war.

MASS MEDIA. A French intellectual writing to a friend in Paris from Athens in 1837 A.D. noted the following: "Greece has one court of Appeal, three streets, four museums, five trees, six bakeries, seven habitable houses, eight associations and nineteen newspapers!" In this respect there has been a regression. There are actually 15 national newspapers in Greece of which four are morning ones with a circulation of 42,062 and 11 are evening papers with a circulation of 605,802 (February 1992) throughout the country. Most papers are of the tabloid format. In recent years there has been a significant upsurge of interest in the Sunday press. In 1992 there were 13 newspapers selling 832,616 copies on Sundays. Of the daily press, the conservative *Eleftheros Typos* sold most copies, i.e., 147,526 a day on average in 1992, while the socialist paper *Ta Nea* came second with an average of 139,166 a day. A success story in the financial press has been the liberal daily *Kerdos* ("Profit") which is widely read by the business community, and is profitable and very informative. Its owner is a self-made business tycoon in his mid-forties named Thomas Liakounakos. He started at the age of 18 with a mere $2,000 in his pocket and is now in charge of a conglomerate with a turnover of $60 million per annum and interests in international trade, computers the media, health care, fashion, and the construction industry.

Press freedom is constitutionally guaranteed and jealously guarded. There was always freedom of the press in Greece except in periods of dictatorship during which the muzzling of the newspapers was always experienced as a personal affront by the Greeks. Despite these attitudes, however, the circulations are low compared to the rest of Europe. The reason is that Greek society is still very much an oral society since ancient times. The Greeks love conversation, what they call *kouvenda*, a mixture of dialogue, gossip, and small talk by means of which the speakers and listeners satisfy their curiosity and derive amusement. Those shunning *kouvenda* find themselves socially isolated much like the *idiotes* or private persons in ancient Athens who ended up being labeled idiots.

In the electronic media, developments have been rapid and momentous. The first state radio station in Greece began broadcasting in 1936 while the first state television station began in 1966. The state monopoly in radio and television was absolute until it collapsed in 1989. Ever since, commercial stations (both radio and television) have been thriving while the state stations have witnessed a steady and apparently irreversible decline. State broadcasting is financed by the license fee, advertising revenue, and the state budget which covers deficits. There are actually five state radio stations covering the whole of the country, and 21 regional ones as well as three state television channels. The "5th program" of Greek Radio broadcasts round the clock in 15 languages and caters mainly to the millions of Greeks abroad.

Supervision, control and enforcement of a Code of Practice is the prerogative of a 15-member National Radio and Television Council which was set up in 1989 with the express mandate to grant operating licenses to applicants for new radio and Television stations. Pending before the Council at the end of 1992 were 1,250 applications for radio stations (most of which had been broadcasting anyway) and 82 applications for Television stations (of which about 40 have also been operating without a proper license). Applications were screened and licenses, i.e., the distribution of frequencies according to certain criteria (non-interference with air control operations, military communications, etc.) were granted in July 1993. Such regulation is expected to put an end to the unlicensed chaos which prevailed for four years. The root of the problem lies in the fact that when the decision was taken in 1989 that the Greek state should no longer rule the airwaves no regulatory mechanism was in place to cope with the explosion of a hitherto unmet demand.

MAVROKORDATOS, ALEXANDROS (1791–1865). Representative of the English tradition in early Greek parliamentary politics. He was born in Constantinople to a prominent Phanariot (''Phanari'' was a section of the city inhabited by well-to-do Greeks) family that had produced several functionaries in the Ottoman Porte and the administration of the Danubian principalities. Mavrokordatos studied in Italy and spent time in Wallachia (now part of Romania) before joining in the Greek War of Independence (q.v.) as a leading political figure. He became prime minister on several occasions during the rule of King Otto Wittelsbach (q.v.). He, more than any other of his contemporaries, was a staunch believer in the British model of parliamentary rule and of liberal democracy.

MEGALI IDEA. A term (meaning ''Grand Idea'') used in a Greek Parliament debate of 1844 to describe Greece's post-independence irredentist aspirations. Since over three-fourths of Greeks at the time resided outside the realm of the Hellenic Kingdom, it became the policy of most governments to unite and incorporate all territories on which the unredeemed lived. In 1864, the Ionian islands (q.v.) became part of the Greek state. Thessaly (q.v.) and a section of Epirus (q.v.) followed in 1881. During the Balkan Wars and the First World War (qq.v.), Greece reached its present size (with the exception of the Dodecanese ceded to Greece by the 1947 Paris treaty). The ''Megali Idea'' expired in 1922 after the Asia Minor debacle. Since that time Greece has upheld the territorial status quo in the Balkans and the Aegean.

MERKOURI, MELINA (1922–1994). Born in Athens (q.v.) in 1922 into a political family, Melina Merkouri started life as an actress and became known in Greece with her first film *Stella* (1955). She won international acclaim with the film directed by her husband-to-be Jules Dassin *Never on Sunday* (1960). Other successes include *Topkapi,* another Dassin film.

In the late 1960s, Melina Merkouri campaigned vigorously in Europe and the United States against the Colonels' regime in Greece, and was deprived of her citizenship as a result. Upon the junta's demise she returned to Greece, became an active member of PASOK (q.v.), was elected a member of Parliament in 1977 and appointed minister of culture in 1981, a post she retained until PASOK lost office in 1989. She died May 6, 1994.

METAXAS, IOANNIS (1871–1941). Officer, politician, and dictator. Born in the island of Cephalonia, he studied at the Military Academy of Athens and Berlin. An admirer of Germany and a supporter of King Constantine I (q.v.) during the great "schism" between the Crown and Prime Minister Sophocles Venizelos (q.v.), he resigned from the army in 1920. Although a critic of Greece's Anatolian campaign, he was implicated in a military coup against the Plastiras-Gonatas government in 1923 and had to flee the country. He was the first prominent royalist to recognize the Greek Republic in 1924 and became actively involved in parliamentary politics since. He was appointed Minister of War and then Prime Minister in a caretaker government by King George II (q.v.) after the restoration of the monarchy and the elections of 1935. Backed by the King he became dictator on 4 August 1936. When faced with an Italian ultimatum to allow passage of Axis troops through Greece on 28 October 1940, he chose to refuse and by so doing he expressed the will of an entire nation. Greek resistance and victory against a Fascist attack from Albania became Greece's finest hour during the Second World War (q.v.).

METHODIUS see CYRIL AND METHODIUS

MIAOULIS, ANDREAS (1769–1835). Admiral of the insurgents during the Greek War of Independence (q.v.). Born in the island of Hydra, he made his name by breaching the British continental blockade during the Napoleonic War. Between 1821 and 1827, he conducted a successful war against the Ottoman navy and disrupted sea communications between the Porte in Constantinople and the Greek mainland.

MINERAL WEALTH. More than 30 kinds of minerals and ores are extracted in Greece. The main ore, in terms of value, is bauxite of which deposits are found in the mountains of Central Greece (q.v.) (Mount Parnassus in particular). It is partly exported and partly used locally to produce alumina. Greece is among the main bauxite-producing countries in Europe. Proved reserves in mainland Greece amount to 40 million tons and probable deposits are estimated at twice that amount. Other important ores are magnesite (12 percent of world production), chromite, and nickel. There are huge deposits of asbestos in Greece as well as high quality marbles known from antiquity. Magnesite in Euboea and Lesbos, chromites in Euboea, iron pyrites and emery in Naxos, barite in Melos, lead and zinc in Central Greece, sulphur in Melos and Nisyros, manganese and antimony in Northern Greece and Chiosas, as well as perlite and pumice stone are also extracted in modest amounts.

About 10 percent of Greece's consumption of crude oil is produced locally (from an offshore platform near the island of Thassos in the Northern Aegean) while the 36 million tons of lignite mined in Greece every year—from an estimated 3 billion ton of deposits—are used almost exclusively (96%) for electricity production. Mineral areas contribute some 5 percent to GNP and some 16 percent to the value of exports. Mining and quarrying contribute only 1.5 percent to the country's GNP but substantially more to the dollar value of exports (6 percent in 1990). The extraction of minerals was hard hit by the difficulties of the 1980s as many companies went into public ownership to avoid bankruptcy while others went bankrupt.

MISTRA. Eight kilometers west of Sparta in the Peloponnese (q.v.) a purely medieval town in ruin is to be found, a kind of Byzantine Pompei with beautifully preserved churches, monasteries, palaces and some of the finest examples of fourteenth and fifteenth century Byzantine architecture. An impregnable fortress which dominates the town, it was built in 1249 by William II de Villehardouin, Prince of Achaea. The Frankish nobleman tried in this way to protect his "Duchy of Sparta" from bands of marauding Slavs. Ten years later William was defeated and taken prisoner by the Byzantine emperor, Michael Palaiologos, who managed to recapture Constantinople from the Latins in 1261.

For the next two centuries (1262–1460) Mistra developed into a center of both learning and the arts with a reputation as "the descendant of the ancient Hellenic city states showing the same intellectual vivacity and bustle" (Steven Runciman: *The Last Byzantine Renaissance*). Mistra's culture combined awareness of the Greek past, the Greek language, and scholarship with the flowering of Byzantine art. With the decline of the Byzantine Empire, Mistra became the focal point of an intellectual revival which was more Hellenic than Christian. Amongst the most brilliant of Greek scholars was the philosopher George Gemistos (1360–1407) or Plethon (to call him by his hellenized pen-name), who argued that Plato should be preferred to Aristotle. He moved to Mistra—on the advice of the wise and kindly Emperor Manuel—because in Constantinople where he taught at the university he infuriated the Church establishment with his rationalistic Platonism.

Mistra fell to the Turks in 1460. From 1687 to 1715 it was in the hands of the Venetians and prospered thanks to its silkworm industry. Upon the return of the Turks Mistra rapidly declined. After the refounding of Sparta in 1834 by the newly independent Greek kingdom, Mistra was abandoned. It was saved for posterity by the restoration work of the French School of Archaeology in 1896–1910. The last 30 families living there were moved by the Greek archaeological service in 1952 and wholesale reconstruction was further pursued by Greek experts. Beautifully restored Mistra today attracts visitors from all over the world.

MITSOTAKIS, (CONSTANTINOS) KONSTANTINOS (1918–). Born in Chania, Crete (q.v.), Mitsotakis studied law at Athens University and began to practice in 1941. During the German occupation of Crete he joined the resistance, was imprisoned and condemned to death by the occupation forces but was spared through an exchange of prisoners. He was continuously elected deputy in Parliament since 1946 and served as minister in several Liberal and coalition cabinets.

Mitsotakis appeared as the major contender for the leadership of the Center Union (q.v.) in the mid-1960s but his clash with the party's leader Georgios Papandreou (q.v.) in the crisis of 1965, made him a persona non grata in the liberal camp. During the Colonels' dictatorship he was initially interned and then escaped abroad. After the fall of the regime he founded for a while his own party and then joined Karamanlis's New Democracy (q.v.). In 1984, he was elected president of the party after the death of Evangelos Averoff. He became Prime Minister in 1990.

Mitsotakis was always in line with western foreign positions and opposed Andreas Papandreou's (q.v.) anti-western declaratory politics. He resigned from his position as head of the New Democracy party after his electoral defeat on 10 October 1993.

MODERN GREEK see LANGUAGE

MONASTICISM. The word defines the tendency of Christians to live alone (from the Greek verb *monazein* which means exactly that) or to form coenobitic communities living secluded from the world under religious vows. Most Orthodox theologians agree that monasticism is crucial in order to understand Eastern spirituality as such: mystical, Christocentric and sacramental. One point must be made at the outset: monasticism was and is a lay movement which probably originated from groups of early Christians living together and wishing to lead a dedicated, austere life away from the turbulence of the "century."

St. Anthony is regarded as the father of this movement starting in 270 A.D. in Egypt. A rich farmer, he gave away his possessions and removed himself from the world first to an empty tomb and then to the desert. His *askesis* (training) consisted in isolation, prayer and fasting. His adversaries were the demons who tempted him first with his former comforts, then with lascivious desires, finally with frightening visions of wild beasts. When he emerged at the age of 55 (c. 306 A.D.) victorious from his encounter with the powers of evil, he was transfigured and legend has it he did not age and had acquired the gift of teaching and healing the sick. These extraordinary events induced many to set up monasteries in the desert. St. Anthony died in 356 A.D. at the age of 105 having become a much sought-after sage and healer. All in all a remarkable career for an Egyptian farmer who never learned any Greek and remained illiterate to the end of his long life. Those following in his footsteps did not all become hermits, a vocation for the disciplined few. They followed Anthony's younger contemporary Pachomius (he died in 346 A.D.) who organized the communal (coenobitic) form of monasticism and devised the necessary Rule to ensure its good functioning.

Monasticism posed a threat to the established Church in the Byzantine Empire because the monk could in no way be controlled: he was a Christian who followed Christ's injuction as he understood and interpreted it. He did not seek perfection through the Church but outside it. However, the rigors of monastic life and the appeal of a life of meditation in silence restricted, somewhat, the influence of the monks on the affairs of the Church and the state. More serious for the Byzantine economy was the withdrawal of manpower and the low productivity of the monastic lands. On the other hand, there were never any "monastic orders" in the East which could acquire serious influence and challenge the authority of the Church.

Some Emperors could not tolerate monks. Constantine V for instance loathed them so much that he called them the "unmentionables." He persecuted them, forced some of them to marry, secularized many monasteries and even threatened to banish them and blind them (a common enough form of punishment in those days).

Monasticism, however, emerged greatly strengthened from the iconoclastic troubles. It had added new martyrs to the calendar of the Orthodox Church. The monasteries themselves thrived. Thanks to a system devised by Basil II, which made it possible to assign a monastery to a lay patron (known as *characticarios*) for his lifetime, the economics of monasticism improved dramatically. Such privatization literally worked wonders which can still be admired today. The most splendid religious buildings of the Middle Byzantine period happen to be monastic. In today's Greece, Hosios Loukas, Nea Moni on Chios, and Daphni display a level of craftsmanship nowhere to be found in any episcopal or parish church.

The notion that monastic life led to fanaticism, intolerance and—at best—narrow-mindedness is an oversimplification. Monks with unlimited time to spare, away from secular distraction (*perispasmos*) and eager to achieve deification (*theosis*), read avidly, copied patiently a great variety of different texts, and achieved serenity having assuaged the beasts of desire, anger, sorrow, and fear. Virtue, it is true, they saw mainly in negative terms.The obsessive revulsion from the material world made them acutely distrustful of their five senses ascribing all pleasures to the work of the Devil. They were hostile to outspokenness (*parrhesia*) and had no sense of humor. Christ, it seems, had never laughed in his lifetime. At the most, one could allow oneself to smile, as did the Syrian Saint Julian Sabas when he heard news of the death of Julian the Apostate, the emperor who tried to restore paganism. See also MOUNT ATHOS.

MOUNT ATHOS (HOLY COMMUNITY OF). The area in Halkidiki known as Mount Athos or Holy Mount (Aghion Oros) comprises 20 large monasteries (but no convents, as women are banned) which form since 1926 a monastic republic governed by the Synod or "Holy Community" with its headquarters at Karyes on the central western side of the peninsula. All monasteries are represented in the Synod. The Greek state authorities appoint a civil commissioner who is responsible for law and order. In dogmatic matters, though, Mt. Athos takes guidance from the Ecumenical Patriarchate in Constantinople. Heterodox or schismatics are not tolerated. All monks, whatever their nationality or ethnic background, become Greek subjects. Beside the monasteries there are also some hermits living dangerously above alarming precipices in huts and caves only accessible by decaying ladders.

The monasteries contain invaluable murals, documents, icons and Christian relics of stunning beauty which can be seen and admired by male visitors. In 1963, the 1000th anniversary of the monastic community was officially celebrated. It is noteworthy that the incursion of Latins, Catalans (1307), Serbes (1346) and Turks did not permanently damage Mt. Athos. Thanks to its resourceful diplomacy, the Mt.

Athos monastic republic remained the spiritual centre of Orthodoxy (q.v.) during the 400-year long Ottoman rule. In the days of its greatest expansion it is said to have housed some 40,000 monks. The oldest of the ruling monasteries, the Great Lavra, has by itself produced 26 patriarchs and more than 144 bishops.

In the first quarter of the twentieth century the number of monks started to decline, a trend which became more pronounced as no more novices were allowed by the militantly atheistic regimes of eastern Europe to come to the monastic community. At the same time fewer and fewer Greeks made the ascent to the Mountain. While at the start of the century there were on Athos some 7,500 monks, in 1971, their number had shrunk to 1,145 and these were almost all old men. However, even during this difficult period there were signs of continuing Athonite spirituality. St. Silouan (1866–1938), proclaimed a saint in 1988, though of peasant background, left behind him at the Russian monastery of St. Panteleimon deeply moving poetic meditations published in many languages. Fr. Joseph (died in 1959), a Greek, gathered around him a group of disciples and perfected with them the practice of "mental" or "inner" prayer (*noera prosefchl*) considered to be a significant contribution to Orthodoxy.

Suddenly and unexpectedly a new chapter of Athonite history began to take shape in the 1970s and 1980s. By 1990, 1,500 monks were resident on the Mountain. What was remarkable was the age structure of this population. In 1971, the great majority of the then 1,145 monks were over 60. By 1990, the majority of the 1,500 or more were under 40. Many of those are highly educated and talented people, writers, thinkers, and confessors.

This revival has been attributed to the emergence of gifted abbots who drew towards them a number of high caliber recruits and also by the stresses and strains of modern city life which drives young people to the peaceful spiritual haven of the Mountain.

Outside Athos there is also the celebrated monastery of St. John the Theologian (the Evangelist) on the island of Patmos, founded by St. Christodoulos in 1088. One of the outstanding monks here in the present century was Fr.

Amphilochios (1888–1970), already widely revered as a saint. He was an ecologist, long before this had become fashionable. "Whoever does not love trees, does not love Christ," he used to say.

MUSIC. When Greece became independent in 1830, its musical tradition was twofold: the "demotic" (q.v.) songs—strongly influenced by ecclesiastical music—which had originated in the post Byzantine history of the Greek people and the mainly Italian school of the Ionian islands (q.v.) which had escaped Turkish rule. Greece was thus cut off from the classical European musical tradition during the very centuries (sixteenth to nineteenth) which saw the blossoming of this musical renaissance in the West. While the technique of polyphony was perfected in the West, the Greek Orthodox Church (q.v.), resistant to change in music as in everything else, remained monophonic without any instrumental accompaniment. Monophonic music developed into the unique "Byzantine chant." Moreover, there was no court in medieval Greece to encourage music appreciation, no concert going bourgeoisie, no locus for musical creation. Perforce the sounds which emerged were developed by a blend of psalmodic melody and folk songs called *tragoudia,* a word which stems directly from the ancient Greek term of *tragodia* (tragedy).

These folk songs were monodic, modal, with a variety of rhythms, of limited range sometimes extending no more than the interval of a fifth or a fourth, a feature making notation in the modern western system almost impossible. Most songs are unaccompanied. When they do have an accompaniment it is used to keep the rhythm or to form a complex harmonic texture completely independent of the monody and always improvisatory.

Some musicologists, experts on modern Greek music, such as Professors Thrasyvoulos Georgiadis and Samuel Baud-Bovy have insisted that the 7/8 time found throughout Greece in the folk music is derived from the heroic hexameter in which the Homeric epics were recited. The circular folk dance called *syrtos* is known to have existed in the first century A.D. The music which prevailed during the long centuries of Ottoman rule was heard in marriage ceremonies, various festivities and courtship rites. After Greece became free, the folk tradition divides into the older demotic klephtic songs of the countryside and a new type of popular songs heard in prisons, slums, as well as in the hashish dens, generally known as *rebetiko* (q.v.).

When Greece was freed, many Greeks living in Europe returned home and became emissaries of European musical culture. Ioannis Capodistrias (q.v.), the first governor and King Otto Wittelsbach (q.v.), the first monarch established bands, imported the first pianos, introduced music teaching in schools, and invited musicians from Germany, Italy, and the Ionian islands to perform in Athens (q.v.). As opera was introduced many musical schools were founded and orchestras organized while a variety of choirs, musical societies, and later musical stage productions emerged. Greece became in this way aware of a musical heritage which was totally imported. It is in this climate that Greek composers started to make their appearance.

Among the better known representatives of the European (mainly Italian) school were Pavlos Karrer (1829–1896); Nicholas Montzaros (1796–1873), who wrote the music for the national anthem; Napoleon Labelette (1864–1932); and the creator of the Greek opera, Dionysios Lavrangas (1860–1941). With Manolis Kalomiris (1883–1962), a native of Smyrna, Romantic and Wagnerian in his orchestration, the European and the folk traditions merge. Prominent Greek composers who wove demotic themes and melodies into western musical forms were Marios Varvoglis (1885–1967), who evolved his own style influenced by French Neoclassicism, Georgios Sklavos (1888–1976) and Antiochos Evangelatos (1903–1981). All these composers, deeply influenced by their musical studies abroad, wrote music where Classicism, Romanticism, Neoclassicism, and Impressionism can easily be traced. Their efforts to express the austere monodic folk song in a totally alien European idiom had only limited success.

Working in the field of modern avant-garde music, Yannis Christou (1926–1970) transformed the whole concept of musical background to ancient tragedy. In the same line,

Nikos Skalkotas (1904–1949), a gifted composer who died in his prime, became internationally known for his brilliant use of Greek demotic tunes (of which his "Greek Dances" are the best known). In his original modernist compositions, Ianni Xenakis (q.v.) has won international acclaim for his complex mathematically patterned musical creations. Both Skalkotas and Xenakis did not, however, work from within the Greek musical tradition. Like Stravinsky and Bella Bartok they brought something of their countries' music into the European tradition.

-N-

NAVARINO. Presently a town on the western Peloponnesian (q.v.) coast with a population of 2,107. It is located near Kalamata and known for its arcaded streets built by the French in 1829 close to an old Byzantine castle. Navarino became famous several times in Greek history. It was in the Bay of Navarino that the Athenians trapped the Spartans in 425 B.C. and where an abortive Russian expedition had landed in 1770. But its greatest glory came in the nineteenth century through the battle that took place there on 20 October 1827 and secured the independence of Greece.

By 1827, the Greek War of Independence (q.v.), already in its sixth year, had reached a decisive turning point. A new vigorous force which had already made its appearance two years before, in the person of the Egyptian ruler Ibrahim Pasha, became of great importance to the outcome of the Greek Revolution. Ibrahim Pasha, leading a powerful army, was since 1825 devastating the Peloponnese by giving the Greeks a simple choice: submit to the Prophet or die. The Pasha had nothing personal against the Greeks. He was simply after the Ottoman Empire's territories in the Middle East. Sensing that the Empire was crumbling he fought the Sultan's battles for him to gain strength, from which position he could hope to seize the Sultan's title. His ruthlessness, however, raised an alarm in the West. Greek captives, it was reported, were being sold as slaves in Cairo while genocide was threatened throughout the Greek mainland.

George Canning, the British Foreign Secretary, then made the first diplomatic move for a joint intervention against the hordes of Ibrahim. "Though he was a Tory by tradition," wrote H.A.L. Fisher, in his *History of Europe* (Arnold, London, 1936, p. 88) "and a member of a Tory government, he was not prepared to see the most illustrious corner of Europe and the original home of its civilization settled by a population of fellaheen and negroes. Rather than acquiesce in the extermination of the Greeks he invited the intervention of the powers." Meanwhile the Greeks themselves did not remain idle. In May 1827, the charismatic Greek leader Theodoros Kolokotronis (q.v.) won the battle of morale with his slogan "fire and axe against those who kowtow" against Ibrahim Pasha's offer of amnesty and money to Greeks who would lay down their arms and submit. To people utterly exhausted by six years of relentless fighting this was a tempting proposition. Kolokotronis convinced his fellow Greeks they could win and urged them not to give up. This forced the hand of Ibrahim who by his gruesome "barbarization project" brought western public opinion to a boiling point.

The framework for an intervention existed. The Treaty of London signed in July 1827 by France, Britain, and Russia recommending limited home rule for the Greeks in the Peloponnese provided for a "peaceful blockade" in Greek waters if the Sultan and his Egyptian allies failed to accept the Treaty's terms. The Sultan, however, in high spirits after Ibrahim's initial "successes," rejected the terms of the Treaty, defied the Powers and ordered the Turkish and Egyptian fleets to maintain a supply route for Ibrahim so that he might finish off the unyielding Greeks.

An allied fleet was therefore sent to Greece under British Admiral Sir Edward Codrington. His instructions were somewhat vaguely worded. The fleets were instructed to secure an armistice without engaging in hostilities, an ambivalent policy described by Foreign Secretary Canning as one of "peaceful interference." The aim was clear, the method not. "Save the Greeks from destruction, if possible without a battle" were the orders given. For hours the European admirals tried to convince the Egyptians to go home quietly, leaving the Greeks to their emasculated home rule. Then Ibrahim committed the fatal (to him) error of showing disrespect to the British flag when during the negotiations an Egyptian ship shot the occupants of a British open boat sent to parley. By dusk the same day the Egyptian fleet was annihilated. The Turks and their allies were warned not to fire ever again on a ship or boat of the Allied Powers. The hulks of their sunken ships can be clearly seen off Pylos when the sea is calm. The Egyptians, beaten, went home; the Turks, chastened, conceded defeat.

The Tsar and the French were delighted by the outcome, Metternich called it a "terrible catastrophe" and the Duke of Wellington, who became prime minister soon afterwards, referred to it as "the untoward event" in the "Speech from the Throne" at the opening of Parliament in January 1828. The independence of Greece, was proclaimed in 1829 and recognized by the Ottoman Empire in 1832. The first Greek nation-state in the long history of Greece was thus born.

NEW DEMOCRACY. The party is the direct descendant of the pre-junta National Radical Union, founded and led by Constantinos Karamanlis (q.v.), the most influential figure in postwar Greek politics. After the change of regime, Karamanlis and his New Democracy party won both the 1974 (54.3 percent of the vote) and 1977 (41.8 percent) elections. In April 1980, Karamanlis was elected President of the Republic by Parliament and was replaced as head of the party and Premier, by George Rallis.

Karamanlis's own political transformation, after his departure from politics in 1963, determined New Democracy's general orientation. A staunch anti-communist and supporter of NATO (q.v.) in the 1950s and early 1960s, he reflected accurately the change in mood of the public upon his triumphant return in 1974. This change was implemented as follows: 1) closer ties with western Europe and the European Community (q.v.); 2) improvement of relations with the Communist Balkans and the Soviet Union; 3) Scrupulous respect of parliamentary and press opposition highlighted by the legalization of the Communist Party.

Entry into the European Community, achieved in January 1981 after tortuous negotiations, was the hallmark of Karamanlis's pursuit of an "organic Greek presence in the West." A guarantee for parliamentary democracy and a peaceful deterrent to Turkish provocations were in his estimation the most important by-products of EC membership. His Balkan multilateralism and his 1979 trip to Moscow were to a great extent motivated by his concern for Greek security. Although he claimed that Greece, after the 1974 Turkish assault on Cyprus (q.v.), had no choice but to assume full control of her armed forces and withdraw from the military arm of NATO, he acknowledged the necessity of sustaining friendship with the United States (q.v.) and Western Europe and insisted that facilities in Greece provided to the Americans should be governed by considerations of mutual advantage.

In spite of New Democracy's efforts to modernize its stance from paternalistic conservatism to moderate liberalism, the elections of 1981 proved that PASOK (q.v.) was the more successful of the two in appealing to centrist voters. In the past, ruling party and state went hand in hand and it was only through New Democracy's own repudiation of repressive measures against rural and urban opposition that bolder voters were encouraged to try their luck with PASOK. The electoral defeat of October 1981, although in no sense abject since the party won 35.9 percent of the vote, generated a minor panic in its ranks which led to the choice of Evangelos Averoff as its new leader.

In August 1984, the leadership of the party was offered to Constantinos Mitsotakis (q.v.). A one time Center-Union (q.v.) party deputy who had clashed with Georgios Papandreou (q.v.), Mitsotakis was unpopular with centrist voters and a personal enemy of Andreas Papandreou (q.v.). The 1985 elections were therefore conducted with considerable invective by both sides. Although ahead in the 1989 elections, an electoral law that was unfavorable to the victor prevented Mitsotakis from forming a government until 1990. Even then New Democracy secured a majority in Parliament based on one deputy. By the summer of 1993 the government's austerity policy took its toll. It was voted down in Parliament and lost the elections of 10 October to PASOK.

NEWSPAPERS see MEDIA.

NORTH ATLANTIC TREATY ORGANIZATION (NATO). Greece's accession to the North Atlantic Treaty Alliance was initially obstructed by Britain's concept of Western defense in the Near East and the opposition of certain Scandinavian countries to an overextension of NATO's primary aims. When Greece and Turkey (q.v.) dispatched combat forces to South Korea in 1950, they were acting as members of the United Nations but their motives were in fact to override objections to their entry into NATO. For Greek politicians of the Liberal coalition government which pressed for Greek membership, NATO not only provided an additional guarantee against Balkan communism, it also constituted a door to a community of democratic European states and an institutional link to the United States (q.v.). In September 1951, NATO foreign ministers in Ottawa approved Greece's full membership.

-O-

ONASSIS, ARISTOTLE (1908–1975). Tanker tycoon, airline operator, and man of the world. His business success, enormous fortune and extravagant life-style turned Aristotle Onassis into a figure of international repute whose every move was covered by the world media.

He was born in Smyrna, Turkey. In 1922, when the Turks massacred the Greeks of Smyrna, the Onassis family escaped to Athens (q.v.). In 1923, young Aristotle emigrated to Buenos Aires, did odd jobs, saved like mad, and built up a small tobacco business. In 1933, he came to Europe and bought in mid-slump six 10,000-ton Canadian ships. In 1934, he built his first tanker in Sweden. In 1946, he married Tina Livanos, daughter of the doyen of Greek shipping tycoons. In 1949, he built more tankers in Hamburg. He created Olympic Airways in the 1950s, having obtained from the Greek government an agreement on his terms. He made his fortune by realizing after the Second World War (q.v.) that oil would become of prime importance and that oil companies would not be able to run their own tanker fleets at competitive rates while at the same time increasing oil production. Onassis thus became one of the great carriers without whom great producers would be lost.

His personal life was no less flamboyant than his business career. In the 1960s, his tumultuous affair with Maria Callas (q.v.) soon moved the Onassis story from the gossip columns to the first page of the popular press. In 1968, he married Jacqueline Bouvier Kennedy. The marriage proved a disaster and not just on the financial side. He lost his grip, drank too much, and after the death of his son and heir Alexander—who was killed in a freak plane crash—he became depressed and died in 1975.

The Onassis Foundation he set up to commemorate his son is a tribute to civic virtue. Every year, the Foundation offers two prizes, named "Olympia" and "Athinai" respectively, which consist of a silver plaque and a scroll, each accompanied by a sum of $50,000. The "Olympia" prize is for "persons or organizations who contribute to the solution of ecological or environment problems" while the "Athinai" prize is given for "contributions to the rapprochement of peoples and the respect of human dignity."

ORTHODOX CHURCH. The Holy Orthodox Catholic Apostolic Eastern Church, to give it the official name it uses itself, is the historical representative of (most of) eastern Christendom. It is sometimes called the Greek Orthodox Church which is confusing because the great majority of its members are not Greek and because the Greek Church (q.v.), as such, is a distinct national autocephalous church on a par with the Russian, the Bulgarian, the Serbian, and others. It calls itself Holy, for obvious reasons, Orthodox which means "true belief," Catholic from the Greek word *catholiki* meaning universal, Apostolic because it was established by the Apostles and Eastern because it took root in eastern Europe. The Western Church calls itself Roman Catholic.

The Orthodox Church, consists of 1) those churches which, having accepted all the decrees of the first seven ecumenical councils (q.v.), agree on doctrine and remain in full communion with one another, and 2) such churches as have derived from these by missionary activity or by abscission without loss of communion.

Unlike Protestantism, Orthodoxy insists upon the hierarchical structure, upon the Apostolic Succession and the traditions—not just the Bible—upon the need for an episcopate and a full-time priesthood. Unlike Roman Catholicism, which insists on the supremacy and the universal jurisdiction of the Pope, the Orthodox Church is run by five Patriarchs (and has proposed—to no avail—to acknowledge the Pope as "primum inter pares," i.e., first among equals) and stresses the infallibility of the Church as a whole. The Orthodox Church is thus collegial, not monarchical, and believes it is infallible because Christ and the Holy Spirit cannot err when manifesting themselves in a charismatic institution which sees itself as a continued Pentecost.

The divisions which have brought about the present fragmentation of Christendom occurred in three main stages at intervals of roughly five hundred years. The first came about in the fifth and sixth centuries when the Oriental Churches, as they are known today, separated from the main body of the Christian Church. These Oriental Churches fall into two groups: 1) The Church of the East ("Assyrian," "Nestorian," "Chaldean," "East Syrian") which covers mainly Christians in Iran and Iraq; and 2) the five Non-Chalcedonian Churches, also called Monophysite, which cover the Middle East, Armenia and Ethiopia. The second division, conventionally dated to the year 1054, separated Eastern Orthodoxy from Roman Catholicism and is called the Schism (q.v.). The third division, between Rome and the Reformers in sixteenth century Europe, does not concern Orthodoxy directly.

The Orthodox Church, in contrast to all the other forms of Christianity, was not born of a scission from the Christian mainstream but represents a gradual and uninterrupted development from the original Pentecost to the present day. The Orthodox emphasis on tradition thus conveys the essence of an institution whose task is to preserve the doctrine uncorrupted as a treasure, a cherished monument, and hand it down pure, immaculate to new generations. When describing the Eastern Churches, Roman Catholicism, or the Protestant faiths, the historian can immediately identify the new version by the fact that it was new in relation to something older, i.e., the corpus from which it stemmed. Not so with Orthodoxy which proceeded naturally from the Pentecostal illumination without any break in continuity.

A comprehensive picture of the Orthodox around the world today and the Churches they belong to is given by the English Orthodox bishop Timothy Ware in his book, *The Orthodox Church,* which has been a valuable source of information to many. Orthodox Christians, defined as those baptized as such, are distributed as follows among the four ancient Patriarchates:

Constantinople	6,000,000
Alexandria	350,000
Antioch	750,000
Jerusalem	60,000

The heads of Patriarchates, however, small the size of their flock, are called Patriarchs. There are also nine other auto-cephalous Churches (as the national Churches are called):

Russia	50–85,000,000
Serbia	8,000,000
Romania	17,000,000
Bulgaria	8,000,000
Georgia	5,000,000
Cyprus	450,000
Greece	9,000,000
Poland	750,000
Albania	210,000 in 1944

All except Poland and Albania are in countries where the Christian population is entirely or predominantly Orthodox. The Churches of Greece and Cyprus are Greek; four of the others—Russia, Serbia, Bulgaria, Poland—are Slav. The heads of the Russian, Romanian, Serbian and Bulgarian Churches are known by the title Patriarch; the head of the

Georgian Church is called Catholicos-Patriarch; the heads of the other Churches are called either Archbishop or Metropolitan.

There are in addition several Churches which, while self-governing in most respects, do not possess full independence. These are termed "autonomous" but not "autocephalous."

Czechoslovakia	100,000
Sinai	900
Finland	52,000
Japan	25,000
China	10,000–20,000

The Orthodox Church is therefore a family of mostly self-governing Churches held together by unity of faith and community of sacraments. The Patriarch of Constantinople has no right to interfere in the internal affairs of other Churches. His position resembles somewhat that of the Archbishop of Canterbury in the worldwide Anglican community. All Orthodox accept and profess the teachings of Jesus Christ and the Apostles and the authoritative decisions of the Ecumenical Councils (q.v.) which have created the living tradition. They also belong to the Orthodox Church. Orthodoxy (q.v.) is not a private faith. Bishops must be unmarried, while priests and deacons must not contract a second marriage. All priests preach the word and perform the six sacraments—baptism, confirmation, penance, eucharist, matrimony and unction of the sick. Bishops alone can administer the seventh, the sacrament of orders.

During the 400-year long Ottoman rule the Orthodox Church preserved the faith and the Greek language (q.v.) while providing a parallel organization to the alien rule. Modern neo-Orthodox thinkers regard this secular task as subaltern and insist that the Orthodox message is much more than a survival kit for oppressed nationalities or an ethical code for character improvement. They often accuse the Greek Church (q.v.) of conventionalism and degeneration into an administrative hierarchy subordinate to the secular state. In their eyes, the true aim of a Christian life is salvation through faith, vigil, prayer and almsgiving.

ORTHODOXY. The main feature of Orthodoxy it that its Christianity is woven into tradition, perceived as living continuity within the Christian Church as it took shape from the day of the Pentecost. It was on that day, that the Apostles were said to have been filled with the Holy Spirit as "there appeared to them tongues like flames of fire, divided among them and resting on each one" (Acts ii, 2–4).

This Pentecostal feeling is very much alive in the Orthodox Church (q.v.) whose members aspire at achieving gradual *theosis* or deification of each individual. Though the development of the Orthodox body of beliefs has occurred in history, its truth—the Church claims—is eternal, vouchsafed by the sanctity of the Bible and the weight of tradition which is the witness of the Holy Spirit in action throughout history.

God has never been an abstraction for the Orthodox Christian. He is a person but not *one* person. To be precise, He is three persons. Father, Son and Holy Spirit, each of whom "dwells" in the other by virtue of a never ceasing movement of love. God is thus not just a unity but a union. Trinitarian theology rests on certain basic principles considered fundamental. The Father is unbegotten and has His source and origin only in Himself. The Son, though coequal to the Father and coeternal with Him, has his source and origins in the Father from whom he is begotten from all eternity—"before all ages" as the Creed says. Jesus, the incarnate god, was born of woman when he was made flesh but before taking human form He existed from all eternity in Heaven as a person. The distinctive characteristic of the third person in the Trinity is procession. The Holy Spirit has His origin in the Father but is not begotten by Him. He proceeds (*ekporevetal*) from the Father from all eternity. It is precisely at this point where the western view of the Trinity clashes with that of the East.

The Roman Catholic view, as expressed many centuries before the schism (q.v.) by St. Augustine of Hippo (360–440 A.D.)—who distinguished two different hinds of procession of the Holy Spirit from the Father and the Son—has the Holy Spirit proceeding eternally from the Father and the Son (*filioque* in Latin). Orthodox theologians have at times held that the Spirit may perhaps be deemed to proceed through *(dia)* the Son but not from *(ek)* the Son as the Doctrine of "Double Procession" postulates. Orthodoxy, in other words rejects the *"filioque"* as far as this applies to eternal procession, i.e., in terms of relations within the Trinity existing from all eternity. However, it agrees with the West that in practical terms, i.e., as far as the mission of the Spirit in the word is concerned, He is sent by the Son and is indeed the "Spirit of the Son." Evidence for the Orthodox position is educed from the Scripture. John XV, 26 has Christ say: "When the comforter has come, whom *I will send to you* from the Father—the Spirit of truth, *who proceeds from the Father,* will bear witness to Me." Christ is the one who actually sends the Spirit but the Spirit Himself, as a Trinitarian person, proceeds from the Father. So the Bible teaches, and so Orthodoxy believes. The West, on the other hand, insists on the "double procession," i.e., on the eternal procession from Father and Son.

The trouble with the *filioque* seems to be that it can lead to a fusing of the Father and the Son into one person since they both become from all eternity the sources of the Spirit. Therefore, the Western view by overemphasizing the unity of God at the expense of His Trinitarian diversity, and by demoting the Holy Spirit creates—according to some Orthodox theologians—a religion fostering authoritarianism and centralization. Western theologians reply that this interpretation is unfair because it pushes Filioquism to extremes. By the same token, they reply, the eastern view, if stretched, could lead to the absurdity of tritheism, i.e., three gods. There is hope that the present-day dialogue between Orthodox and Roman Catholics may lead to an understanding on this thorny question, since on the basics there seems to be a large degree of agreement.

On free will, the Orthodox are on the side of the angels, so to speak. They take very seriously Paul's words: "we are fellow workers (*synergoi*) with God" (I. Corinthians iii, 9).

Synergy, cooperation is the prerogative of free persons. Slaves can only obey or rebel.

For St. Augustine of Hippo (354–430 A.D.), the founding father of western Christianity, the Fall was a catastrophic event. Adam's descendants—he said—are under a "harsh necessity" of committing sin. His notion of "original guilt" is still accepted in a mitigated form by Roman Catholics. It is, however, not shared by the Orthodox who do not think that humans have automatically inherited Adam's guilt together with his mortality but acquire it only if by their own free choice they decide to imitate Adam. Christianity broke from Judaism not so much on the issue of love (both Deuteronomy and Leviticus contain the words. "Love thy neighbor") as on the question of original Sin (Jews believe we are born with pure souls) and its corollary, i.e., the possibility of Man's redemption offered as a choice—but not certainty—through the atoning death of God's own son.

In the West, the tide of Christian opinion ran strongly in favor of Augustinian pessimism, authoritarianism and dogmatic intolerance. Faced with seemingly incomprehensible disasters the West European medieval Christians may have felt reassured that ultimate responsibility went back to Adam and that their rulers would ensure their salvation by promoting the Truth and fighting Error. Guilt, especially so far removed, is easier to bear than helplessness. As for the Orthodox, they tried with varying success to cope with their enormous difficulties without ever establishing institutions such as the Holy Inquisition or the Index, i.e., without systematically burning people and/or books. One reason for this is that Christ's appearance in the world and His teaching of love has always been of crucial importance to Orthodoxy.

To pursue the issue of differences between East and West it is important to dispel a misunderstanding. It is misleading to assert—as some have done—that the East focuses on the Risen Christ, while the West is more concerned with Christ Crucified. The East certainly celebrates the Resurrection with much greater jubilation than the West but it does not distinguish between Christ's martyrdom and His glorification. The Orthodox see Christ as a suffering God. Behind his broken flesh they discern the Triune God, seeing even Golgotha as a Theophany. The Crucifixion is thus not separated from the Resurrection as happens in the West. The Cross is not just an emblem of pain but a symbol of victory. The Orthodox worshipper is encouraged both to sympathize with the Man of Sorrows and to adore the triumphant King of Kings. The difference is one of approach. Where Orthodoxy sees Christ the Victor, whether on the cross or Risen, the late medieval and post-medieval West concentrates more on Christ the victim.

OTTO WITTELSBACH, KING (1815–1867). Second son of King Ludwig I of Bavaria, Otto was chosen to become the first King of the new Greek state in 1832. During the early years of his reign, state affairs were managed by a three-man regency council. In 1843, Otto was faced with a popular uprising and demands for a constitution which he was obliged to grant. In 1844, Greece became a constitutional monarchy. Otto's irredentist exploits and his pro-Russian position during the Crimean War won him the displeasure of France and Britain. In 1862, he and his wife Amalia were forced to abandon throne and country. As an individual he was well liked and few doubted his good intentions towards his subjects and his kingdom, but in terms of statesmanship he fell short of popular expectations.

OTTOMAN RULE (1453–1821). The cultural survival and development of the Greek Orthodox (q.v.) people under Ottoman rule depended on the educational infrastructure of the Patriarchate of Constantinople and was defined by the openings that Moslem conquest allowed their Christian subjects. Exclusion from ownership of land and from the military profession, the burden of taxation reserved for ''nonbelievers,'' the frequent enslavement of Christians, and the extraction of a ''child levy'' to man the cadres of the Ottoman infantry and the civil service, left little margin for improving the lot of Greeks other than that provided by commerce and finance.

In the eighteenth century the routes of trade with the West brought into the Balkans enlightenment and revolutionary ideas. Such figures as Rhigas Fereos and Adamantios Korais (qq.v.), and secret revolutionary societies such as the Philiki Etairia (Society of Friends), became the harbingers of the subsequent War of Independence (q.v.) against Ottoman rule.

In 1770, the Greeks rose against the Sultan following encouragement and promises of assistance by the Russians. The "Orlov" rising, however, with little aid from Russia, was violently suppressed by the Ottoman forces. It took the Greeks 50 years before they attempted the 1821 War for Independence.

-P-

PALAMAS, KOSTIS (1859–1943). A Romantic poet. Born in Patras two years after the death of Solomos (q.v.), Palamas came from a distinguished family of educators and intellectuals. His formative years coincided with the explosion of the romantic movement which in Greece was not simply the free expression of individual emotion unconstrained by the discipline of consciously held principles and purposes, but also a nationalist aspiration for the restoration of former Byzantine splendor, associated with a belief in the "popular values" as preserved in folklore (q.v.), superstitions, and the deep recesses of the national psyche. He developed a Romantic humanism of his own making borrowing ideas from Goethe, Romain Rolland, Victor Hugo, Leconte de Lisle, the Parnassians, and the Symbolists. Nietzsche impressed him with his radical critique of existing cultures and the dichotomy between the Apollonian and the Dionysian forces in man and the universe.

Palamas attempted a major synthesis of all such disparate influences "in a poem which integrates all my ideas," as he said about his "Dodecalogue of the Gypsy." The central figure, a moral and cultural "Agonistes," very much molded on Zarathustra, is a gypsy uncontaminated by civilization, "untaught by any father / unknown by any mother / by no caress enslaved," who loves the earth, hates the cities, is strong, unattached, and seeks redemption through his own means.

Palamas's ideas and soul-searching are very much of his

day and age. Some of his works are still read and taught as examples of an exalted poetical imagination. His works of literary criticism are still very much appreciated: It was he who "discovered" Kalvos (q.v.) and who contributed to a deeper understanding of Solomos. He undoubtedly helped shape an idiom of declamatory poetry of some quality. His style, has not, however, endeared him to younger generations suspicious of romantic verbosity.

PANGALOS, THEODOROS (1878–1952). An important military figure of the interwar period who briefly became a dictator. Pangalos studied at the Military Academy and in Paris. He was a leading member of the Military League of 1909. In 1916, he joined the revolt in Thessaloniki. In 1917, he was appointed Chief of the Personnel Department at the Ministry of Army Affairs. In 1918–20 he was Chief-of-Staff to Paraskevopoulos's GHQ in Macedonia and in Asia Minor. An ambitious and able politically-minded General, he engineered the trial of the six royalist ministers and became dictator in 1925. He was overthrown by Georgios Kondylis (q.v.), Zervas and Dertilis and was imprisoned.

PAPADOPOULOS, GEORGIOS see COLONELS' COUP AND REGIME

PAPAGOS, ALEXANDROS (1883–1955). Military commander and politician. Born in Athens (q.v.) into a prominent royalist family, Papagos studied in the Brussels Academy and joined the cavalry in 1906. He stood by the monarchy throughout its long controversy with Eleftherios Venizelos (q.v.). He was dismissed by the Venizelos government from the army in 1917. In 1921, he was given a cavalry command in Asia Minor and, in 1923, was dismissed again for aiding the Leonardopoulos-Gargalidis coup. He was readmitted in 1927 by the "Ikoumeniki" (all-party) government and worked quietly for the restoration of the King. In 1935, with other officers he pressed Panaghis Tsaldaris (q.v.) to resign, thus assisting Georgios Kondylis (q.v.) to assume power. He was Commander-in-Chief of the Greek armed forces during the Greek-Italian War (see SECOND WORLD WAR) (1940–

41) and became the Commander of the successful campaign against the communist forces in the last phase of the Greek Civil War (1949). He ran for politics after retirement and was Prime Minister between 1952–55 and head of the Greek Rally party, which he founded.

PAPANASTASIOU, ALEXANDROS (1878–1936). Influential socialist politician of the interwar period. Having studied political economy and philosophy in Berlin, Papanastasiou on his return to Athens (q.v.) founded the group of Sociologists. A champion of land reform in Thessaly, he was elected deputy in 1910, and joined the Liberal Party in 1917–1920, becoming Minister of Communications and holding other posts. In 1922, he was imprisoned after issuing the "Republican Manifeso." Papanastasiou left the Liberal Party to found the Republican Union (Dimokratiki Enosis). In 1924, as Prime Minister, he proclaimed the Republic. Throughout his life he upheld the cause of the less privileged.

PAPANDREOU, ANDREAS (1919–   ) Academic and politician. Born in Chios, while his father Georgios Papandreou (q.v.) was prefect of the island, Andreas studied at Athens University and got his Ph.D. from Harvard where he worked as an assistant. He became Professor of Economics at the University of Minnesota in 1951 and Professor at Berkeley in 1955. While in the United States, he was associated with the Stevenson liberals. He returned to Greece with his children and American wife in 1961 and headed the Center for Economic Studies in Athens (q.v.). Papandreou was elected deputy of Achaia in 1964 and served as Minister of the Presidency and Alternate Minister of Coordination in his father's Center Union (q.v.) government between 1964–65. He was briefly detained during the 1967 dictatorship and allowed to leave the country, after pressure was exerted by President Johnson on the junta. He founded the Panhellenic Resistance Movement (PAK) abroad and returned to Greece two months after the collapse of the military regime to head the Panhellenic Socialist Movement (PASOK) (q.v.). He was elected to Parliament between 1974–90 and was Prime Minister between 1981–89.

A politician of considerable influence over his constituency, Andreas (as he was known to friends and foes) introduced new concepts in Greek foreign policy such as a predilection for nonalignment and the Third World. His brand of populist socialism led him to oppose entry into the European Community (q.v.). Once in office, however, he became a strong supporter of European institutions and relied heavily on their funds to promote his distributive and electorally very rewarding economic policies. He was back in power as Prime Minister after his electoral success of 10 October 1993.

PAPANDREOU, GEORGIOS (1888–1968). Prominent politician of the center. Born in the Peloponnesian village of Kalentzi, he studied law in Athens (q.v.) and political science in Germany. He was appointed prefect of the island of Lesvos in 1915 and served as minister in governments of the Liberal Party (q.v.) throughout the interwar period. During the Axis occupation he was imprisoned and fled to the Middle East to head the Greek government in exile. After the repatriation of his government and the liberation of Greece from the occupation forces, he was faced with the Communist insurrection of December 1944.

Papandreou wandered politically before he became the rallying force of the wide coalition that made up the Center Union (q.v.) party. Although his main task was to defeat Constantinos Karamanlis's (q.v.) ruling party in 1963, he was associated with efforts to liberalize the state and became the object of devotion for an assortment of followers. He resigned from his position as Prime Minister after clashing with King Constantine II (q.v.) in 1965. The Colonels' coup (q.v.) of April 1967 was partly motivated by the likelihood that Papandreou would have won the impending elections.

PAPANIKOLAOU, GEORGIOS (1883–1962). Discoverer of the "Pap smear" test. Born in Euboea , he studied medicine at the University of Athens and pursued graduate studies in Germany. Papanikolaou made his career in the United States and taught at Cornell University. In the 1920s he developed the smear test which became a standard method of detecting cervical cancer. He was nominated for the Nobel Prize in medicine but did not receive it. In 1932, he became an honorary member of the Athens Academy.

PASOK (PANHELLENIC SOCIALIST MOVEMENT). PASOK was founded in 1974 as a continuation of Andreas Papendreou's (q.v.) Panhellenic Liberation Movement (PAK) which operated during the junta period (see COLONELS' COUP AND REGIME). Unlike most traditional Greek political formations (with the exception of the Communist Party [q.v.]), it has become a mass party with grassroots organizations and regional committees relying on influential professionals rather than local bosses and patrons for its regional representation. This reflects one of the major changes in the structure of Greek political life. Still, the party's founder, Andreas Papandreou, commanded from the outset unquestioned authority over a compliant party apparatus and was effectively in charge of most of its activities.

National independence, popular sovereignty, and social liberation, constituted the main points of PASOK's ideology which has been described as leftist populist, combining national pride with faith in the general will. In practical terms, PASOK drew the bulk of its constituency from among those who felt that they had missed out on the development bonanza of the late 1960s and the 1970s. Although the Greek farmer of today has little in common with his impoverished counterpart of the past, PASOK successfully exploited the grievances of the peasants and those of their disoriented kin who crowd the large cities.

The realization of popular sovereignty and social liberation depends, according to PASOK, on securing national independence since the relation between these three fundamental goals is seen as a "linear succession of stages." Thus the party capitalized on the resentment that the average Greek felt against dependence on the great powers.

Andreas Papandreou initially rejected the evolutionary tactics of Social Democracy and considered western tolerance of Eurocommunism as an effort of the industrial north to pacify its own working class. He called on all "nonaligned'' Mediterranean countries to join forces against great power influence and maintained that Greece should pursue its self-interest and reject foreign patronage.

Throughout the winter and spring of 1981, Papandreou conducted a low key campaign against the New Democracy (q.v.) government, hoping perhaps to reconcile PASOK with a constituency disappointed by the ruling party but still sensitive to memories of social upheavals. During his campaign, he played down his opposition to the European Community (q.v.) and promised to submit to the verdict of a fairly conducted referendum over membership. A rift between the more radical Executive Bureau of the party and its moderate parliamentary representatives underlined the predicament of a movement split between radical purism on the one hand and the need to gain wider support among a liberal sector of the electorate on the other.

The Socialist government's first years in power evolved under difficult circumstances. Economic adversities mounted and PASOK's initial euphoria was considerably toned down into pragmatism by the end of 1983. Although the normal period of grace expired and austerity measures became a feature of government policy, the public appeared less demanding than under New Democracy. The explanation could be sought in the sobering effect of the recession or the contention that socialist policy is somehow more bearable as it is not supposed to enhance private gain but promote social justice. Criticism from the puritan wing of the movement, against foreign policy compromises that dilute PASOK's promises of nonalignment and withdrawal from NATO (q.v.), grew less audible during the mid-1980s.

The election of 1985 gave PASOK a significant margin (45.82 percent and 172 deputies in Parliament). The illness of Papandreou, however, and his absence from the administration of power during the summer of 1988 was the beginning of a period of political crisis with allegations of scandals and financial corruption. The elections of June 1989 took their toll on PASOK which lost power with 38 percent of the vote. It returned to power after the elections of 10 October 1993, where it won 47 percent of the vote.

PELOPONNESE. The southernmost extremity of the Balkan peninsula surrounded by water and joined with mainland Greece by a narrow isthmus is called the Peloponnese, i.e., the island of Pelops as the ancient Greeks called it. Its medieval name is Moreas meaning in Greek mulberry-tree, of which there is a profusion in the Peloponnese. It has an area of 21,739 square kilometers and a population of 1,077,003. The largest city is Patras (pop. 172,763), followed by Kalamata (45,090). Two-thirds of the peninsula are covered by mountains the highest of which is Taygetus (2,404 meters).

The economy is based on agricultural production (olives, citrus fruit, wine, currants), tourism (q.v.) (relics of the Mycenean era, Olympia, Epidaurus and the stunning Byzantine ghost town of Mistra [q.v.] are all places of great interest) and extraction of minerals (of which lignite in the Megalopolis area of Arcadia is systematically mined to fuel power plants).

The Peloponnese has always played an important role in Greek history. The ancient city of Mycenae dominated early civilization with a high degree of culture but with tragedy for the kings and queens of the house of Atreus. The early recorded history of the Peloponnese deals with the rise of Sparta. After the Macedonian conquest, Corinth came to prominence. The Greek culture and language in the region survived successive waves of rulers such as Romans, Franks, and Turks, as well as incursions of Slavis in the sixth century. The War of Independence (q.v.) in 1821 started in the Peloponnese.

PLASTIRAS, NIKOLAOS (1883–1953). Officer and politician of the liberal center. After serving in the Balkan Wars (q.v.) and in Epirus, Plastiras joined the Venizelist movement in 1916, winning rapid promotion for distinguished service in Macedonia (q.v.) and the Ukraine. As a Colonel and Regimental Commander in Asia Minor, he remained in the army at the front after November 1920, despite his known Venizelist loyalties. Leader of the revolution of September 1922, Plastiras pursued thereafter an active political career until his death. He became Prime Minister between 1951–52.

POETRY (MODERN). Professor Trypanis in his *Mediaeval and Modern Greek Poetry* (Clarendon Press, 1951) states that "in the last 100 years much greater and more original poetry has been written in Greece than in the fourteen centuries that preceded them."

It is always intriguing to notice how artistic fermentation in a particular place and time produces a pleiad of outstanding poets, or painters or musicians without any forward warning or detectable reason for that matter. Athens in the Golden Age, Florence at the time of Dante, the London of Shakespeare, the Vienna of Mozart, the Paris of the Impressionists, the Dublin of Yeats and Joyce are dubbed "miracles" only because they remain unexplained, not because they are in any way "abnormal." Greece, and more especially Athens (q.v.) has witnessed a kind of cultural flowering since it became the capital of Greece. Unfortunately, this has remained little known outside the country mainly because of the hitherto low status of modern Greek as a "less important" language. However, the increasing number of students who master it are immediately attracted to the culture.

In fact, Solomos, Kalvos, Palamas Sikelianos, Cavafy, Seferis, and Elytis belong to a modern tradition that hold its own in the twentieth century with the Anglo-American tradition of Pound, Eliot, Auden and their post-modernist successors. The Greek diaspora (q.v.) is well represented in modern Greek poetry. Cavafy lived in Liverpool and wrote some verse in English before he became a Greek poet from Alexandria. Solomos was an Italian poet before he learned to write limpid Greek verse. Jean Moreas wrote in French and the Nobel prize winner Seferis, an itinerant diplomat, wrote most of his poems while posted abroad.

In terms of quantity, Greece, with a population less than a fifth of Great Britain, nonetheless produces annually a greater volume of published poetry. On average, Greece sees two new volumes of poetry published daily. Poetry remains a natural part of popular life in a way that has long ceased to be the case in the West. Oral poetry is very much alive in Crete (q.v.) where peasants continue to learn by heart long passages of the 10,000-odd lines of Kornaros's seventeenth-century epic, the *Erotokritos*. Couplets from it are sometimes printed on the back of the tear-off sheets of calendars found in Greek homes. Memory is also reinforced by spontaneous composition. The Cretan *mantinades* (rhyming couplets for every occasion) and the ritual lament of the dead, the *moirologhia,* still flourish in many rural areas.

Surrealist poetry took a particular form in Greece. Surrealism as it emerged in France was an attempt at overthrowing bourgeois values and the crass materialism of the Third Republic. It aimed to scandalize by way of preposterous public displays, obscenities and manifestos couched in violent antiestablishmentarian and antichauvinist language. In Greece the movement remained purely artistic and never rejected "Greekness" (q.v.). In an interview in 1972, the Nobel prize winner Elytis explained that in order to present the true face of Greece and not simply the image of it such as the Europeans wanted to see, he and his generation "had to destroy the tradition of realism and the prejudices that have reigned since the Renaissance." Greek surrealists such as Empirikos and Engonopoulos tried to transcend Realism by discovering new associations and thereby enriching the poetical idiom with bold innovative imagery and language.

A question often asked and diversely answered is to what extent this poetic florescence stems from its "Greekness." Each reader will have to make up his own mind on this issue. The rich local linguistic resources and tradition do of course play a significant part in this revival but so do painful experiences of national survival, interruptions, discontinuities, fervent aspirations partly fulfilled, a talent to enjoy life and mourn for its loss without losing hope, the ability to remember without succumbing to history and dream without succumbing to despair. All such feelings, aspirations, notions, beliefs, and ideas have been variously invoked to explain the "poetic temperament" of so many modern Greeks, both prolific writers and avid consumers of verse. There is no definitive answer and there need not really be one. Poetry is important. Meta-poetry can wait.

POLLUTION, AIR. The capital of Greece has been cruel to modern Athenians who often wake up in the morning to see their city in the throes of a kind of smog or "cloud" (*nefos* in Greek) containing particles of SO, NOx, CO^2 and hydrocarbons damaging to buildings and persons alike. This is due to the fact that Athens (q.v.) is surrounded by mountains producing inversion effects while the ventilation potential is low. The causal factors of the "cloud" are in order of significance: emissions by cars (64 percent), industry (20 percent), and central heating (16 percent). The Greek government has introduced strict controls on all three sources of air pollution. The levels of pollutants are measured daily by means of eight automatic and three semi-automatic air pollution monitoring stations in Athens. The air quality standards which Greece strives to achieve are those adopted by the European Community (EC) (q.v.). Measurements in 1990 showed that air pollution in Athens was within the prescribed limits for SO, smoke, and lead, whereas the values of NOx were above the limit in the center. A system of alert-levels, triggers off the appropriate response.

The most drastic measures concern restriction of car traffic. In 1989, an incentive scheme was introduced to encourage the replacement and purchase of "clean" cars with catalytic converters using lead-free petrol. This has been very successful and has already had a significant impact on the Athenian *nefos*.

Greece has adopted the EC policies aiming at the stabilization of carbon dioxide emissions throughout the Community at 1990 levels by the year 2000. Though Greece accounts for a minimal portion of the global CO^2 emissions it is of course seriously threatened by the impact of the greenhouse phenomenon involving a possible change of climate. Measures are taken to promote energy conservation and efficient use of fuels with low CO^2 emissions, avoidance of excessive use of fertilizers, as well as prevention of forest fires (q.v.).

POLLUTION, WATER. Water is of prime importance to Greece, a country for which the sea has been a life-line since the mist of times while the few rivers that do exist on her territory have been a prime source of wealth. In fact, water in Greece is scarce but rather clean. Small concentrations of phosphates and nitrates have, however, been detected in the Evros and the Axios Rivers and on a seasonal basis in other rivers and lakes, sometimes leading to eutrophication. Fish farming may have increased the level of ammonia—a catabolic product of fish. Greece, with its enormous coastline (approximately half the coastline of the entire African continent) is especially concerned with seawater pollution.

The coastal waters are much cleaner than would be expected, given that most of the population and the economic activities are concentrated with 20–25 kilometers of the coast. An increase in oil consumption as well as in the traffic density of tankers and cargo ships in Greek waters have multiplied the sources of marine pollution. In the gulfs where the major cities lie such as Saronikos (Athens-Piraeus), Thermaikos (Thessaloniki), Patraikos (Patras), and Pagasitikos (Volos), problems of water pollution do occur which have necessitated the adoption of appropriate measures. The coastal waters have, on the whole, withstood, this onslaught rather well. In 1993, Greece gained the first place in numbers of clean coasts and beaches as identified by the EC "Blue Flag" system. In fact, Greece obtained 237 "Blue Flags," more than any other EC country.

Systematic checks and measurements have proven to the entire satisfaction of the European Community (q.v.) authorities that 97 percent of the areas where swimming is allowed are perfectly adequate in terms of the EC's specifications while 84 percent of these areas are deemed to be in excellent condition according to the most stringent EC standards. An extensive program for the protection of the marine environment (in the framework of ENVIREG) has been under way for some years, while a plant, under construction in the Athens (q.v.) area, is being equipped with a biological treatment unit. The Saronikos Gulf which functions as the dumping place of most of the pollutants generated by the Athens-Piraeus conurbation—housing over three million people and 65 percent of industrial activity of Greece—is remarkably clean. With few local exceptions, the Saronikos water is suitable for bathing and shellfish production. Among the exceptions are a number of areas in the vicinity of the major untreated waste water outfalls. Fishing and shellfish production have been forbidden in these areas. The affected parts of the gulf are mostly in Elefsis Bay, where serious turbidity has been observed, along with the disappearance of some seabed organisms.

However, even if cleanliness is next to godliness, it is also a result of legislation properly enforced. Greece conforms strictly to all international agreements and conventions such as OILPOL 54/62 against operational pollution by steamships, MARPOL 73/78 against accidental pollution, the resolutions of the London Dumping Convention and the regulations imposed on their members by international organizations such as the International Maritime Organization United Nations Environment Program, etc. National legislation and most importantly Law 743/77 on ''the protection of marine environment,'' based on the ''Polluter Has to Pay'' principle, is biting. Polluters can be imprisoned for up to five years and have to pay large fines up to 150 million drachmae (about $500,000) while Greek seamen involved in polluting crimes risk losing their license to work. Any damage done has, of course, to be compensated in full by the polluter.

POPULATION. When Greece first emerged as a nation-state in 1830 with territory comprising only the Peloponnese and Central Greece (qq.v.) its population was 2,600,000 and by 1928 it had risen to 6,200,000, partly as a result of the acquisition of new territories, the Ionian islands, Thessaly, Epirus, Macedonia, Crete (qq.v.) and the Dodecanese. Before that, there was an influx of ethnic Greeks, refugees from Russia as a result of the 1917 Revolution and from Bulgaria as a result of the convention supplementing the Treaty of Neuilly of 1919 which provided for a voluntary exchange of populations.

The largest number of refugees came, though, after the catastrophy of Asia Minor when over a million ethnic Greeks harassed, destitute and forlorn arrived in the islands of the Aegean, Piraeus and Thessaloniki glad to have at least saved their lives. As a result, the population of Athens (q.v.) alone nearly doubled between 1920 and 1928, the city being encircled by shanty towns which bore (and still bear) such nostalgic names as ''Nea Ionia'' or ''Nea Smyrni.''

Emigration has always acted in Greece as a brake on population growth—whose rate has never been particularly high—the most active periods have been 1911–15 (when nearly 130,000 persons left), 1955–60 (160,000) and the 1960s (830,000). After the Second World War (q.v.) there was a rush to the cities as well as a rush abroad (mainly to Germany). Emigration has virtually stopped by now. Regional development and tourism have retained many people in the countryside who would otherwise have migrated to the cities in search of employment. Increasing prosperity as well as large scale emigration abroad of Greek women of child-bearing age in the 1960s have produced a fall in the birth rate.

Today Greeks number 10,264,186 souls according to provisional figures of the 1991 census, of which some 70 percent live in urban or semi-urban centers. Vital statistics are comparable to those of developed European countries. Deaths are 8.5 and births 16.1 per 1,000 annually giving a natural annual increase of 7.6 per 1,000. Mainly as a result of emigration the net annual growth in population fell in the 1980s from 1 percent in 1980 to 0.1 percent in 1988. Life expectancy is 72.2 years for males, and 76.4 for females. The population is aging rapidly, a fact which weighs heavily on welfare and social security services. In 1981, some 15 percent of the population were over 65, a figure which is likely to rise to 35 percent by the end of the century. Infant mortality remains at 11 per 1,000 live births, a high rate for western Europe. To counter these trends the government is generally subsidizing families with large numbers of children.

-R-

RADIO see MEDIA

REBETIKO. A form of popular music consisting of a song accompanied by a string instrument called *bouzouki* very much like the ancient lyre. The composer and the performer are, most of the time, one and the same person, a fact which does not encourage specialization as happened in the West.

The *rebetiko* music originated in the poor quarters of Athens, Piraeus, and Thessaloniki after the influx of refugees from Asia Minor. The songs are usually nostalgic and sad, portraying the sadness of life and unrequited love. The often very sophisticated melodic line and the extraordinary variations required of the *bouzouki* players have made this form of entertainment very popular with Greeks and even with foreign tourists. Amongst the most famous representatives of the genre are Markos Vamvakaris (1905–1972) and Vassilis Tsitsanis (1915–1984).

The *rebetiko* tradition inspired two gifted modern Greek composers who became well known abroad: Manos Hadjidakis (1925–   ), known from the music he wrote for the film *Never on Sunday,* and Mikis Theodorakis (1924–   ) of *Zorba the Greek* fame.

Rebetiko music is monodic, i.e., there is only one musical line, the melody is without harmony or counterpoint. The explanation most commonly offered is that the Islamic world ruling Greece for 400 years knows no harmony while the Orthodox liturgy, an integral part of Greek life under the Ottoman rule, does not allow for instrumental music. The reason given by the Church is that man must praise God with his own voice, not with lifeless instruments. Early Greeks, Christians remembered in horror, used instruments such as the pipe and the drum to drive themselves as worshipers to orgiastic frenzies. Over the centuries, the Orthodox Church (q.v.) has perfected choral singing of great difficulty and intricacy.

The model system used is the Turkish *makam* whereby the octave is not divided up into whole tones and half-tones of the European major and minor scales but into a variety of intervals of different sizes many of which sound out of tune to western ears.

REFUGEES (1922–1923). The defeat of the Greek forces in Asia Minor caused a wholesale expulsion of the Greek population from Turkey. Close to a million-and-a-half refugees were exchanged for half-a-million Moslems and converged on Greece, a country of barely five million. The effect of this sudden influx on Greek society, economy and politics, cannot be exaggerated. Although the economy bore the strain of their settlement for decades after their arrival and their shanty neighborhoods in Athens (q.v.), and Thessaloniki remained in a deplorable condition throughout the interwar period, the urban settlers provided a huge working force for a growing industry and skills for the commercial sector. The rural refugees were settled mainly in Macedonia and Thrace (qq.v.) and were given lands abandoned by the Moslems who went to Turkey.

The addition of about 300,000 voters to a total of 800,000 voting population in Greece, played a decisive role in interwar politics, favoring mainly the Venizelist camp and republican tendencies. The urban refugees also provided support and leadership for the Communist Party (q.v.).

RELIGION see CYRIL AND METHODIUS; ECUMENICAL COUNCILS; GREEK CHURCH; HESYCHASM; ICONO-CLASM; MONASTICISM; ORTHODOX CHURCH; OR-THODOXY; SCHISM

RITSOS, YANNIS (1909–1991). Prolific poet who was interested in drawing, music, literature, and communism. Ritsos was born in Monemvasia, in the Peloponnese (q.v.), and in 1925 moved to Athens (q.v.) where he suffered his first attack of tuberculosis. He spent more than four years in various sanatoria, an experience which marked him both physically and psychologically. In 1936, while in Thessaloniki, he witnessed an attack by the mounted police against striking tobacco workers of which 12 died after having been fired upon. Deeply moved as a poet and as a left-wing militant— which he had by then become—he wrote the "Epitafios" (Epitaph), a heroic lament of a mother over her son's body. During the Nazi Occupation, he took part in the resistance movement and, during the Civil War, he was exiled to various Aegean islands together with thousands of his fellow communists.

In 1945, Ritsos began working on his other long poem called "Romiossini" (Greekness) where he celebrates the bravery of Greek resistance fighters from the Byzantine frontiersman Dighenis Akritas to the modern guerrilla. He was among the first to be arrested when the Colonels' junta took power in April 1967 and was later released for health reasons. He died in 1991 having witnessed the crumbling of communism.

Ritsos is an uneven poet as invariably happens with those who write too much. His published work from his first collection in 1944 to his last poems written in 1988 fill some 5,000 pages of poetry, not including his translations of Mayakovsky, Ehrenbourg, Hikmet and some short stories in prose. He displays enormous versatility and a prodigious register ranging from the lyrical vignette to long poems sometimes including elements of drama. He is fluent, but often repetitive; his imagery is profuse, but often less than original. The lyric quality of his verse is, of necessity, spread thin on the ground. Towards the end of his career he used shorter forms and tried to develop a terser, more meditative style.

Although Ritsos's work verges on propaganda and sometimes even steps into it quite blatantly (as with his poem on the death of Stalin and the one celebrating the Soviet invasion of Czechoslovakia in 1968), he was master of his own house in terms of style, never espoused the theory of "socialist realism," and sometimes even disagreed with the party line. His poetry has been translated into 20 languages, but since the collapse of communism, his public has shrunk significantly both in Greece and abroad.

-S-

SCHISM. The breach of unity of the visible Christian Church, conventionally thought to have occurred in the eleventh century, resulting in the creation of the Roman Catholic Church in the West as a distinct and separate church, out of communion with the Orthodox Church (q.v.).

When Cardinal Humbert and two other legates of the Pope entered the Church of Aghia Sophia in Constantinople one sunny afternoon on the 12th of July in the year of the Lord 1054, it was clear that they had not come to pray. They placed a Papal "Bull of Excommunication" upon the altar and left while the cardinal shouted: "Let God look and judge." The incident is conventionally considered to mark the great schism between Eastern and Western Christianity.

There were two main points of difference. One was theological and concerned the *"filioque,"* i.e., the procession of the Holy Spirit both from Father and Son according to the Latins, only from the Father according to the Byzantines. The other was organizational. What was the place of the Pope to be in the scheme of things? He was at the top, the absolute ruler, he enjoyed full powers (*plenitudo potestatis*), said the Latins. He could be the first among equal Patriarchs, while dogmatic questions would continue to be solved by Ecumenical Councils (q.v.), said the Byzantines. These two issues were never resolved although there were repeated efforts to paper over differences or to ignore them.

Political developments accentuated the differences. In the West, the total collapse of the Roman Empire and the emergence of a plurality of warring chiefs served greatly to strengthen the autocratic structure of the Western Church. By force of circumstance the Popes were thus driven to issue commands to secular rulers and assume responsibilities which went far beyond anything the Greek Patriarchs were ever asked to do. In the East, there was a strong secular head, the Emperor, to uphold order and enforce law, thus allowing bishops to develop a sense of equality among them and base the Church on collegiality, not monarchy, as in the West.

Orthodoxy (q.v.) has the Church guardian of an eternal truth, in service not so much to advance the human condition as to ensure salvation and participation in the Kingdom of God which is not of this world. Therefore the Church, a bulwark against falsity and heresy, must be protected from corrosion by the "spirit of the age" and upheld as keeper of the true faith while its rites and forms of worship must reflect its love of tradition and its will never to defect. Roman Catholicism sees the Church as a leaven in the world, properly active in all human concerns, a force to alleviate want and oppression as well as a light to illuminate men's minds.

The two differing attitudes need not have led to mutual anathemas and confrontation as the present respect and courtesy of disagreement between the Pontiff and the Patriarch of Constantinople show. In the Middle Ages, however, such doctrinal differences were impossible to overcome and increasingly difficult to live with.

SECOND WORLD WAR (1939–1945). Greece was drawn into the war when Italian troops crossed the borders of Albania and violated Greek territory on 28 October 1940. The Greek counter-offensive pushed the Italians deep into Albania and the Greek army maintained the initiative throughout the winter. During the campaign the head of the Greek government, Ioannis Metaxas (q.v.), resisted inadequate British support which would have provoked a German intervention. After his death in February 1941, King George II (q.v.) was persuaded that the forces Britain was able to deploy in the Greek theater merited total Greek commitment to the Allied cause.

Between 5 April and the end of that month the Germans overran both Yugoslavia and Greece. What could be salvaged of the Greek army was evacuated to Crete (q.v.). When Crete fell under an airborne attack at the end of May, the King and his government-in-exile were established in London and Cairo for the duration of the war. The Greek armed forces in Egypt participated in the major Allied campaign against the Germans. In occupied Greece (Thrace and part of Macedonia were annexed by Bulgaria) the hardships suffered by the population under the Axis forces swelled the ranks of the resistance and made the Communist-controlled EAM-ELAS a formidable factor in wartime developments. Enemy occupation and a subsequent Civil War between Communist and anti-Communist forces, compounded the heavy price that the Greeks paid for their participation in the Second World War.

SEFERIS, GEORGE (1900–1971). The poet, Nobel prize winner, critic and diplomat George Seferiadis, or Seferis as he called himself, was born in Smyrna, where he spent his childhood. He came to Greece with his family at the age of 22, fleeing the wanton destruction and killings perpetrated by the Turks against the Christian population. Vivid images of despair have been haunting his poetry ever since: homes destroyed, people forced to march towards unknown destinations, camps, wreckage, and boats capsizing under the load of too many panic-stricken refugees fleeing their burning city. Such images often appear in his poems on a background of broken statues, Venetian forts, Byzantine churches, rocks, olive trees, and the luminous blue of the Aegean atmosphere. A ship full of harried forlorn passengers traveling hopefully if aimlessly is to him a recurrent symbol of a world without direction fleeing one evil without clear guidance as to how to avoid the next. ''What are they after, our souls traveling on the deck of decaying ships?,'' he will wonder in his ''Myth of History'' (*''Mythistorima''*).

The family settled in Athens where young Seferis studied law before going to Paris where he enrolled at the Sorbonne. He graduated in 1924, joined Greece's foreign service in 1926 and had a distinguished career as a diplomat.

While a vice-consul in London in 1931, he read extensively and was influenced by the works of Ezra Pound and T.S. Eliot. He spent the next 20 years writing poems deeply influenced by T.S. Eliot such as *''Strophe''* (''Turning Point'') in 1931, *''I Sterna''* (''The Cistern'') in 1932 and, later, *''Mythistorima''* (''Myth of History''). In 1951, when he was Counsellor at the Greek Embassy in London, he actually met T.S. Eliot. After their last conversation, just before Seferis left for Beirut where he was posted in 1952, Eliot told him: ''I am glad I met a real poet.'' Seferis received his Nobel prize in 1963 for ''his outstanding lyric poetry which inspires a profound feeling for the Hellenic world of culture,'' in the words of the citation.

His poetry and his works of literary criticism display such a depth of empathy with situations and people, such a precise intellectual domination over his material and such a vast assimilated culture of European poetry and literature that many people predicted he would be more praised than read. This did not happen. His books are, as they have always been, poetic best-sellers with particular appeal to the young.

SHIPPING. As one might expect of a nation living so close to the sea, the Greeks have since ancient times displayed their nautical skills. The rugged terrain, the huge coastline and the innumerable islands make sea transport all important for the country. Upon its creation as a nation-state in 1830 Greece had 1,050 sailing vessels with a total tonnage of 30,600. By 1871, the Greek fleet had 6,135 vessels and close to 440,000 tons. In the late nineteenth century the Greek merchant marine shifted to steam. The first steamboat was acquired in 1862. By the beginning of World War I (q.v.), the Greek fleet possessed 475 steamboats of which it lost 360 during the hostilities. By 1925, prewar tonnage was restored and 14 years later it had doubled. On a per capita basis the Greek merchant marine was, in 1939, the sixth in the world. During World War II (q.v.) the Greeks lost 78 percent of their vessels. It took them more than a decade to recoup these losses. The modern Greek merchant fleet was built up after the war and became the largest in the world during the 1970s. In March 1992, it reached 53.9 million gross registered tons of which about half were under the Greek flag (25 million).

Greek shipping is up to 95 percent involved in bulk trade and is therefore heavily dependent on carrying cargo between third countries. Greeks specialize in the tramp trade where the pickings are rich and the risks great. Shipping firms are thus very vulnerable to international crises, especially oil crises. However, Greek shipowners have shown remarkable skills in diversifying their trade ahead of crises and refurbishing their fleets with newer, more versatile vessels. A severe limiting factor to the industry's expansion is the scarcity of qualified seamen since the ones at work sign up on average for only six months a year and abandon their career at the age of 40. The merchant navy employs some 100,000 Greek seamen, i.e., some 3 percent of the total working population. A further 2 percent are employed in ancillary services.

Greece possesses a total of 444 ports of which 123 are capable of handling vessels (cargo or passenger) of international size. In 1990, the government cut taxes and made revictualling in Greek ports tax free in an effort to attract new vessels to the Greek flag.

SIKELIANOS, ANGELOS (1884–1951). An original, if somewhat grandiloquent and highly idiosyncratic poet, born in the island of Lefkas, whose extravagant ideas are as much remembered as his work. He published his poems under the general title: *Lyrical Life (Lyrikos Vios)*. He has also written unplayable tragedies such as *Dighenis, Christ in Rome,* and

Daedalus. Like Eliot he saw the modern world as a "waste-land." The Greek poet, however, saw escape only by reverting to the values of pre-Socratic thinkers, the world of Delphic oracles, and Eleusinian mysteries. He was attracted to ancient Greek cults and believed they could be resuscitated in all their dark mystic beauty.

His first important poem, "The Visionary," already contained the seeds of his exalted pantheistic doctrine. In it he glorifies man's body and blood as part of the dance and rhythm of life in general. He was obsessed by the notion of a lost unity (of life and matter, earth and sky, feminine and masculine) which could, he believed, be achieved once again. In his "Consciousness of Woman" he maintains that the eternal principles at the core of life are somehow reflected in the rites of the marriage ceremony in Greek villages. He goes much further than his contemporary romantic lovers of folklore (q.v.) in that he believed one could find ancient truths, and answers to modern problems, in the Greek villages. Such was the depth of his convictions that he tried to put them into practice by organizing a center of learning at Delphi (q.v.) financed by his wealthy and devoted American wife.

Delphi was chosen because Sikelianos considered it the spiritual fount of Orphic wisdom and inspiration. Students at the center would gradually move from folklore to the ancient cultures themselves. The "Delphic Idea," as it was dubbed, was launched in the form of two "Delphic Festivals," one in 1927 and another in 1937. They were hailed by enthusiasts in Athens (q.v.) but failed to attract seekers of infinity. The project was aborted by the poet himself, lest it became a tourist attraction. The idea of reviving ancient Greek rituals in modern context has thus been abandoned. This particular form of ancestor worship known in Greece as *archaiolatreia* died with this inspired poet vibrant with ideas of another time.

SOLID WASTE. In Greece, as in other countries, increasing prosperity allows people to buy more objects and makes them throw more away. In the Greece of the 1990s, the estimated quantity of household waste is 0.95 kg per person per day. The well-known trend that as countries become richer they progressively discard more paper is true of Greece too, where paper is by far the most important item in the domestic rubbish bin. Legislation everywhere has typically attacked air and water pollution (qq.v.) first and solid waste afterwards. This is true of Greece as well. One reason is that substances that are lethal if inhaled, imbibed, or touched may do little harm when safely confined to a well-run tip. The responsibility for collection and transport of waste lies in Greece, with local authorities, who use the landfilling method for disposal, in most cases without pre-treatment. There are 5,000 such landfill areas throughout Greece of which only a few operate according to proper specifications for controlled sanitary disposal of wastes. In some areas this creates problems such as fires, odors, and pollution of surface waters. Greece has been implementing since 1992 an ambitious investment program aiming to reduce waste production at the source, and to improve the operation of landfills in use.

Solid waste is increasingly perceived as a serious issue because it tends to be the pollution problem to which other problems are eventually reduced. The first step is to regulate solid waste disposal so that it is not done illegally in an environmentally harmful way. This is more or less ensured in Greece where the absence of heavy industry has so far spared the environment from any toxic and dangerous wastes. Recycling—with the exception of 60,000 tons of used oils which are recycled every year to be used as fuel—is in its infancy. The distinction between "waste" (to be dumped) and "residual matter" (to be recycled) which has concentrated the minds of experts in other countries, has therefore not had to be—as yet—seriously considered in Greece. Probabilities are that recycling will not visit Greece soon as it is anyway on the wane everywhere because it is not profitable.

Although Greeks have become increasingly more hostile to the idea of living near a rubbish dump the government is doing its best to resolve the political problem of opening new landfills of high standards with the assistance of the European Community (EC) (q.v.). Until recently European countries have been far more willing than the United States for the public sector to pay the greater part of the costs of cleaning up. Where the private sector has been legally liable for the costs of doing so, liability has been much more limited than in America. In March 1993, the EC Commission published a very tentative paper on remedying environmental damage favoring "strict" liability in which negligence does not have to be proved. It has not been received well by industry.

SOLOMOS, DIONYSIOS (1798–1857). The "national poet of Greece," as he has been officially recognized, Dionysios Solomos is one of the most outstanding products of the nineteenth-century Septinsular culture. He was born in Zakynthos, the illegitimate son of a wealthy aristocrat and his maidservant. Legitimacy and the title of count were conferred on him late in life when his father married his mother shortly before his death in 1807. The following year he went to Italy where he studied literature. In 1818, he returned to Zakynthos—by then a British protectorate—and wrote Italian verse while at the same time becoming deeply involved with the Greeks' struggle for independence. In 1823, he wrote his famous "Hymn to Liberty" whose first four stanzas eventually became the lyrics of Greece's national anthem. His other, much more thoughtful and sophisticated works such as "The Woman of Zakynthos" and the fragmentary "Lambros" were appreciated mainly by the cognoscenti of the Anglo-Ionian-Corfiote society. The "Free Besieged," on which he toiled for almost two decades, deals with the desperate exodus of Greeks from the city of Missolonghi during which most perished. In spite of his unceasing efforts this elegiac poem was never entirely completed.

Solomos was a perfectionist who became a self-taught master of the demotic (q.v.) language and never stopped trying to better himself. By mining the wealth of the spoken tongue, the folk songs and the literary works written in seventeenth-century Cretan demotic idiom, Solomos shaped the language of modern Greek poetry. In his uncompleted work "Dialogos" he uses the Baconian formula: "First submit to the language of the people and then, if you are able, master it." He maintained that freedom is in the spirit, not the letter which, he said, must be common to enable the exchange of ideas. He strongly believed in Dante's precept "nutriciam imitans," i.e., that one should write in the language of one's nurse. His views were not popular with the linguistic establishment made of "purists." Even his "Hymn to Freedom," written in 1823 and which became the national anthem after the expulsion of King Otto (q.v.) (1862), ran the danger of being replaced by another "of a nobler language."

In 1849, he was awarded the Gold Cross of the Knight of the Savior and the title of "national poet" in spite of his predilection for the demotic language and the fact that his major works consist of incomplete poems such as "The Cretan," "Porfyras" and—as mentioned—"The Free Besieged." His overriding quest for perfection has left us many variant readings for literally hundreds of individual lines. Students of modern Greek poetry usually start with Solomos, poet who managed to reconcile the spiritual with the material, the classical with the romantic, in a unique way.

SOPHOULIS, THEMISTOKLIS (1860–1949). Liberal politician who inherited the leadership of Sophocles Venizelos's (q.v.) party. Born in the island of Samos to a prominent family, Sophoulis studied archaeology in Athens and Germany. His political career began in 1990 when he was elected a member of the parliament of independent Samos. In 1912, he took part in an armed operation to set the island free from the last vestiges of Turkish influence. He participated in the revolt of 1916 on the side of Venizelos and became the Minister of Interior in the Thessaloniki government. In 1917, he became President of Parliament and, in 1924, headed a government that lasted for three months. President of Parliament again between 1926 and 1928, he became Minister of Army Affairs in Venizelos's 1928 government. After the latter's death, he assumed the leadership of the Liberal Party (q.v.). He was Prime Minister during the Greek Civil War (see SECOND WORLD WAR) (1947–49).

STOCKBREEDING. Greece is unsuitable for efficient stockbreeding because of its climate and lack of pastures. This is particularly true of bovine breeding. As a result, meat imports cover about 20 percent of annual consumption. Traditionally, Greeks bred free ranging sheep and goats, as they still do, especially in mountain areas. There are about 12 times more sheep and six times more goats than cattle bred in the country.

The best known Greek dairy product is a cheese called "feta" made of sheep's milk, which has of late become quite popular abroad.

STOCK EXCHANGE see INDUSTRY (MANUFACTURING)

-T-

TAKIS, VASILAKIS (1925–). Artist of international reputation. Takis was born in Athens (q.v.) but later established himself in Paris. He is best known for his mobile electrical contraptions. In 1958, he made his mark with his "Telemagnetic" sculptures and, in 1968, he was granted a fellowship at the MIT Center for Advanced Visual Studies in Cambridge, Massachusetts. He has exhibited widely and has been commissioned with various public works of art by the French government.

TELEVISION see MEDIA

THESSALY. This region lies in the eastern part of continental Greece bordering Macedonia in the north, Epirus in the west, Central Greece in the south, and the Aegean (qq.v.) in the east. Covering an area of 14,037 square kilometers and with a population of 731,230, Thessaly is one of the most fertile areas in Greece. It is also one of the hottest places in Europe during the summer and consists of a vast plain surrounded by several mountains among which is Mount Olympus (the seat of the 12 gods as ancient Greeks believed). The largest towns are Larissa (pop. 113,426) and Volos (106,142). The Thessalian plain is drained by the Peneus River (205 kilometers). Its main income comes from farming. The major crops are cereals, cotton and sugar beets. The most attractive sights in

Thessaly are the Meteora (a word which means in Greek "floating in mid air") monasteries near Kalambaka perched on high rocks and almost inaccessible by ordinary means.

Thessaly was ruled by an oligarchy in ancient Greece and came successively under Macedonian and then Roman rule. In the twelfth century it became the center of a Bulgar-Vlach kingdom known as Great Wallachia. The Turks conquered it in 1389 and ceded it to Greece in 1881. By the acquisition of Thessaly, Greece secured an area with traditions deep in the Greek past. Even during the long Ottoman occupation of the area, Greeks had formed the majority of the Thessalian population, and Greek had been the official language. Important for the economic future of the whole country was the richness and vastness of the area. Dominated by the more than 3,000-meter high Mount Olympus, the vast Thessalian plain was destined to contribute notably to the Greek economy of the future with its large production of tobacco and grain. Nearby, the slopes of Mount Pelion next to its twin, Mount Ossa, were destined to provide some of the wood much needed by the country. The capital, Larissa had long been a crossroads for communication between northern and central Greece and was to be an even more important junction in the future.

THRACE. The northeastern part of continental Greece bordering Macedonia (q.v.) to the west, Bulgaria to the north, Turkey to the east, and the Aegean Sea (q.v.) to the south is called Thrace. Its total area, including the island of Samothrace, is 8,578 square kilometers. The largest town is Alexandroupolis (39,283 pop.). Thrace is dominated by the range of the Rodope Mountains (2,278 meters) which form the natural border with Bulgaria. Between this range and the sea lie the plains of Xanthe and Komotini. The natural border with Macedonia is the Nestos River and with Turkey the Evros River. Thrace became Greek in 1920.

Thrace's far eastern location brought it early under Ottoman control. It remained particularly subject to their influence. After capturing the area in the mid-fourteenth century, the Ottomans held it for over 500 years before it was turned over to newly created Bulgaria in 1878, after the Russo-

Turkish War. The Bulgarians controlled Thrace until 1919, when, as a result of the defeat of the Central Powers at the close of World War I (q.v.) Bulgaria was required to cede the western part of the area to Greece. In that same year a first exchange of populations took place. Greeks residing in Bulgaria who wanted to return to Greece were exchanged for an equal number of Bulgarians wishing to leave their residence in western Thrace for Bulgaria. There is a sizeable Moslem minority (over 100,000) living in Thrace as the area was exempted from the exchange of populations between Greece and Turkey according to the provisions of the Treaty of Lausanne (1923).

The economy of Thrace is similar to that of eastern Macedonia relying mainly on tobacco, sugar beet, and cotton. The traditional silk production of the Evros region has been all but annihilated by synthetic fiber production.

TOURISM. Greece started to attract visitors who wanted to see its archaeological sites as early as the nineteenth century. The trend continued with ups and downs until the outbreak of the Second World War (q.v.). In 1938, there were 90,333 tourist arrivals in Greece. They were to be the last for a long time.

After the war the picture changed because the Greek government for the time built a substantial infrastructure enabling tourists to enjoy the clean waters, the beaches, the antiquities and the climate at a reasonable cost.

In 1966, tourist arrivals passed the million mark for the first time. The present figure—considered by many as having reached saturation point—is eight million with the British and Germans being the most numerous. The Greek Tourist Board (EOT by its Greek acronym) is trying to spread this influx in space (relieving Corfu, Rhodes and Myconos of almost intolerable pressure) and in time (so that arrivals cover the whole season and not just the month of August). There has been a marked development of winter tourism in recent years. Mount Parnassus near Delphi, Karpenisi in Central Greece and Mount Vermion in western Macedonia have started to acquire a good reputation internationally as winter resorts.

Tourism is very important to Greece in economic terms. Tourist earnings were estimated to be 3.7 percent of GDP, though the actual contribution is probably much higher since 10 percent of the work force is said to be directly or indirectly involved in this industry.

TRIKOUPIS, HARILAOS (1832–1897). An important statesman and reformer. Trikoupis was born in Nafplion, the son of a prominent Greek politician and historian, Spyridon Trikoupis. He studied law at the University of Athens and Paris and served as First Secretary in the Greek Embassy in London. In 1863, he was elected deputy by the Greek community in England and, in 1865, by his Messolonghi constituency. He became Minister of Foreign Affairs in the Koumoundouros government of 1866. Prime Minister for the first time in 1882, he dominated Greek politics for almost a quarter of a century.

Trikoupis was probably the most important Greek politician of the nineteenth century. A champion exponent of parliamentary politics in the liberal tradition, he created the extensive infrastructure that was responsible for Greece's subsequent economic development. Unlike his major political opponent, Theodoros Diliyannis (q.v.), he believed that modernization of the state took precedence over irredentist adventures. Trikoupis was also aware that his country could not fulfill its aspirations regarding Ottoman-held territories with solid Greek populations without foreign implication and support. Although a prudent administrator, he contracted foreign loans to finance his public works which led the country to bankruptcy.

TSALDARIS, PANAGHIS (1868–1936). Leader of the Populist Party, and political opponent of Sophocles Venizelos (q.v.). Born in Corinth, Tsaldaris studied law in Athens (q.v.), Berlin, and Paris. He was Minister of Justice in the Gounaris cabinet of February 1915 and was later exiled for his royalist stand. He became a Minister of Interior in the Rallis government of November 1920. After the execution of Dimitrios Gounaris in 1922, he became the de factor leader of the anti-Venizelist Populist Party. In 1927, he was the Minister of Interior in the "Ikoumeniki" (all-party) government and became Prime Minister in 1932. An honest politician and staunch parliamentarian, his moderate position placed him at odds both with the Venizelist and royalist extremists.

TSATSOS, KONSTANTINOS (1899–1987). Statesman and scholar. Tsatsos was born in Athens (q.v.) in a family of scholars and politicians. He studied law at Athens University and worked as an aid to Eleftherios Venizelos (q.v.) during the deliberations of the Sevres treaty. After serving in the Greek army between 1920–23, he studied philosophy of law in Heidelberg along with Panayotis Kanellopoulos (q.v.) and Ioannis Theodoracopoulos. The three became influential exponents of the Heidelberg school of thought in Greece.

In 1929 he was awarded a Ph.D. degree in law from Athens University and became a Professor of Philosophy of Law at that institution. He was interned during the Metaxas (q.v.) dictatorship for his liberal ideas. He resumed his teaching after the German invasion of Greece but was sacked by the occupation government. He subsequently became involved in the resistance and was obliged to flee to the Middle East.

After the war, Tsatsos taught briefly at Athens Law School but resigned from his post in 1946 to run for office. In 1949, he became Minister of Education and later, as the life-long friend of Constantinos Karamanlis (q.v.), he served in many ministerial posts. He was a prolific writer and one of the more important idealist philosophers of contemporary Greece. After the fall of the Colonels' regime, he was elected President of the Republic by Parliament and served from 1975–80.

TURKEY, RELATIONS WITH. Although both countries entered NATO simultaneously in 1951 and cooperated within the western alliance, the Cyprus (q.v.) issue began to create tensions in the mid-1950s. In 1955, a mob in Istanbul demanding the annexation of Cyprus by Turkey, destroyed Greek houses, shops, and churches causing an exodus of the Greek population.

In 1959, Prime Minister Constantinos Karamanlis (q.v.) and Turkish Premier Menderes, meeting in Zurich drafted an agreement for the creation of an independent Cyprus. The integrity and constitution of the state were guaranteed by Britain, Greece, and Turkey. A few years later, following an attempt by President Makarios III (q.v.) to amend the constitution, fighting broke out between the two communities.

The Turkish invasion of Cyprus in 1974 determined relations between Greece and Turkey for the next two decades. Besides this pending problem there are other issues that constitute serious sources of tension between the two states: 1) the Aegean, continental shelf; 2) the control of air traffic over the Aegean; 3) the allocation of operational responsibility of the Aegean air space within NATO; 4) the militarization of the Greek islands; 5) the Turkish Aegean army and its fleet of landing craft; 6) the breadth of Greek air space and its constant violations by Turkish fighters; and 7) the Moslem minority of Thrace (q.v.) and the dwindling Greek minority of Istanbul.

TYCOONS. The phenomenal success of Greek shipping (q.v.) due to a combination of business acumen by shipowners, high expertise and loyalty by officers and crews, minimal interference by the unions and help by the state does produce a regular crop of tycoons whose personal fortune and life-style have prompted extensive coverage by the international press. One of the wealthiest and best known magnates is Stavros Niarchos (83), living in St. Moritz, Switzerland. He is reputed to be worth $4 billion, is a known art lover and a former rival of Aristotle Onassis (q.v.). They were both married to the same woman, Christina Livanos, coming from yet another shipping dynasty. Others in this category are Yannis Latsis (82), the London-based tycoon reputedly worth $2 billion, a generous contributor to the Tory party, friend of British royals and very close to the royal family of Saudi Arabia where he amassed most of his fortune. Vardis Vardinoyannis (59) is based in Athens (q.v.) and owns a newspaper and a football club. He has been the target of an attack by an elusive terrorist group calling itself the "17th November." Others in this category include George Lemos (81), George Livanos (64) and numerous members of the Goulandris family. Most rich shipowners are not publicity seeking and donate substantial sums to charities in their native islands of Andros and Chios.

-U-

UNITED NATIONS RELIEF AND REHABILITATION ADMINISTRATION (UNRRA). An organization established in 1943 by the allies of the Second World War (q.v.) to meet immediate needs of liberal states. Allied countries that had not experienced occupation were to raise a levy based on their rational incomes to provide funds for relief of their less fortunate allies. Aid was primarily extended to Greece as well as Albania, China, Czechoslovakia, Poland, and Yugoslavia. The list of beneficiaries later included countries that had been on the side of the enemy such as Austria, Finland, Hungary, and Italy. Also aided were Ethiopia, Byelorussia, and Ukraine in a limited field.

UNRRA was given the status of a sovereign state and the total amount placed at its disposal aggregated $4 billion.

UNITED STATES, RELATIONS WITH. The Greek War of Independence (q.v.) was influenced by the same enlightenment principles that inspired the American War of Independence and the first democratic constitution of Greece had drawn from the liberal heritage of eighteenth-century revolutions. There is furthermore an absence of an aristocratic tradition in both American and Greek society, which encourages the conviction of the man in the street that all human beings are created equal and are therefore entitled to pass valid judgement on their leaders.

The two countries fought for the same cause in two World Wars as well as in the Korean war. At the end of the Second World War the United States became the major protector of Greece. The Truman Doctrine of 12 March 1947 and the Marshall Plan of 5 June 1947 provided security guarantees and aid to a devastated country.

Clouds in Greek-American relations appeared whenever American foreign policy was faced with a choice between the Greek and the Turkish position on Cyprus (q.v.) or whenever the US acted as an arbiter between Greece and Turkey. Furthermore, the US government lost points in Greece during the years of its support for the Greek military regime (1967–74). The 1974 Turkish invasion of Cyprus, perpetrated with allied weaponry despite the ban imposed by American laws on such use, provoked a Congressional embargo on supplies of arms to Turkey. Successive administrations, however, undermined what could have been a tool of decisive pressure on Turkey to withdraw its forces from the island. The embargo was finally lifted in 1978 and the Turkish troops are still in Cyprus.

In 1976, following the conclusion of a Defense Cooperation Agreement (DCA) between the US and Turkey, the Greek government was quick to initial an agreement that established a 7:10 ratio of US military aid to Greece and Turkey. Maintaining this ratio, which according to Greece's views guarantees the balance in the Aegean (q.v.), has become a doctrine of Greek foreign policy. The extension of free aid to Turkey has in fact undermined the ratio, but in principle it has not been abandoned.

Although the advent of PASOK (q.v.) caused strain on US-Greek relations, the Papandreou government signed a Defense and Economic Cooperation Agreement (DECA) in 1983 which guaranteed the operation of American bases in Greece. The Mitsotakis government improved relations between the two states but American policy in the Balkans in the early 1990s deviated from Greece's support of the status quo in the region.

-V-

VENIZELOS, ELEFTHERIOS (1864–1936). Dominant political figure. Born in Chania Crete, Venizelos studied law in Athens (q.v.). He entered Cretan politics in 1889 and became a leading figure in the revolutionary movement for unification of the island of Crete (q.v.) with Greece. His opposition to Prince George, High Commissioner of Crete, won him a national reputation. From the moment he arrived in Greece in

1910, at the invitation of the Military League, until his death in exile in 1936, he dominated Greek politics. Founder and leader of the Liberal Party (q.v.), which became the rallying point of many distinguished political figures including Georgios Kafandaris (q.v.), Alexandros Papanastasiou (q.v.), Themistoklis Sophoulis (q.v.), and Georgios Papandreou (q.v.).

During his first term in power (1910–14), Venizelos reformed the state apparatus, education and the economy. Through an intricate network of alliances he was responsible for Greece's territorial enlargement during the Balkan Wars and the First World War (qq.v.). His commitment to Greece's participation on the side of the Triple Entente caused a "national schism" between his followers and the supporters of King Constantine I (q.v.). The legacy of the "schism" bedeviled Greek politics throughout the interwar period.

During his last term in office (1928–33), Venizelos managed to extricate Greece from its Balkan isolation by concluding bilateral treaties with Romania, Italy, Turkey, and Yugoslavia.

Although he possessed a personality that aroused strong sentiments among friends and foes, he was without a doubt the most important political figure in modern Greek history.

VENIZELOS, SOPHOCLES (1894–1964). The son of Eleftherios Venizelos (q.v.), Sophocles was born in Chania, Crete (q.v.). He entered the Military Academy in 1910 and saw action in the subsequent wars. He resigned from the officer corps in 1920 and was elected member of parliament. During the Second World War (q.v.) he became Prime Minister of the government-in-exile and served as Prime Minister and minister in several postwar governments. As Minister of Foreign Affairs in 1951 he was instrumental in bringing Greece into NATO (q.v.).

Venizelos was one of the main forces behind the foundation of the Center-Union Party (q.v.) which won the elections of 1963 and 1964. Although the natural heir of his father in the leadership of the Liberal Party (q.v.), he was always prepared to give way to other politicians in order to serve moderation and cooperation within the liberal camp.

VERGHINA. The name of Verghina was given to a village in western Macedonia (q.v.), 64 kilometers west of Thessaloniki, built in 1923 by refugees from Asia Minor on the site of the ancient city of Aigai which Perdikkas, founder of the Macedonian dynasty, made his capital.

Verghina acquired world fame when the Greek Professor of Archaeology Manolis Andronikos (q.v.) discovered there the royal tombs of Philip of Macedon, father of Alexander the Great. The interior of the tomb contains a superb fresco, the first example of a fourth century B.C. fresco ever to be unearthed. In the press conference he gave an 11 November 1977, Professor Andronikos showed the magnificent objects he found, indicative of the high status of the person buried there. Among them were five miniature ivory heads depicting Philip II, his wife Olympias, his son Alexander and his parents Amyntas and Eurydice. In the chamber there was a sarcophagus which contained a coffer made of solid gold weighing 11 kilograms. The lid was delicately decorated with the 16-point radiating star, the emblem of the Macedonian Kings. Inside the coffer was a diadem also worn by Macedonian royalty, a shield made of gold and ivory, a pair of greaves of which one was smaller than the other (Philip was lame), a helmet, a superb breast plate and a long staff made of bamboo, cloth and ivory, obviously the royal scepter. Massive and elaborate marble doors seal the underground burial places. The contents of the tombs now form a stunning exhibition at the Archaeological Museum in Thessaloniki.

These extraordinary finds which shook the archaeological world confirmed what the English historian Professor Hammond had been saying for years, namely that the capital of the kingdom of Macedon was located in Verghina and not in Pella as was commonly believed. Further excavations showed hundreds of tombs of ordinary Macedonians all bearing Greek names, as well as their fathers' (always ritually named on tombstones). Typical names found on the site are, for instance, Alkimos, Antigonos, Drykalos, Evkseinos, Iraklidis, Kleagoras, Leandros, Lyssanias, Menandros, Nikostratos, Pevkolaos, Proksenos, Pierion, Philstos, Philoras, Vereniki, and Xenocrati. These not only mean something in Greek (Alkimos for instance is the Homeric term for a strong, valiant man) but are widespread throughout the Greek world. Similar finds were later made at Dion by Professor Pantermalis.

-W-

WAR OF INDEPENDENCE (1821–1828). War broke out in March 1821 almost simultaneously in the Danubian principalities of Romania under an officer of the Russian army, Alexander Ypsilantis, and the Peloponnese (q.v.) in southern Greece. The Danubian outbreak had the significance of a general Balkan uprising against Ottoman oppression according to the vision of Rhigas Fereos (q.v.). The rising in the Peloponnese was in keeping with Greek national aspirations and the revival of hellenism in its birthplace.

Whereas the campaign in Romania failed dismally and Ypsilantis spent the rest of his life in an Austrian prison, the war in the Peloponnese and the maritime islands off its coast was crowned with success. In the battle of Dervenakia in 1822, the commander of the Greek forces, Theodoros Kolokotronis (q.v.), destroyed an Ottoman army of 30,000 men.

An important factor in the Greek victories of the first two years was the role of the fleet in the Aegean commanded by admiral Andreas Miaoulis, who managed to prevent the reinforcement of the Ottoman garrisons of the Peloponnese by sea. The rough terrain of the hinterland gave the Greek irregulars with their guerilla tactics of a definite advantage. Once, however, the first Greek governments were established and constitutions were drafted according to French Revolution prototypes, a civil war broke out between different localities and factions. Thus, the warlords of central Greece joined forces with the islanders against the notables of the Peloponnese.

Civil strife among the Greeks allowed the Ottomans to invite the Egyptian forces under General Ibrahim to quell the rebellion. The naval Battle of Navarino (q.v.) in October 1827, between a joint Russian, British, and French squadron and an Ottoman-Egyptian force, ended with the destruction of the latter. By the spring of the following year, Russia declared war against the Porte and marched its forces against Constantinople. The treaty of Adrianople (1829) obliged the Sultan to recognize the autonomy of Greece which, thanks to British-Russian antagonism, was soon transformed into independence. The limited borders of the new state included only 800,000 Greeks out of an estimated total of four million under Ottoman rule. The first President of the independent Greek state was Count Ioannis Capodistrias (q.v.), former Foreign Minister of the Russian Czar.

WARS see BALKAN WARS; FIRST WORLD WAR; SECOND WORLD WAR: WAR OF INDEPENDENCE.

WATER MANAGEMENT. Water is of paramount importance to Mediterranean countries. Greece is not dry, but water is lacking where it is most needed, i.e., near the large cities. Water management is therefore costly because sophisticated waterworks are needed to ensure storage during high rainfall seasons as well as efficient distribution from water-rich to water-deficient areas. The purity of surface and underground water resources has been at risk from urban and industrial wastes, intensive use of fertilizers and pesticides as well as from sea water penetration along the coast. High European Community (q.v.) support prices for crops needing irrigation, such as cotton and maize, which have produced a drop in groundwater levels leading to increasing salinization in intensely cultivated areas in Thessaly (q.v.).

This is what prompted, during the last decade, a series of measures to increase the use of groundwater for drinking purposes (it stood at 66 percent in 1990) while closely monitoring the whole process of water supply so as to avoid drawdown, loss of pressure, and salinization of some aquifers. As for agriculture the aim is not necessarily to increase the water supply but to encourage farmers to use less wasteful irrigation methods. Where tourism has replaced agriculture (q.v.)—as for instance in the islands—the problems are serious as per capita demand rises sharply from 100 liters daily at a moderate hotel to more than 600 liters at a luxury resort.

Ensuring the water supply for the Athens-Piraeus conurbation became a major concern for the government in 1992 and early 1993 because of the dramatic decline in rainfall. The Mornos reservoir had been satisfactorily covering the needs of the population. A run of dry winters, however, together with rising consumption (swimming pools and well tended gardens are no longer a rarity in suburbia) and losses from an aging distribution network had shrunk reserves to a dangerous all-time low. Though the 80 liters daily per capita consumed by Athenians is low by European standards the water company sounded the alarm, and managed to reduce it by 30 percent. In the meantime a vigorous drilling program is under way while work on a dam project to divert water from the Evinos River in Central Greece (q.v.) into the Mornos artificial lake is well under way. Once this project is completed, in 1996, the problem will be solved for the foreseeable future. See also POLLUTION, WATER; SOLID WASTE.

-X-

XENAKIS, IANNIS (1921–   ) Composer, mathematician, engineer and architect. Steeped in classical Greek thought and literature from a tender age, Xenakis brought to his musical talent a perfectionism and an attention to detail he says were due to his classical upbringing. He joined the left-wing resistance movement during the Nazi occupation, took music lessons from a Russian pianist, and never stopped reading Plato. In 1945, during the Communist December uprising in which he took part, he was hit by mortar fire, lost an eye and broke his cheekbone. Xenakis escaped to Paris where he has worked ever since as an architect and composer.

Xenakis is best known as a composer of modern music. Messian, whom he met, told him to do three things: "compose-work-listen." He has done just that. He has also challenged all traditional concepts in music only to replace them with an ideom based on mathematics, information theory, systems analysis, and experimental psychology. He starts composing by making graphs and complex calculations. His works have been labeled "meta-music." In deference to ancient Greece he gives his pieces ancient Greek names such as "Oresteia" or "Polytopon." While his music has deeply impressed the cognoscenti of modern music it has not so far had much appeal for ordinary concertgoers. As an architect, he has worked with Le Corbusier. In 1983, he became a member of the French Academy.

INTRODUCTION TO THE BIBLIOGRAPHY

This bibliography on Modern Greece (1821–1993), with few exceptions, contains only titles in English. If we had attempted to include a comprehensive collection in other western European languages (let alone Greek) the space allocated for this exercise would have been wholly inadequate. For the same reason we have decided to confine our articles in English to those published in journals and periodicals between 1978–1993 and to such topics as politics, international affairs, and defense.

Readers versed in Greek can consult the monumental nineteenth-century bibliography of D. Ginis and V. Mexas, *Elliniki Vivliographia 1800–1863,* 3 vols. Athens 1939, 1941, 1957 (and its many supplements), and the *Elliniki Vivliographia,* an annual publication of the National Library of Greece, 1930–1938, 10 vols. A twentieth-century bibliography is being compiled by K. Delopoulos. Also see the bilingual (Greek-English) *Bulletin of Greek Bibliography,* Hellenic Federation of Publishers and Booksellers, a trimonthly edition, first published in 1991. Editor: Vassiliki Stratis.

Unpublished dissertations are not included in this collection. For a bibliography of theses produced in British universities, see Rousos Koundouros, *On Greece and Cyprus: Theses Index in Britain (1949–1974),* London, 1977. The most inclusive catalogue for American university dissertations is produced by University Microfilms, Ann Arbor, Michigan.

A thorough analysis of the current bibliography and historical research on Greece is provided by Alexander Kitroeff, ''Continuity and Change in Contemporary Greek Historiography,'' in *European History Quarterly,* Vol. 19 (1989), pp. 269–298. Mary Jo Clogg and Richard Clogg, *Greece,* World Bibliographical Series, Vol. 17 (Clio Press, 1980), and Heinz A. Richter, *Greece and Cyprus Since 1920* (Wissenschaftlicher Verlag Nea Hellas, 1984), constitute the two most useful bibliographical guides on the subject.

A work which has become a source of inspiration for scholars who came of age in the 1970s and early 1980s is John A. Petropulos's *Politics and Statecraft in The Kingdom of Greece 1833–1843* (Princeton, 1968). The book includes an in-depth analysis of the social forces that led to the Greek War of Independence, 1821–1830. John S. Koliopoulos's *Brigands with a Cause: Brigandage and Irredentism in Modern Greece 1821–1912* (Oxford, 1987), is an excellent sample of social history that draws from the Petropulos example and furthers research into primary archival material on the nineteenth and early twentieth century.

The period of Greek history which has drawn the greatest interest of researchers, following the Greek War of Independence, has been the Second World War, occupation and Civil War (1940–1949). The most important reader on the subject is John O. Iatrides (ed.), *Greece in the 1940s. A Nation in Crisis* (University Press of New England, 1981), and the best eyewitness account is provided by C. M. Woodhouse, *Apple of Discord* (London, Mayflower Press, 1948).

John K. Campbell, *Honour Family and Patronage* (Oxford, 1964), has been the guiding influence in a series of works in social anthropology that dealt with Greece. Nicos P. Mouzelis, *Modern Greece. Facets of Underdevelopment* (Macmillan, 1978) contains a theoretical framework for approaching the sociology of Greece as well as a compilation of important Greek works that appeared in the 1970s. In the realm of international politics, the Hellenic Foundation for European and Foreign Policy (ELIAMEP), an independent institution that attracts prominent scholars in the field, has produced basic works on Greek foreign policy and defense: A. Alexandris, T. Veremis, P. Kazakos, C. Rozakis et al, *Greek-Turkish Relations 1923–87* (in Greek) (Athens, Gnosi-ELIAMEP, 1988); Yannis Valinakis, K. Ioakimidis, P. Kitsos et al, *The Defense Policy of Balkan States* (in Greek) (Athens, Papazissis Publishers-ELIAMEP, 1991); and G. Mourtos, I. Laganis, G. Harvalias et al, *Balkan Developments* (in Greek) (Athens, Gnosi, 1994).

The most useful general readers on modern Greece are John Campbell and Philip Sherrard, *Modern Greece* (Ernest Benn, 1968) and Richard Clogg, *A Short History of Modern Greece,* (Cambridge, 1979).

CONTENTS OF BIBLIOGRAPHY

BOOKS (1821–1993)

    I. General
       a. General Information
       b. Journals and Yearbooks
   II. History
       a. Before 1821
       b. Nineteenth Century
       c. Twentieth Century
  III. Politics
  IV. Economy
   V. Society
  VI. Diaspora
 VII. Education
VIII. Religion
  IX. Law
   X. Culture
       a. Art
       b. Literature
       c. Music
       d. Folklore

ARTICLES (1978–1993)

1. Foreign Policy
2. The European Community, NATO, and the Mediterranean
3. Greek-Turkish Relations
4. Cyprus
5. Internal Affairs

BOOKS

I. GENERAL

a. General Information

Admiralty. Naval Intelligence Division. *Greece* (Geographical Handbook Series). 3 vols. London: 1944.

Brown, Anne, and Helen Dudenbostel. *Greece: A Selected List of References.* Washington, D.C.; Library of Congress, 1943. 101p.

Clogg, Richard and Mary Jo. *Greece.* Oxford: Clio Press, 1980. 224p.

Dimaras C. Th., C. Koumarianou, and L. Droulia (eds.). *Modern Greek Culture: A Selected Bibliography (in English, French, German, Italian).* Athens: A.N.H.C.I.A.S.E.E.S, 1974. 119p.

Divo, Jean-Paul. *Modern Greek Coins, 1828–1968.* Zurich: Bank Leu, 1969. 100p.

A Fresh Look at Greece, The Country and the People. Athens: General Secretariat for Press and Information, 1988. 224p.

Greece. A Portrait. Athens: Research and Publicity Center, 1979. 191p.

Grothusen, Klaus-Detlev (ed.). *Griechenland.* Südosteuropa-Handbuch, Göttingen: Vandenhoeck & Ruprecht, 1980.

Hall, G.K. *Catalog of the Gennadius Library, American School of Classical Studies, Athens.* Boston: 1968.

―――. *Catalog of the Modern Greek Collection at the University of Cincinnati.* Boston: 1978.

Horecky, Paul. *Southeastern Europe: A Guide to Basic Publications.* Chicago: Chicago University Press, 1969. 755p.

Horecky Paul, and David Kraus (eds.). *East Central and Southeast Europe: A Handbook of Library and Archival Resources in North America.* Oxford: Clio Press, 1976, 468p.

Howe, Robin. *Greek Cooking.* London: Andre Deutsch, 1960. 282p.

Huxley, Anthony, and William Taylor, *Flowers of Greece and the Aegean.* London: Chatto and Windus, 1977. 185p.

Kitromilides, Paschalis, and Marios Evrivides. *Cyprus* (World Bibliographical Series), Vol. 28. Santa Barbara: Clio Press, 1982. 193p.

Koundouros, Roussos. *On Greece and Cyprus: Theses Index in Britain (1949–1974).* London: Greek Press and Information Office, 1977. 23p.

Leyton, Evro. *The Modern Greek Collection in the Harvard College Library.* Harvard Library Bulletin, Vol. 19, No. 3, 1971. 221p.

Pantelouris, E.M. *Greece: An Introduction.* Moffat, Scotland: Blue Acre Books, 1980, 1987. 217p.

Richter, Heinz. *Greece and Cyprus Since 1920: Bibliography of Contemporary History.* Heidelberg: Wissenschaftlicher Verlag, 1984. 437p.

Rossides, Eugene (ed.). *American Hellenic Who's Who 1990.* Washington, D.C.: American Hellenic Institute, Inc., 1990. 401p.

Schuster, Mel. *The Contemporary Greek Cinema.* Metuchen, New Jersey: Scarecrow Press, 1979. 368p.

Stikas, George. *Flowers of Greece.* Athens: Papeco, 1984. 158p.

Swanson, Donald. *Modern Greek Studies in the West: A Critical Bibliography of Studies on Modern Greek Linguistics, Philology and Folklore, in Languages Other than Greek.* New York: New York Public Library, 1960. 93p.

Walton, Francis. *The Greek Book, 1476–1825.* Athens: Dixième Congrès International des Bibliophiles, 1977. 46p.

Weintraub, D., and M. Shapira. *Rural Reconstruction in Greece: Differential Social Prerequisites and Achievements During the Development Process.* Beverly Hills, California; London: Sage Publications, 1975. 80p.

Who's Who—Epitomo Viographico Lexico. Athens: Metron, 1992. 603p.

b. Journals and Yearbooks

Balkan Studies. Thessaloniki, Greece: Institute of Balkan Studies, First Volume, 1960.

Byzantine and Modern Greek Studies. Oxford, 1975.

Cambridge Papers in Modern Greece (KAMPOS), Cambridge, 1993.

Epitheorisis Koinonikon Erevnon: The Greek Review of Social Research. Athens: Social Science Center, 1969.

Epsilon: Modern Greek and Balkan Studies. University of Copenhagen, Department of Modern Greek and Balkan Studies, 1987.

Hellenic Review of International Relations. Thessaloniki, The Institute of Public International Law, 1981.

Hellenika: Jahrbuch fuer die Freunde Griechenlands. Ausgaben Neugriechische Studien Bochum, 1964.

Journal of Modern Greek Studies. Baltimore: Johns Hopkins University Press, 1985.

Journal of Modern Hellenism. New York, 1985.

Journal of the Hellenic Diaspora. New York: Pella, 1974.

Mandatophoros: Bulletin of Modern Greek Studies. Amsterdam: Byzantijns-Nieuwgrieks Seminarium, University of Amsterdam, 1972.

Modern Greek Society: A Social Science Newsletter. Providence, Rhode Island, 1973.

Modern Greek Studies Yearbook. University of Minnesota, 1985.

Scandinavian Studies in Modern Greek. Gothenburg, Sweden, 1977.

The South-East European YEARBOOK. Athens: Hellenic Foundation for European and Foreign Policy (ELIAMEP), 1988.

II. HISTORY

a) Before Independence

Clogg, Richard. *The Movement for Greek Independence 1770–1821: A Collection of Documents.* London: Macmillan; New York: Barnes & Noble, 1976. 232p.

Hadjiantoniou, George. *Protestant Patriarch: The Life of Cyril Lucaris (1572–1638), Patriarch of Constantinople.* London: Epworth Press, 1961. 160p.

Nicol, Donald. *Meteora: The Rock Monasteries of Thessaly.* London: Chapman & Hall, 1963. 210p.

Papadopoullos, Theodore. *Studies and Documents Relating to the History of the Greek Church and People Under Turkish Domination.* Brussels, 1952. 507p.

Runciman, Steven. *The Fall of Constantinople.* Cambridge: Cambridge University Press, 1965. 256p.

————. *The Great Church in Capitivity: A Study of the Patriarchate of Constantinople from the Eve of the Turkish Conquest to the Greek War of Independence.* Cambridge: Cambridge University Press, 1968. 455p.

Stavrianos, L.S., *The Balkans Since 1453.* New York: Holt, Rinehart and Winston, 1965. 970p.

Topping, P.W. *Studies in Latin Greece, A.D. 1205–1715.* London: Variorum, 1977. 394p.

Vacalopoulos, Apostolos. *History of Macedonia 1354–1833.* Thessaloniki: Institute of Balkan Studies, 1973. 758p.

Zakythinos, D.A. *The Making of Modern Greece: From Byzantium to Independence.* Oxford: Blackwell; Totowa, New Jersey: Rowman & Littlefield, 1976. 235p.

b) Nineteenth Century

Bower, Leonard, and Gordon Bolitho. *Otho I. King of Greece: A Biography.* London: Selwyn & Blount, 1939. 263p.

Clogg, Richard (ed.). *The Struggle for Greek Independence: Essays to Mark the 150th Anniversary of the Greek War of Independence.* London: Macmillan; Hamden, Connecticut: Archon Press, 1973. 259p.

Dakin, Douglas. *British and American Philhellenes.* Thessaloniki: Institute for Balkan Studies, 1955. 245p.

―――. *The Greek Struggle for Independence, 1821–1833.* London, Batsford; University of California Press, 1973. 344p.

―――. *The Unification of Greece 1770–1923.* London: Ernest Benn; New York: St. Martin's Press, 1972. 344p.

Diamandouros, Nikiforos et al. (eds.). *Hellenism and the First Greek War of Liberation (1821–1830).* Thessaloniki: Institute for Balkan Studies, 1976. 237p.

Dontas, Domna. *Greece and the Great Powers 1863–1875.* Thessaloniki: Institute for Balkan Studies, 1966. 223p.

Driault, E., and M. Lhéritier. *Histoire Diplomatique de la Grèce de 1821 à nos Jour.* Paris, 1926.

Economopoulou, Marietta. *Parties and Politics in Greece 1844–55.* Athens, 1984. 333p.

Hussey, J.M. *The Finlay Papers: A Catalogue.* London: Thames & Hudson, 1973. 200p.

Jelavich, Charles. *Language and Area Studies: East Central and Southeastern Europe: A Survey.* Chicago: Chicago University Press, 1969. 483p.

Jenkins, Romilly. *The Dilessi Murders.* London: Longman, 1961. 190p.

Kofos, Evangelos. *Greece and the Eastern Crisis 1875–1878.* Thessaloniki: Institute for Balkan Studies, 1975. 283p.

Koliopoulos, John. *Brigands with a Cause.* Oxford: Clarendon Press, 1987. 342p.

Levandis, John. *The Greek Foreign Debt and the Great Powers 1821–1898.* New York: Columbia University Press, 1944. 137p.

Lidderdale, H.A. *The Memoirs of General Makriyannis 1797–1864*. London: Oxford University Press, 1966. 234p.

McGrew, William. *Land and Revolution in Modern Greece 1800–1881*. Kent, Ohio: Kent State University Press, 1985. 339p.

Michalopoulos, D. *Vie Politique en Grèce Pendant les Années 1862–69*. Athens, 1981. 264p.

Papadopoulos, G.S. *England and the Near East 1896–1898*. Thessaloniki: Institute for Balkan Studies, 1969. 300p.

Petropulos, John-Anthony. *Politics and Statecraft in the Kingdom of Greece 1833–43*. Princeton, New Jersey: Princeton University Press, 1968. 646p.

Pratt, Michael. *Britain's Greek Empire: Reflections on the History of the Ionian Islands from the Fall of Byzantium*. London: Rex Collings, 1978. 206p.

Prevelakis, Eleftherios. *British Policy Towards the Change in Dynasty in Greece 1862–63*. Athens, 1953. 194p.

Woodhouse, C.M. *The Battle of Navarino*. London: Hodder & Stoughton, 1965. 191p.

———. *The Greek War of Independence: Its Historical Setting*. London: Hutchinson, 1952. 167p.

c) Twentieth Century

Alastos, Doros. *Venizelos: Patriot, Statesman, Revolutionary*. London: Lund Humphries, 1942. 304p.

Alexander, G.M. *The Prelude to the Truman Doctrine British Policy in Greece 1944–1947*. Oxford: Clarendon Press, 1982. 299p.

Alexandris, Alexis. *The Greek Minority of Istanbul and Greek-Turkish Relations 1918–1974.* Athens: Center for Asia Minor Studies, 1983. 391p.

Alexandris, Alex et al. *Greek-Turkish Relations, 1923–1987* (in Greek). Athens: Gnosi, ELIAMEP, 1988. 733p.

Argenti, Philip. *The Occupation of Chios by the Germans and Their Administration of the Island: Described in Contemporary Documents.* Cambridge: Cambridge University Press, 1966. 375p.

Augustinos, Gerasimos. *Consciousness and History: Nationalist Critics of Greek Society 1897–1914.* Boulder, Colorado: East European Quarterly, 1977. 183p.

Auty, Phyllis, and Richard Clogg (eds.). *British Policy Towards Wartime Resistance in Yugoslavia and Greece.* London: Macmillan; New York: Barnes & Noble, 1975, 308p.

Averoff, Evangelos. *Lost Opportunities: The Cyprus Question.* New Rochelle, New York: Aristide Caratzas, 1982. 440p.

Baerentzen, Lars (ed.). *British Reports on Greece.* Copenhagen; Museum Tusculanum Press, 1982. 214p & 4 maps.

Baerentzen, Lars, John Iatrides, and Ole Smith (eds.). *Studies in the History of the Greek Civil War 1945–49.* Copenhagen: Museum Tusculanum Press, 1987. 324p.

Barker, Elizabeth. *British Policy in South-east Europe in the Second World War.* London: Macmillan, 1976. 320p.

Barros, James. *The Corfu Incident of 1923: Mussolini and the League of Nations.* Princeton, New Jersey: Princeton University Press, 1965. 339p.

———. *The League of Nations and the Great Powers: The Greek-Bulgarian Incident, 1925.* Oxford: Clarendon Press, 1970. 143p.

Bitzes, John. *Greece in World War II to April 1941.* Kansas: Sunflower University Press, 1989. 214p.

Blinkhorn, Martin, and Thanos Veremis (eds.). *Modern Greece: Nationalism and Nationality.* Athens: ELIAMEP, SAGE, 1990. 172p.

Browning, Robert (ed.). *The Greek World-Classical, Byzantine and Modern.* London: Thames and Hudson, 328p.

Buckley, Christopher. *Greece and Crete 1941.* London: H.M. Stationery Office, 1952. 311p.

Byford-Jones, W. *The Greek Trilogy: Resistance-Liberation-Revolution.* London: Hutchinson, 1945. 270p.

Calvocovessi, P., R. Clogg, and D. Dakin et al. *Greece and Great Britain During World War I.* Thessaloniki: Institute for Balkan Studies, 1985. 257p.

Campbell, John, and Sherrard, Philip. *Modern Greece,* London: Ernest Benn, 1968. 426p.

Cassimatis, Louis. *American Influence in Greece 1917–1920.* Kent, Ohio: Kent State University Press, 1988. 300p.

Casson, Stanley. *Greece Against the Axis.* London, 1941.

Cervi, Mario. *The Hollow Legions: Mussolini's Blunder, 1940–1941.* London: Chatto & Windus, 1972. 336p.

Chandler, Geoffrey. *The Divided Land: An Anglo-Greek Tragedy.* London: Macmillan, 1959. 214p.

Clogg, Richard. *A Concise History of Greece.* Cambridge: Cambridge University Press, 1992. 257p.

————. *A Short History of Modern Greece.* Cambridge: Cambridge Univeristy Press, 1979. 242p.

———— (ed.). *Greece in the 1980s.* London: Macmillan, 1983, 270p.

Close, David. (ed.). *The Greek Civil War 1943–1950.* London: Routledge, 1993. 265p.

Couloumbis, Theodore, John A. Petropoulos, and Harry J. Psomiades (eds.). *Foreign Interference in Greek Politics: An Historical Perspective.* New York: Pella Publishing Co., 1976. 171p.

Cruickshank, Charles. *Greece 1940–1941.* London: Davis-Poynter, 1976. 206p.

Curtright, Lynn. *Muddle, Indecision and Setback: British Policy and the Balkan States, August 1914 to the Inception of the Dardanelles Campaign.* Thessaloniki: Institute for Balkan Studies, 1986. 214p.

Dakin, Douglas. *The Greek Struggle in Macedonia, 1897–1913.* Thessaloniki: Institute for Balkan Studies, 1966. 538p.

Dalven, Rae. *The Jews of Ioannina.* Philadelphia: Cadmus Press, 1990. 227p.

Essays in Memory of Basil Laourdas. Thessaloniki, 1975. 645p.

Eudes, Dominique. *The Kapetanios: Partisans and Civil War in Greece, 1943–1949.* London: New Left Books, 1972. 381p.

Fleischer, Hagen. *Im Kreuzschatten der Mächte Griechenland 1941–1944.* Vol. I & II. Frankfurt: Peter Lang, 1986. 819p.

Fleming, Amalia. *A Piece of Truth.* London: Jonathan Cape, 1972. 257p.

Forbes-Boyd, Eric. *Aegean Quest: A Search for Venetian Greece.* London: Dent, 1970. 203p.

Gerolymatos, Andre. *Guerilla Warfare and Espionage in Greece 1940–47.* New York: Pella, 1992. 398p.

Hamson, Denys. *We Fell Among Greeks.* London: Jonathan Cape, 1946. 221p.

Higham, Robin. *Diary of a Disaster. British Aid to Greece, 1940–41.* Lexington: University Press of Kentucky, 1986. 269p.

Higham, Robin, and Thanos Veremis (eds.). *The Metaxas Dictatorship: Aspects of Greece 1936–1940.* Athens: ELIAMEP, 1993. 242p.

Hondros, John. *Occupation and Resistance: The Greek Agony 1941–44.* New York: Pella Publishing, 1983. 340p.

Hourmouzios, Stelios. *No Ordinary Crown: A Biography of King Paul of the Hellenes.* London: Weidenfeld & Nicolson, 1972. 375p.

Housepian. Marjorie. *Smyrna 1922: The Destruction of a City.* New York: Harcourt, Brace & World, 1968. 275p.

Iatrides, John (ed.). *Ambassador MacVeagh Reports: Greece, 1933–47.* Princeton, New Jersey: Princeton University Press, 1980. 769p.

Jones, Howard. *A New Kind of War: America's Global Strategy and the Truman Doctrine in Greece.* Oxford: Oxford University Press, 1989. 327p.

Keeley, Edmund. *The Salonika Bay Murder, Cold War Politics and the Polk Affair.* Princeton, New Jersey: Princeton University Press, 1989. 395p.

Kitroeff, Alexander. *The Greeks in Egypt, 1919–1937: Ethnicity and Class.* Oxford: Middle East Centre, 1989. 209p.

Koliopoulos, John. *Greece and the British Connection 1935–1941.* Oxford: Clarendon Press, 1977. 315p.

Kondis, Basil. *Greece and Albania 1908–1914.* Thessaloniki: Institute for Balkan Studies, 1976. 151p.

Koumoulides. John. (ed.). *Greece in Transition: Essays in the History of Modern Greece, 1821–1974.* London: Zeno, 1977. 334p.

Kousoulas, George. *Revolution and Defeat: The Story of the Greek Communist Party.* London: Oxford University Press, 1965. 306p.

Leeper, Reginald. *When Greek Meets Greek.* London: Chatto & Windus, 1950. 244p.

Leon, George. *Greece and the Great Powers, 1914–1917.* Thessaloniki: Institute for Balkan Studies, 1974. 521p.

————. *The Greek Socialist Movement and the First World War: The Road to Unity.* Boulder, Colorado: East European Quarterly, 1976. 204p.

Llewellyn-Smith, Michael. *Ionian Vision: Greece in Asia Minor, 1919–1922.* London: Allen Lane, 1973. 401p.

Mackenzie, Compton. *Aegean Memories.* London: Chatto & Windus, 1940. 419p.

————. *First Athenian Memories.* London: Cassell, 1931. 402p.

————. *Greek Memories.* London: Cassell, 1932. 455p.

Mager, K. *Istoria tou Ellinikou Typou.* 3 vols. Athens: A. Dimopoulos, 1957.

Marder, Brenda. *Stewards of the Land: The American Farm School and Modern Greece.* New York: Columbia University Press, 1979. 234p.

Matthews, Kenneth. *Memories of a Mountain War: Greece, 1944–1949.* London: Longman, 1972. 284p.

Mayes, Stanley. *Makarios: A Biography.* London: Macmillan, 1981.

Mazower, Mark. *Greece and the Inter-War Economic Crisis.* Oxford: Clarendon Press, 1991. 334p.

McNeil, William Hardy, *Greece: American Aid in Action, 1947–1956.* New York: Twentieth Century Fund, 1957. 240p.

————. *The Greek Dilemma: War and Aftermath.* London: Gollancz, 1947. 240p.

————. *The Metamorphosis of Greece Since World War II.* Chicago: University of Chicago Press: Oxford, Blackwell, 1978. 264p.

Mercouri, Melina. *I Was Born Greek.* London: Hodder & Stoughton, 1971. 224p.

Miller, William. *Greece.* London: Benn, 1928. 351p.

Mitrakos, Alexander. *France in Greece During World War I.* Boulder, Colorado: East European Monographs, 1982. 258p.

Myers, E.C.W. *Greek Entanglement.* London: Hart-Davis, 1955. Second edition, Gloucester: Alan Sutton Publishing Ltd., 1985. 290p.

O'Ballance, Edgar. *The Greek Civil War 1944–1949.* London: Faber & Faber; New York: Praeger, 1966. 237p.

Pallis, A.A. *Greece's Anatolian Venture and After.* London, 1937.

Palmer, Alan. *The Gardeners of Salonika: The Macedonian Campaign 1915–1918.* London: Andre Deutsch, 1965. 286p.

Papacosma, Victor. *The Military in Greek Politics: The 1909 Coup d'Etat.* Kent, Ohio: Kent State University Press, 1977. 254p.

Papastratis, Procopis. *British Policy Towards Greece During the Second World War 1941–44.* Cambridge: Cambridge University Press, 1984. 274p.

Pentzopoulos, Dimitri. *The Balkan Exchange of Minorities and Its Impact upon Greece.* Paris, The Hague: Mouton, 1962. 293p.

Petsalis Diomidis, Nikos. *Greece and the Paris Peace Conference 1919.* Thessaloniki: Institute for Balkan Studies, 1978. 399p.

Queen Frederica. *A Measure of Understanding.* London: Macmillan, 1971. 270p.

Richter, Heinz. *British Intervention in Greece. From Varkiza to Civil War 1945–1946.* London: Merlin, 1985. 573p.

———. *Griechenland zwischen Revolution und Konterrevolution 1936–1946.* Frankfurt, 1973.

Sarafis, Marion. *Greece: From Resistance to Civil War.* Nottingham: Spokesman, 1980. 142p.

Sarafis, Stefanos, *ELAS: Greek Resistance Army.* London: Merlin Press, 1980. 556p.

Sciaky, Leon. *Farewell to Salonica: Portrait of an Era.* London: W.H. Allen, 1946. 213p.

Smith, Peter, and Edwin Walker. *War in the Aegean.* London: William Kimber, 1974. 304p.

Smothers, Frank, William Hardy McNeill, and Elizabeth Darbishire McNeil. *Report on the Greeks: Findings of a Twentieth Century Fund Team which Surveyed Conditions in Greece in 1947.* New York: Twentieth Century Fund, 1948. 226p.

Spourdalakis, Michalis. *The Rise of the Greek Socialist Party.* London: Routledge, 1988. 331p.

Stasinopoulos, Arianna. *Maria: Beyond the Callas Legend.* London: Weidenfeld, 1987, 329p.

Stavrakis, Peter. *Moscow and Greek Communism 1944–49.* Ithaca: Cornell University Press, 1989. 243p.

Stewart, I.McD.G. *The Struggle for Crete 20 May–1 June 1941: A Story of Lost Opportunity.* London: Oxford University Press, 1966. 518p.

Sweet-Escott, Bickham. *Baker Street Irregulars.* London: Methuen, 1965. 278p.

Toynbee, Arnold. *The Western Question in Greece and Turkey.* New York: Howard Fertig, 1970. 408p.

———. *The Western Question in Greece and Turkey: A Study in the Contact of Civilizations.* London: Constable, 1922. 420p.

Vacalopoulos, Apostolos. *A History of Thessaloniki.* Thessaloniki: Institute for Balkan Studies, 1972. 153p.

Veremis, Thanos. *Greek Security Considerations: A Historical Perspective.* Athens: Papazissis, 1980. 128p.

Vlavianos, Haris. *Greece 1941–49: From Resistance to Civil War.* London: Macmillan, 1992. 350p.

Vryonis, Speros. *The Decline of Medieval Hellenism in Asia Minor and the Process of Islamization from the Eleventh Through the Fifteenth Century.* Berkeley: University of California Press, 1986. 532p.

Vukmanovic, Svetozar. *How and Why the People's Liberation Struggle of Greece Met with Defeat.* London: Merlin Press, 1985. 144p.

Wittner, L.S. *American Intervention in Greece, 1943–1949.* New York: Columbia University Press, 1982.

Woodhouse, C.M. *Capodistria: The Founder of Greek Independence.* London: Oxford University Press, 1973. 544p.

———. *Modern Greece: A Short History.* London: Faber & Faber, 1977. 332p.

———. *The Struggle for Greece 1941–1949.* London: Hart-Davis, MacGibbon, 1976; Brooklyn Heights, New York: Beekman/Esanu, 1979. 324p.

Xydis, Stephen. *Greece and the Great Powers 1944–1947: Prelude to the "Truman Doctrine."* Thessaloniki: Institute for Balkan Studies, 1963. 758p.

Zervos, Stella Reader. *One Woman's War: A Diary of an English Woman Living in Occupied Greece 1939–1945.* Athens: Centre Academic Press, 1991. 123p.

III. POLITICS

Alford, Jonathan (ed.). *Greece and Turkey. Adversity in Alliance.* London: Gower, 1984. 151p.

Aliboni, Roberto (ed.). *Southern European Security in the 1990s.* London: Pinter Publishers, 1992. 147p.

Amen, Michael Mark. *American Foreign Policy in Greece 1944–1949: Economic, Military and Institutional Aspects.* Frankfurt am Main: Peter Lang, 1978. 310p.

Argyropoulos, Alexander. *Greece-Turkey: An Annotated Collection of Articles, 1986–1989.* Athens: ELIAMEP-Papazissis Publishers. 1990. 150p.

Attalides, Michael (ed.). *Cyprus: Nationalism and International Politics.* Edinburgh: Q Press, 1979. 226p.

————. (ed.). *Cyprus Reviewed.* Nicosia: Zavalis, 1977. 277p.

Bahcheli, Tozun. *Greek-Turkish Relations Since 1955.* Boulder, Colorado; Westview Press, 1990. 216p.

Barker, Elisabeth. *Macedonia: Its Place in Balkan Power Politics.* London, New York: Royal Institute of International Affairs, 1950. 129p.

Barkman, Carl. *Ambassador in Athens.* London: The Merlin Press, 1989. 297p.

Brown, James. *Delicately Poised Allies: Greece and Turkey.* London: Brassey's. 1991. 184p.

Carmacolias, Demetrios. *Political Communication in Greece, 1965–1967: The Last Two Years of a Parliamentary Democracy.* Athens: National Center of Social Research, 1974. 167p.

Chaconas, Stephen-George. *Adamantios Korais: A Study in Greek Nationalism.* New York: Columbia University Press, 1942. 181p.

Chipman, John (ed.). *NATO's Southern Allies: Internal and External Challenges.* London: Routledge, 1988. 399p.

Clogg, Richard. *Parties and Elections in Greece.* Durham, North Carolina: Duke University Press, 1987. 268p.

————. (ed.). *Greece Under Military Rule.* London: Secker & Warburg: New York: Basic Books, 1972. 272p.

Constas, D. (ed.). *The Greek Turkish Conflict in the 1990s.* London: Macmillan, 1991. 279p.

Couloumbis, Theodore. *Greek Political Reaction to American and NATO Influence.* London: Yale University Press, 1966. 250p.

————. *The United States, Greece and Turkey. The Troubled Triangle.* New York: Praeger, 1983. 232p.

Couloumbis, Theodore, and Sallie M. Hicks (eds.). *U.S. Foreign Policy Toward Greece and Cyprus: The Clash of Principle and Pragmatism.* Washington, D.C.: Center for Mediterranean Studies and American Hellenic Institute, 1975. 161p.

Couloumbis, Theodore, and John O. Iatrides (eds.). *Greek-American Relations: A Critical Review.* New York: Pella, 1980. 263p.

Couloumbis, Theodore, J.A. Petropoulos, and H.T. Psomiades (eds.). *Foreign Interference in Greek Politics.* New York: Pella, 1976. 171p.

Couloumbis, Theodore, and Y. Valinakis (eds.). *The CFE Negotiations in Vienna and Their Impact on Southeastern Europe.* (in Greek.) Athens: ELIAMEP, 1991. 236p.

Crawshaw, Nancy. *The Cyprus Revolt: An Account of the Struggle for Union with Greece.* London: George Allen & Unwin, 1978. 447p.

Danopoulos, Constantine. *Warriors and Politicians in Modern Greece.* Chapel Hill, North Carolina: Documentary Publications, 1984. 225p.

Deane, Philip. *I Should Have Died.* London: Hamish Hamilton. 1976.

Eaton, Robert. *Soviet Relations with Greece and Turkey.* Athens: ELIAMEP, 1987. 52p.

Featherstone, Kevin, and Dimitrios Katsoudas (eds.). *Political Change in Greece: Before and After the Colonels.* London: Croom Helm, 1987. 301p.

Gianaris, Nicholas. *Greece and Turkey: Economic and Geopolitical Perspectives.* New York: Praeger, 1988. 204p.

Hellenic Foundation for Defense and Foreign Policy. *Greek-Turkish Relations and Cyprus.* (in Greek.) Athens, 1986. 222p.

―――. *International Treaties from Lausanne (1923) to Paris (1947).* (in Greek.) Athens, 1987. 72p.

―――. *The Iran-Iraq War and its Impact on the Eastern Mediterranean.* (in Greek.) Athens, 1988. 105p.

―――. *Security Issues of Cyprus-Part I.* (in Greek.) Athens, 1989. 122p.

―――. *The Seven-to-Ten Ratio in U.S. Aid to Greece and Turkey.* (in Greek.) Athens, 1988. 105p.

―――. *Yugoslavia Today.* (in Greek.) Athens, 1990. 121p.

Helsinki Watch, *Denying Human Rights and Ethnic Identity: The Greeks of Turkey.* New York: Human Rights Watch, 1992. 54p.

Hitchens. Christopher. *Cyprus.* London: Quartet Books, 1984. 192p.

Iatrides, John. *Revolt in Athens: The Greek Communist "Second Round," 1944–1945.* Princeton, New Jersey: Princeton University Press, 1972. 340p.

―――. (ed.). *Greece in the 1940s. A Nation in Crisis.* London: University Press of New England, 1981. 444p.

Ioakimidis, Panayotis. *A Greek Strategy for the Creation of a New Europe* (in Greek). Athens: ELIAMEP, 1990.

Ioannides, Christos. *In Turkey's Image: The Transformation of Occupied Cyprus into a Turkish Province.* New Rochelle, New York: Caratzas, 1991. 254p.

Jecchinis, Christos. *Trade Unionism in Greece: A Study in Political Paternalism.* Chicago: Roosevelt University, Labor Education Division, 1967. 205p.

Kariotis, Theodore (ed.). *The Greek Socialist Experiment: Papandreou's Greece 1981–1989.* New York: Pella, 1992. 346p.

Kitromilides, Paschalis. *The Enlightment as Social Criticism, Iosipos Moisiodax and Greek Culture in the Eighteenth Century.* Princeton: Princeton University Press, 1992. 203p.

Kitromilides, Paschalis, and Peter Worsley (eds.). *Small States in the Modern World.* Nicosia: Zavallis Press, 1979. 259p.

Kofos, Evangelos. *The Impact of the Macedonian Question on Civil Conflict in Greece 1943–1949.* Athens: ELIAMEP, 1989. 46p.

———. *Nationalism and Communism in Macedonia.* Thessaloniki: Institute for Balkan Studies, 1964. 251p.

Kohler, Beate. *Political Forces in Spain, Greece and Portugal.* London: Butterworth Scientific, 1982. 281p.

Kuniholm, Bruce. *The Origins of the Cold War in the Near East: Great Power Conflict and Diplomacy in Iran, Turkey and Greece.* Princeton: Princeton University Press, 1980, 485p.

Legg, Keith. *Politics in Modern Greece.* Stanford: Stanford University Press, 1969. 367p.

Macridis, Roy. *Greek Politics at a Crossroads.* Stanford: Hoover International Studies, 1984. 72p.

Markesinis, Basil. *The Theory and Practice of Dissolution of Parliament: A Comparative Study with Special Reference to the United Kingdom and the Greek Experience.* Cambridge: Cambridge University Press, 1972. 283p.

Mavrogordatos, George. *Rise of the Green Sun: The Greek Election of 1981.* London: King's College, 1983. 63p.

————. *Stillborn Republic, Social Coalitions and Party Strategies in Greece 1922–1936.* Berkeley: University of California Press, 1983. 380p.

Meynaud, Jean. *Les Forces Politiques en Grèce.* Paris: Etudes des Science Politiques, 1965, 574p.

Mouzelis, Nicos. *Politics in the Semi-Periphery.* London: Macmillan, 1986. 284p.

Munkman, C.A. *American Aid to Greece: A Report on the First Ten Years.* London: Methuen; New York: Praeger, 1958. 306p.

Papandreou, Andreas. *Democracy at Gunpoint: The Greek Front.* London: Andre Deutsch, 1971. 388p.

Papandreou, Margaret. *Nightmare in Athens.* Englewood Cliffs, New Jersey: Prentice-Hall, 1970. 390p.

Penniman, Howard. *Greece at the Polls: The National Elections of 1974 and 1977.* Washington, D.C.: American Enterprise Institute, 1981. 220p.

Pepelasis, Adamantios (ed.). *Greece.* New York: Harper & Brothers, 1961. 500p.

Poulantzas, Nikos. *The Crisis of the Dictatorships: Portugal, Greece, Spain.* Atlantic Highlands, New Jersey: Humanities Press, 1976.

Reddaway, John. *Burdened with Cyprus: The British Connection.* Weidenfeld & Nicolson, 237p.

Roubatis, Yannis. *Tangled Webs: The U.S. in Greece 1947–67.* New York: Pella, 1987.

Salem, Norma (ed.). *Cyprus: A Regional Conflict and Its Resolution.* London: St. Martin's Press, 1992. 260p.

Spyridakis. Emmanuel. *The "Macedonian Question," an Historical and Diplomatic Review.* Athens: ELIAMEP, 1991. 15p.

Stavrianos, L.S. *Balkan Federation: A History of the Movement Toward Balkan Unity in Modern Times.* Northampton, Massachusetts: Smith College, 1941, 338p.

————. *Greece: American Dilemma and Opportunity.* Chicago: Henry Regnery, 1952. 246p.

Stavrou, Nikolaos. *Allied Politics and Military Interventions: The Political Role of the Greek Military.* Athens: Papazissis, 1977. 196p.

Stearns, Monteagle. *Entangled Allies US Policy Toward Greece, Turkey and Cyprus.* New York: Council on Foreign Relations Press, 1992. 185p.

Stern, Laurence. *The Wrong Horse: The Politics of Intervention and the Failure of American Diplomacy.* New York: Times Books, 1977. 170p.

Stuart, Douglas (ed.). *Politics and Security in the Southern Region of the Atlantic Alliance.* London: Macmillan, 1988. 209p.

Sweet-Escott, Bickham. *Greece: A Political and Economic Survey 1939–1953.* London, New York: Royal Institute of International Affairs, 1954. 207p.

The Athenian, (Roufos, Rodis). *Inside the Colonel's Greece.* London: Chatto & Windus; New York: W.W. Norton, 1972. 215p.

Theodorakis, Mikis. *Journals of Resistance.* London: Hart, Davis MacGibbon, 1973. 334p.

Tsatsos, Constantine. *The Greece of Karamanlis*. London: Doric Publications, 1973. 206p.

Tsoucalas, Constantine. *The Greek Tragedy*. Harmondsworth, England: Penguin, 1969. 208p.

Tsoukalis, Loukas (ed.). *Greece and the European Community*. Farnborough, England: Saxon House, 1979. 172p.

Valinakis, Yannis. *Greece and the CFE Negotiations*. Ebenhausen: Stiftung Wissenschaft und Politik, 1991. 25p.

————. *Greece's Balkan Policy and the "Macedonian Issue."* Ebenhausen: Stiftung Wissenschaft und Politik, 1992, 31p.

Valinakis Yannis et al. *The Defense Policy of Balkan States*. (in Greek.) Athens: Papazissis Publishers-ELIAMEP, 1991. 334p.

Vatikiotis, P. J. *Greece: A Political Essay*. Beverly Hills, California; London: Sage Publications, 1974. 87p.

Veremis, Thanos, and George Tsitsopoulos, G. (eds.). *Greece-Turkey: An Annotated Collection of Articles 1979–1985*. Athens: Papazissis-ELIAMEP, 1987. 252p.

Veremis, Thanos, and Yannis Valinakis (eds.). *U.S. Bases in the Mediterranean: The Cases of Greece and Spain* Athens: ELIAMEP, 1989, 132p.

Vryonis, Speros (ed.). *Greece on the Road to Democracy—from the Junta to PASOK 1974–1986*. New Rochelle, New York: Caratzas, 1991. 402p.

Wilson, Andrew. *The Aegean Dispute*. London: International Institute for Strategic Studies, 1979. 41p.

Xydis, Stephen. *Modern Greek Nationalism*. Washington, London: University of Washington Press, 1969. 207p.

Yannopoulos, George. *Greece and the European Economic Communities: The First Decade of a Troubled Association.* Beverly Hills, California; London: Sage Publications, 1975. 35p.

——— (ed.). *Greece and the EEC Integration and Convergence.* London: Macmillan, 1986. 178p.

IV. ECONOMY

Alexander, Alec. *Greek Industrialists: An Economic and Social Analysis.* Athens: Center of Planning and Economic Research, 1964. 182p.

Break, George, and Ralph Turvey (eds.). *Studies in Greek Taxation.* Athens: Center of Planning and Economic Research, 1964. 250p.

Candilis. Wray. *The Economy of Greece, 1944–66: Efforts for Stability and Development.* New York, London: Praeger, 1968. 239p.

Coutsoumaris, George. *The Morphology of Greek Industry: A Study in Industrial Development.* Athens: Center of Economic Research, 1965. 430p.

Demopoulos, G. *Monetary Policy in the Open Economy of Greece.* Athens: KEPE, 1981.

Freris, A.F. *The Greek Economy in the Twentieth Century.* London: Croom Helm, 1986. 226p.

Georgakopoulos, Theodore. *Economic Effects of Value-added-tax Substitution: Greece.* Athens: Center of Planning and Economic Research, 1976. 312p.

Germidis, Dimitrios, and Maria Negreponti-Delivanis. *Industrialisation, Employment and Income Distribution in Greece: A*

Case Study. Paris: Organization for Economic Cooperation and Development, 1975. 204p.

Halikias, D.J. *Money and Credit in a Developing Economy: The Greek Case.* New York: New York University Press, 1978. 307p.

Hellenic Industrial Development Bank. *Greek Industry in Perspective.* Athens, 1967. 187p.

Kazakos, Panos. *The Relations of Cyprus with the E.C.* (in Greek.) Athens: ELIAMEP, 1990. 143p.

Krengel, Rolf and Dieter Martens. *Fixed Capital Stock and Future Investment Requirements in Greek Manufacturing.* Athens: Center of Planning and Economic Research, 1966. 138p.

Papandreou, Andreas. *A Strategy for Greek Economic Development.* Athens: Center of Economic Research, 1962. 179p.

Pepelasis. Adamantios. *Labour Shortages in Greek Agriculture, 1963–1973.* Athens: Center of Economic Research, 1963, 71p.

Psilos, Diomedes, *Capital Market in Greece.* Athens: Center of Economic Research, 1964. 254p.

Shaw, Lawrence. *Postwar Growth in Greek Agricultural Production: A Study in Sectoral Output Change.* Athens: Center of Planning and Economic Research, 1969. 392p.

Tsoukalis, Loukas. *The European Community and Its Mediterranean Enlargement.* London: George Allen & Unwin, 1981. 273p.

———. *The New European Economy.* Oxford: Oxford University Press, 1991. 333p.

Vouras, Paul. *The Changing Economy of Northern Greece Since World War II.* Thessaloniki: Institute for Balkan Studies, 1962. 227p.

Wallden, Sotiris. *Integration of Southeastern Europe into the World Economy and Balkan Economic Cooperation.* Athens: ELIAMEP, 1990.

Xydis, S. *The Economy and Finances of Greece Under Axis Occupation.* Pittsburg: Hermes Printing Co., 1943.

Zolotas, Xenophon. *Monetary Equilibrium and Economic Development, with Special Reference to the Experience of Greece, 1950–1963.* Princeton, New Jersey: Princeton University Press, 1965, 223p.

———. *The Positive Contribution of Greece to the European Community.* Athens: National Bank of Greece, 1978.

V. SOCIETY

Blum, Richard and Eva M. *The Dangerous Hour: The Lore of Crisis and Mystery in Rural Greece.* London: Chatto & Windus; New York: Scribner's 1970. 410p.

Boulay, Juliet Du. *Portrait of a Greek Mountain Village.* Oxford: Clarendon Press, 1974. 296p.

Campbell, J.K. *Honour, Family and Patronage: A Study of Institutions and Morals in a Greek Mountain Community.* Oxford: Clarendon Press, 1964. 393p.

Dimen, Muriel, and Ernestine Friedl (eds.). *Regional Variation in Modern Greece and Cyprus: Toward a Perspective of the Ethnography of Greece,* New York: New York Academy of Sciences, 1976, 465p.

Eddy, Charles. *Greece and the Greek Refugees.* London: George Allen & Unwin, 1931. 280p.

Friedl, Ernestine. *Vasilika: A Village in Modern Greece.* New York: Holt, Rinehart & Winston, 1963. 110p.

Gage, Nicholas. *Portrait of Greece.* New York: New York Times, 1971. 300p.

Grothusen, Klaus-Detlev. *Südosteuropabandbuch Band III: Griechenland.* Göttingen: Vandenhoeck und Ruprecht, 1980.

Herzfeld, Michael. *Ours Once More: Folklore, Ideology and the Making of Modern Greece.* New York: Pella, 1986. 197p.

King, Francis. *Introducing Greece.* London: Methuen, 1956. 262p.

Lambiri, Ioanna. *Social Change in a Greek Country Town: The Impact of Factory Work on the Position of Women.* Athens: Center of Planning and Economic Research, 1965. 163p.

Lambiri-Dimaki, Jane. *Social Stratification in Greece: 1962–1982.* Athens: Sakkoulas, 1983.

Larrabee, Stephen. *Hellas Observed: The American Experience of Greece 1775–1865.* New York: New York University Press, 1957. 357p.

Loizos, Peter. *The Heart Grown Bitter. A Chronical of Cypriot War Refugees.* Cambridge: Cambridge University Press, 1981, 219p.

Loizos, Peter, and E. Papataxiarchis (eds.) *Contested Identities, Gender and Kinship in Modern Greece.* Princeton, New Jersey: Princeton University Press, 1993.

McNeil, William. *The Metamorphosis of Greece Since World War II.* Chicago: University of Chicago Press; Oxford, Blackwell, 1978. 264p.

Michaelides, Constantine. *Hydra: A Greek Island Town: Its Growth and Form.* Chicago, London: University of Chicago Press, 1967. 93p.

Miller, William. *Greek Life in Town and Country.* London: George Newnes, 1905. 311p.

Moss, W. Stanley. *III Met by Moonlight.* London: Harrap, 1950. 192p.

Mouzelis, Nicos. *Modern Greece: Facets of Underdevelopment.* London: Macmillan; New York: Holmes & Meier, 1978. 222p.

Peristiany, J.G. *Sociology in Greece.* Rome: Instituto Luigi Sturzo, 1968. 263p.

———— (ed.). *Contributions to Mediterranean Sociology: Mediterranean Rural Communities and Social Change.* Paris: Mouton, 1968. 349p.

Sanders, Irwin. *Rainbow in the Rock: The People of Rural Greece.* Cambridge, Massachusetts: Harvard University Press, 1962. 363p.

Sicilianos, Dimitrios. *Old and New Athens.* London: Putnam, 1960. 379p.

Stahl, Paul. *Household, Village and Village Confederation.* New York: East European Monographs. 260p.

Thompson, Kenneth. *Farm Fragmentation in Greece: The Problem and Its Setting, with Eleven Village Case Studies.* Athens: Center of Economic Research, 1963. 263p.

Vlachos, Evangelos. *Modern Greek Society: Continuity and Change: An Annotated Classification of Selected Sources.* Fort Collins: Colorado State University, 1969. 177p.

Walcot, P. *Greek Peasants, Ancient and Modern: A Comparison of Social and Moral Values.* Manchester: Manchester University Press, 1970. 136p.

Weintraub, D., and M. Shapira. *Rural Reconstruction in Greece: Differential Social Prerequisites and Achievements During the Development Process.* Beverly Hills, California; London: Sage Publications, 1975. 80p.

VI. DIASPORA

Bardis, Panos D. *The Future of the Greek Language in the United States.* San Francisco: R and E Associates, 1976.

Bottomley, Gillian. *After the Odyssey: A Study of Greek Australians.* St. Lucia: University of Queensland Press, 1979.

Burgess, Thomas. *Greeks in America.* Boston: Sherman, French, 1913.

Chimbos, Peter D. *The Canadian Odyssey: The Greek Experience in Canada.* Toronto: McClelland and Stewart, 1980.

Contos, Leonidas C. *2001: The Church in Crisis.* Brookline, Massachusetts: Holy Cross Orthodox Press, 1982.

Costopoulos, Michael. *The Greek Community of New York City— Early Years to 1910.* New York: Aristide Caratzas, 1992. 232p.

Cutsumbis, Michael. *A Bibliographic Guide to Materials on Greeks in the United States, 1890–1968.* New York: Center for Migration Studies, 1970. 100p.

Efthimiou, Miltiades B., and George A. Christopoulos. *History of the Greek Orthodox Church in America.* New York: Greek Orthodox Archdiocese, 1984.

Fairchild, Henry Pratt. *Greek Immigration to the United States.* New Haven: Yale University Press, 1911.

Karas, Nicholas V. *The Greek Triangle of the Acre.* Lowell, Massachusetts: Meteora, 1984.

Kourvetaris, G.A. *First and Second Generation Greeks in Chicago.* Athens: National Center of Social Research, 1971. 111p.

Leber, George J. *The History of the Order of Ahepa.* Washington, D.C.: Order of Ahepa, 1972.

Litsas, Fotios K. *A Companion to the Greek Orthodox Church.* New York: Greek Orthodox Archdiocese, 1984.

Marketou, Jenny. *The Great Longing: The Greeks of Astoria.* Athens: Kedros, 1987.

Monos, Dimitri. *The Achievement of the Greeks in the United States.* Philadelphia: Centrum, 1986.

Moskos, Charles. *Greek Americans: Struggle and Success.* Englewood Cliffs, New Jersey: Prentice-Hall, 1980. 162p.

Panagopoulos, E.P. *New Smyrna: An Eighteenth Century Greek Odyssey.* Gainesville: University Press of Florida, 1966.

Papaioannou, George. *From Mars Hill to Manhattan: The Greek Orthodox in America Under Athenagoras.* Minneapolis, Minnesota: Light and Life, 1976. 288p.

Papanikolas, Helen Zeese. *Toil and Rage in a New Land: The Greek Immigrants in Utah.* Salt Lake City: Utah Historical Society, 1974.

Psomiades, Harry, and Alice Scourby (eds.). *The Greek American Community in Transition.* New York: Pella, 1982. 290p.

Saloutos. Theodore. *The Greeks in America: A Student's Guide to Localized History.* New York: Teachers College Press, Columbia University, 1967. 36p.

————. *The Greeks in the United States.* Cambridge, Massachusetts: Harvard University Press, 1964. 445p.

————. *They Remember America: The Story of the Repatriated Greek-Americans.* Berkeley, Los Angeles: University of California Press, 1956. 153p.

Stephanides, Marios. *Detroit's Greek Community.* Lexington, Massachusetts: London: Heath Lexington Books, 1971. 115p.

Tavuchis, Nicholas. *Family and Mobility Among Greek Americans.* Athens: National Center of Social Research, 1972. 191p.

Vatikiotis, P.J. *Among Arabs and Jews: A Personal Experience 1936–90.* London: Weidenfeld and Nicolson, 1991. 166p.

Vlachos, Evangelos. *An Annotated Bibliography on Greek Migration.* Athens: Social Sciences Center, 1966. 126p.

————. *The Assimilation of Greeks in the United States.* Athens: National Center of Social Research, 1968.

————. *The Assimilation of Greeks in the United States with Special Reference to the Greek Community of Anderson, Indiana.* Athens: National Center of Social Research, 1968. 200p.

Vryonis, Speros. *A Brief History of the Greek-American Community of St. George, Memphis, Tennessee 1962–1982.* Malibu: Undena Publications, 1982. 129p.

Xenides, J.P. *The Greeks in America.* New York: George H. Doran, 1922.

Zotos, Stephanos. *Hellenic Presence in America.* Wheaton, Illinois: Pilgrimage, 1976.

VII. EDUCATION

Browning, Robert. *Medieval and Modern Greek.* London: Hutch-inson University Library, 1969. 151p.

Dawkins, R.M. *Modern Greek in Asia Minor: A Study of the Dialects of Silli, Cappadocia and Pharasa, with Grammar, Texts, List Translations and Glossary.* Cambridge: Cambridge University Press, 1916. 695p.

Gennadius, J. *A Sketch of the History of Education in Greece.* Edinburgh: World Federation of Education, 1925. 47p.

Kazamias, Andreas, and Byron G. Massialas. *Greece: Tradition and Change in Education: A Comparative Study.* Englewood Cliffs, New Jersey: Prentice-Hall, 1965. 107p.

Mackridge, Peter. *The Modern Greek Language.* Oxford: Oxford University Press 1985. 387p.

Moustaka, Calliope. *Attitudes Sociometric Status and Ability in Greek Schools.* Paris: Mouton, 1967. 151p.

Newton, Brian. *Cypriot Greek: Its Phonology and Inflections.* The Hague: Mouton, 1972. 186p.

———. *The Generative Interpretation of Dialect: A Study of Modern Greek Phonology.* Cambridge: Cambridge University Press, 1972. 236p.

Ricks, David. *The Shade of Homer: A Study in Modern Greek Poetry.* Cambridge: Cambridge University Press. 192p.

Seaman, David. *Modern Greek and American English in Contact.* The Hague: Mouton, 1972. 312p.

Weintraub D., and M. Shapira. *Rural Reconstruction in Greece: Differential Social Prerequisites and Achievements During the Development Process.* Beverly Hills, California; London: Sage Publications, 1975. 80p.

VIII. RELIGION

Amand, Emmanuel. *Mount Athos: The Garden of the Panaghia.* Amsterdam, 1972. 360p.

Frazee, Charles. *The Orthodox Church and Independent Greece 1821–1852.* Cambridge: Cambridge University Press, 1969. 220p.

Hammond, Peter. *The Waters of Marah: The Present State of the Greek Church.* London: Rockliff, 1956. 186p.

Hasluck, F.W. *Athos and Its Monasteries.* London: Kegan Paul, 1924. 214p.

Sherrard, Philip. *Athos: The Mountain of Silence.* London: Oxford University Press, 1960. 110p.

Ware, Timothy. *The Orthodox Church.* Harmondsworth, England: Penguin Books, 1963. 352p.

IX. LAW

Eddy, Charles. *Greece and the Greek Refugees.* London: George Allen & Unwin, 1931. 280p.

Pazarci, Huseyin et al. *Two Views on Legal Questions Concerning the Greek Islands of the Aegean Sea.* (in Greek.) Athens: Gnosi, ELIAMEP, 1989. 202p.

Rozakis, Christos. *Analysis of the Legal Problems in Greek-Turkish Relations 1973–88.* Athens: ELIAMEP, 1989, 193p.

Rozakis, Christos, and C. Stephanou (eds.). *The New Law of the Sea.* Amsterdam: North Holland, 1983. 354p.

Weintraub D., and M. Shapira. *Rural Reconstruction in Greece: Differential Social Prerequisites and Achievements During the Development Process.* Beverly Hills, California; London: Sage Publications, 1975. 80p.

X. CULTURE

a. Art

Doumanis, O.B., and Paul Oliver. *Shelter in Greece-Oikismoi stin Ellada.* Athens: Architecture in Greece Press, 1979. 173p.

Hadjinicolaou, Nicos. *Theophilos, Kontoglou, Ghika and Tsarouchis: Four Painters of 20th Century Greece.* London: Wildenstein, 1975. 46p.

Joachimides, Christos. *Eight Artists: Eight Attitudes: Eight Greeks, Stephanos Antonakos, Vlassis Caniaris, Chryssa, J. Kounellis, Pavlos, Lucas Samaras, Takis, Costas Tsoclis,* (Introduction). London: Institute of Contemporary Art, 1975. 90p.

Krautheimer, Richard. *Early Christian and Byzantine Architecture.* Harmondsworth, England: Penguin Books, 1965. 390p.

Lidderdale, H.A. *The War of Independence in Pictures: Copies by Demetrios Zographos from Originals by his Father Panayiotis Zographos Commissioned by General Makriyannis and Presented to Her Majesty, Queen Victoria Through her Minister at Athens Sir Edmund Lyons 1839.* Birmingham: University of Birmingham Centre for Byzantine Studies, 1976. 33p.

Lydakis, Stelios. *Geschichte der Griechischen Malerei des 19ten Jahrhunderts (A History of Greek Painting in the 19th Century).* Munich: Prestel Verlag, 1972. 379p.

Phrantziskakis, E.K. *Ellines Zographoi tou 19ou Aiona. (Greek Painters of the 19th Century).* Athens: Commercial Bank of Greece, 1957. 157p.

Rice, David Talbot. *Art of the Byzantine Era.* London: Thames & Hudson. 1963. 286p.

Spender, Stephen. *Ghika: Paintings, Drawing, Sculpture.* London: Lund Humphries, 1964. 69p.

Spiteris, Tony. *Introduction à la peinture néo-hellénique (An Introduction to Modern Greek Painting).* Athens, 1962. 85p.

Travlos, J. *Neoklassiki Arkhitektoniki stin Ellada (Neoclassical Architecture in Greece).* Athens: Commercial Bank of Greece. 1967. 282p.

Tsarouchis, Yannis. *Theophilos.* Athens: Commercial Bank of Greece. 1966. 305p.

b. Literature

Barnstone, Willis. *Eighteen Texts: Writings by Contemporary Greek Authors.* Cambridge, Massachusetts, Harvard University Press, 1972. 187p.

Beaton, Roderick (ed.). *The Greek Novel, AD 1–1985.* London: Croom Helm, 1988. 229p.

Bien, Peter. *Constantine Cavafy.* New York: Columbia University Press, 1964. 48p.

————. *Kazantzakis and the Linguistic Revolution in Greek Literature.* Princeton, New Jersey: Princeton University Press, 1972. 291p.

————. *Nikos Kazantzakis.* New York: Columbia University Press, 1972. 48p.

Calas, Nicolas. *Texts on Poetics and Aesthetics (1929–38)*. New York, 1982.

Cavafy, C.P. *Collected Poems*. Translated by E. Keeley, Philip Sherrard. London: Hogarth Press, 1975. 447p.

———. *The Complete Poems of Cavafy*. Translated by Rae Dalven. New York: Harcourt, Brace & World. 1961. 234p.

———. *Passions and Ancient Days*. Translated by E. Keeley, G. Savidis. London: Hogarth Press, 1975. 68p.

———. *The Poems of C.P. Cavafy*. Translated by John Mavrogordato. London: Hogarth Press, 1952. 199p.

Dimaras, C. Th. *A History of Modern Greek Literature*. London: University of London Press, 1974. 539p.

Doulis, Thomas. *Disaster and Fiction: Modern Greek Fiction and the Asia Minor Disaster of 1922*. Berkeley: University of California Press, 1977. 313p.

———. *George Theotokas*. Boston: Twayne Publishers, 1975. 185p.

Elytis, Odysseus. *The Axion Esti: An International Poetry Forum Selection*. Translated by E. Keeley, G. Savidis. Pittsburgh: University of Pittsburgh Press, 1974. 159p.

———. *The Sovereign Sun: Selected Poems*. Philadelphia: Temple University Press. 1974. 200p.

Friar, Kimon. *Landscape of Death: The Selected Poems of Takis Sinopoulos*. Columbus: Ohio State University Press, 1979. 288p.

———. *Modern Greek Poetry: Translation, Introduction, an Essay on Translation, and Notes*. New York: Simon & Schuster, 1973. 780p.

Jenkins, Romilly. *Dionysios Solomos.* Cambridge: Cambridge University Press. 1940. 186p.

Karanikas, Alexander and Helen. *Elias Venezis.* New York: Twayne Publishers, 1969. 158p.

Kazantzakis, Helen. *Nikos Kazantzakis: A Biography Based on his Letters.* Translated by Amy Mims. Oxford: Cassirer, 1968. 589p.

Kazantzakis, Nikos. *Christ Recrucified.* Translated by Jonathan Griffin. New York: Simon & Schuster, 1954. 470p.

————. *The Fraticides.* Translated by Athena Gianakas Dallas. New York: Simon & Schuster, 1967. 254p.

————. *Freedom and Death.* Oxford: Cassirer, 1956. 472p.

————. *The Last Temptation.* Translated by Peter A. Bien. New York: Simon & Schuster, 1961.

————. *Report to Greco.* Translated by Peter A. Bien. Oxford: Cassirer, 1965. 512p.

————. *Travels in Greece: Journey to the Morea.* Translated by F.A. Reed. Oxford: Cassirer, 1966. 190p.

————. *Zorba the Greek.* Translated by Carl Wildman. New York: Simon & Schuster, 1953. 315p.

Keeley, Edmund. *Angelos Sikelianos.* London: George Allen & Unwin, 1980. 75p.

————. *Cavafy's Alexandria: Study of a Myth in Progress.* Princeton. New Jersey: Princeton University Press, 1977. 196p.

Keeley, Edmund, and Philip Sherrard. *Four Greek Poets: C.P. Cavafy, George Seferis, Odysseus Elytis, Nikos Gatsos.* Harmondsworth, England: Penguin Books, 1966. 110p.

————. *Six Poets of Modern Greece.* New York: Alfred A. Knopf, 1961. 185p.

Levitt, Morton. *The Cretan Glance: The World and Art of Nikos Kazantzakis.* Columbus: Ohio State University Press. 1980. 187p.

Liddell, Robert. *Cavafy: A Critical Biography.* London: Duckworth, 1974. 222p.

Maskaleris, Thanasis, *Kostis Palamas.* New York: Twayne Publishers, 1972. 156p.

Myrivilis, Stratis. *Life in the Tomb.* Translated by Peter A. Bien. Hanover, New Hampshire: University Press of New England, 1977. 325p.

————. *The Mermaid Madonna.* Translated by Abbott Rick. London: Hutchinson, 1959. 288p.

————. *The Schoolmistress with the Golden Eyes.* Translated by Philip Sherrard. London: Hutchinson, 1964. 288p.

Palamas, Kostis. *The Twelve Lays of the Gypsy.* Translated with an Introduction by George Thomson. London: Lawrence & Wishart, 1969. 146p.

————. *The Twelve Words of the Gypsy.* Translated with an Introduction by Frederic Will. Lincoln: University of Nebraska Press, 1964. 205p.

————. *The Twelve Words of the Gypsy.* Translated by Theodore, Ph., George Stephanides, and C. Katsimbalis. Tennessee: Memphis State University, 1975. 314p.

Papadiamantis, Alexandros. *The Murderess.* Translated by George X. Xanthopoulides. London, Athens: Doric Publications, 1977. 167p.

Politis, Linos. *A History of Modern Greek Literature.* Oxford: Clarendon Press, 1973. 338p.

Prevelakis, Pandelis. *The Sun of Death.* Translated by Philip Sherrard. London: John Murray, 1965. 206p.

————. *The Tale of a Town.* Translated by Kenneth Johnstone. London, Athens: Doric Publications, 1976. 119p.

Raizis, M.B. *Dionysios Solomos.* New York: Twayne Publishers, 1972, 158p.

Ritsos, Yannis. *Ritsos in Parentheses.* Translated with an Introduction by Edmund Keeley. Princeton, New Jersey: Princeton University Press, 1979. 175p.

————. *Scripture of the Blind.* Translated by Kimon Friar and Kostas Myrsiades. Columbus: Ohio State University Press, 1979. 251p.

————. *Selected Poems.* Translated by Nikos Stangos. Harmondsworth, England: Penguin Books, 1974. 207p.

Roberts, R.J. "The Greek Press at Constantinople in 1627 and Its Antecedents." *The Library,* vol. 22, no. 1, 1967. 13p.

Roidis, Emmanuel. *Pope Joan.* Translated by Lawrence Durrell. London: Andre Deutsch, 1960. 163p.

Samarakis, Antonis. *The Flaw.* Translated by Peter Mansfield and Richard Burns. London: Hutchinson, 1966. 208p.

Seferis, George. *Collected Poems 1924–1955.* Translated by E. Keeley and P. Sherrard. London: Jonathan Cape, 1969. 490p.

————. *On the Greek Style: Selected Essays in Poetry and Hellenism.* Translated by Rex Warner and Th. D. Frangopoulos with an Introduction by Rex Warner. London: Bodley Head, 1966. 196p.

————. *A Poet's Journal: Days of 1945–51.* Translated by Athan Anagnostopoulos. Cambridge, Massachusetts: Belknap, 1974. 206p.

Sherrard, Philip. *The Marble Threshing Floor: Studies in Modern Greek Poetry.* London: Vallentine, Mitchell, 1956. 258p.

Spencer, Terence. *Fair Greece! Sad relic! Literary Philhellenism from Shakespeare to Byron.* London: Weidenfeld & Nicolson. 1971. 312p.

Taktsis, Costas. *The Third Wedding.* Translated by Leslie Finer, London: Alan Ross, 1967. 303p.

Theotokas, George. *Argo.* Translated by E. Margaret Brooke and Aris Tsatsopoulos. London: Methuen, 1951. 357p.

Trypanis, Constantine. *Medieval and Modern Greek Poetry: An Anthology.* Oxford: Clarendon Press, 1951. 285p.

————. *The Penguin Book of Greek Verse.* Harmondsworth, England: Penguin Books, 1971. 630p.

Tsirkas, Stratis. *Drifting Cities: A Trilogy.* New York: Alfred A. Knopf, 1974. 710p.

Venezis, Ilias. *Acolia.* Translated by E. D. Scott-Kilvert. New York: Vanguard Press, 1957. 260p.

Vikelas, D. *Loukis Laras: Reminiscences of a Chiote Merchant During the War of Independence.* London: Macmillan, 1881. 273p.

c. Music

Butterworth, Katherine, and Sara Schneider (eds.). *Rebetika: Songs from the Old Greek Underworld.* Athens: Komboloi, 1975, 168p.

Dounias, Minos. *Griechenland Volksmusik und Neuere Musik.* Kassal: Barenreiter-Verlag, 1956. 882p.

Holst, Gail. *Road to Rebetika: Musik from a Greek Sub-culture: Songs of Love, Sorrow and Hashish.* Athens: Anglo-Hellenic Publishing, 1977. 175p.

————. *Theodorakis: Myth and Politics in Modern Greek Music.* Amsterdam: Adolf M. Hakkert, 1980.

Papaioannou, John. *European Music in the Twentieth Century.* Edited by Howard Hartog. Harmondsworth, England: Penguin Books, 1961. 336p.

Pym, H. *The Songs of Greece.* London: Sunday Times, 1968. 96p.

Wellesz, Egon. *A History of Byzantine Music and Hymnography.* Oxford: Clarendon Press, 1961. 461p.

d. Folklore

Abbott, G.F. *Macedonian Folklore.* Cambridge: Cambridge University Press, 1969. 372p.

Alexiou, Margaret. *The Ritual Lament in Greek Tradition.* Cambridge: Cambridge University Press, 1974, 274p.

Antoniades, Gault. Anne. *The Anastenaria: Thracian Firewalking Festival.* Athens: Thracian Archives, No. 36, 1954. 22p.

Argenti, Philip. *The Folklore of Chios.* Cambridge: Cambridge University Press, 1949.

Beaton, Roderick. *Folk Poetry of Modern Greece.* Cambridge: Cambridge University Press, 1980. 229p.

Colaclides, Helen. *Folktales of Greece* (Translation). Chicago: University of Chicago Press, 1970. 287p.

Crosfield, Domini. *Dances of Greece.* London: Max Parish, 1948. 40p.

Dawkins, R.M. *Modern Greek Folktales* (Translation). Oxford: Clarendon Press, 1953. 487p.

————. *More Greek Folktales* (Translation). Oxford: Clarendon Press, 1955. 178p.

Johnstone, Pauline. *Greek Island Embroidery.* London: 1961. 58p.

————. *Victoria and Albert Museum: A Guide to Greek Island Embroidery.* (Victoria and Albert Museum). London: H. M. Stationery Office, 1972. 111p.

Kyriakides, Stilpon. *Two Studies on Modern Greek Folklore.* Thessaloniki: Institute for Balkan Studies, 1968. 132p.

Kyriakidou-Nestoros, Alke. "Folk Art in Greek Macedonia." *Balkan Studies,* Vol. 4, No. 1, 1963, 15p.

Lawson, John Cuthbert. *Modern Greek Folklore and Ancient Greek Religion: A Study in Survivals.* Cambridge: Cambridge University Press, 1964. 620p.

Megas, G.A. *Greek Calendar Customs.* Athens: Press and Information Department, Prime Minister's Office, 1958. 159p.

Papadopoulos, S.A. (ed.). *Greek Handicraft.* Athens: National Bank of Greece, 1969. 332p.

Papantoniou, Ioanna. *Ellinikes Phoresies (Greek Costumes).* Nafplion, Greece: The Peloponnesian Folklore Foundation, 1974.

Petrides, Theodore. *Greek Dances.* Athens: Lycabettus Press, 1975. 104p.

Petrides, Theodore, and Elpida, Petridos. *Folk Dances of the Greeks; Origins and Instructions.* Folkestone, England: Bailey Bros. & Swinfen, 1974. 79p.

Rodd, Rennell. *The Customs and Lore of Modern Greece.* London: David Stott, 1892. 305p.

Zora, Popi. *Exhibition of Greek Folk Art Catalogue.* Athens: Ministry of Culture and Sciences. 48p.

ARTICLES

1. FOREIGN POLICY

Analytis, Minas. "Aspects des relations Albanie-Grèce." *Yearbook '91,* The Hellenic Foundation for Defence and Foreign Policy (ELIAMEP), pp. 39–52.

Axt, Heinz-Juergen. "Griechenland in der Europäischen Gemeinschaft. Kosten und Nutzen nach sechsjährigen Mitgliedschaft," *Österreichische Zeitschrift für Politikwissenschaft* 16 (2), 1987, pp. 169–187.

Carpenter, Richard. "Papandreou's Roller Coaster Foreign Policy." *National Review,* April 5, 1985.

Constas, D.C. "Greek Foreign Policy Objectives 1974–1986," *Yearbook '88,* ELIAMEP, pp. 93–128.

Coufoudakis, Van. "Greek Foreign Policy Since 1974: Quest for Independence," *Journal of Modern Greek Studies,* Vol. 6, No. 1, May 1988, pp. 55–75.

―――. "Ideology and Pragmatism in Greek Foreign Policy," *Current History,* December 1981, pp. 426–431.

Couloumbis, Theodore A. "The Crisis in Greek-American Relations," *Greek Accent,* October 1980, pp. 13–16.

―――. "Greece in Global Setting: Towards the Year 2000," *Yearbook '89,* ELIAMEP, pp. 125–136.

Diamandouros, Nikiforos. "The Southern European NICs," *International Organization,* Vol. 40, No. 2, Spring 1986, pp. 547–556.

Dimitras, Panayotes. "Greece's New Isolationism?," *Public Opinion Quarterly,* February–March 1983, pp. 14–16.

Dobratz, Betty. "Foreign Policy and Economic Orientations Influencing Party Preferences in the Socialist Nation of Greece," *East European Quarterly* 21(4), January 1988, pp. 413–430.

Fakiolas, Rossetos. "Changes in Eastern Europe and their Effect on the Greek Economy," *Yearbook '91,* ELIAMEP, pp. 145–161.

Fleischer, Hagen. "Post War Relations Between Greece and the Two German States: A Reevaluation in the Light of the German Unification," *Yearbook '91,* ELIAMEP, pp. 163–178.

Grimmet, R.F. "United States Military Installations in Greece," *Congressional Research Service, The Library of Congress Report,* No. 84–24F, February 16, 1984.

Haas, Richard. "The U.S. and Greece," *Current Policy,* No. 661, February 8, 1985.

Harvalias, George A. "Albanian Irredentism vs Serbian Ethnocentrism (The Kossovo Dispute: Threat to Balkan Regional Stability)," *Yearbook '89,* ELIAMEP, pp. 137–175.

Kofos, Evangelos. "Greece and the Balkans in the '70s and '80s," *Yearbook '90,* ELIAMEP, pp. 193–222.

Lagani, Irene. "Evolutions politiques à Skopje et leurs conséquences eventuelles dans la 'Question Macedonienne,' " *Yearbook '91,* ELIAMEP, pp. 189–207.

Laipson, Ellen. "U.S. Interests in the Eastern Mediterranean. Turkey, Greece and Cyprus," Report prepared for the Subcommittee on Europe and the Middle East of the Committee on Foreign Affairs, U.S. House of Representatives, by the Foreign Affairs and National Defense Division, *Congressional Research Service, Library of Congress,* 98th Congress, 1st Session, Washington, D.C., June 13, 1983, p. 39.

Larrabee, Stephen. "Dateline Athens: Greece for the Greeks," *Foreign Policy,* Winter 1981–82, pp. 158–174.

———. "Papandreou: National Interests Are the Key," *The Atlantic,* March 1983.

———. "Soviet-East European Relations under Gorbachev," *Yearbook '89,* ELIAMEP, pp. 51–66.

Legg, Keith. "Greek Foreign Policy: The Illusion of Change," *AEI Foreign Policy and Defence Review,* Vol. 6, No. 2, 1986, pp. 7–13.

Loulis, John. "Greece Under Papandreou: NATO's Ambivalent Partner," *Institute for European Defence and Strategic Studies,* No. 3, 1985.

———. "Papandreou's Foreign Policy," *Foreign Affairs,* Winter 1984–85, pp. 375–391.

Nachmani, Amikam. "So Near and Yet So Far: Graeco-Israeli Relations," *Mediterranean Historical Review,* Vol. 2, No. 2, December 1987, pp. 223–249.

Noyon, Jennifer, "Greeks Bearing Rifts: Papandreou in Power," *The Washington Quarterly,* Spring 1982, pp. 91–106.

Phillips, J.A. "US-Greek Relations: An Agonizing Reappraisal," *The Heritage Foundation Backgrounder,* July 18, 1985, p. 12.

Pridham, Geoffrey. "Political Parties and Elections in the New Eastern European Democracies: Comparisons with Southern European Experience," *Yearbook '90,* ELIAMEP, pp. 253–268.

Rozakis, Christos. "La politique étrangère grecque 1974–1985: Modernisation et rôle international d'un petit état," *Les Temps Modernes,* December 1985, pp. 861–887.

Schabas, William. "Greece, Eastern Europe, and the Implementation of International Human Rights Norms," *Yearbook '91,* ELIAMEP, pp. 209–223.

Scronias, Vassilis A. "Grèce-U.R.S.S.: Le Paradoxe Commercial," *Yearbook '89,* ELIAMEP, pp. 253–272.

Theodoropoulos, Byron. "On Minorities," *Yearbook '90,* ELIAMEP, pp. 49–54.

Tsitsopoulos, George. "EEC Relations with COMECON," *Yearbook '89,* ELIAMEP, pp. 67–84.

Vatikiotis, P.J. "Aspects of the Gulf Crisis," *Yearbook '90,* ELIAMEP, pp. 55–66.

Vernant, Jacques. "La Politique extérieure de M. Andreas Papandreou," *Défense Nationale,* January 1982, pp. 109–116.

Wallden, Sotiris. "Integration of Southeast Europe into the World Economy and Balkan Economic Cooperation," *Yearbook '90,* ELIAMEP, pp. 279–286.

Yegorov, Boris and Victor Yevgenyev. "USSR and Greece: What Makes for Mutual Understanding and Good-neighborly Relations," *International Affairs,* November 1986, pp. 84–90.

2. THE EUROPEAN COMMUNITY, NATO, AND THE MEDITERRANEAN

Axt, Heinz-Juergen. "Southern Europe and the EC: Divergence and Cohesion," *Yearbook '91*, Hellenic Foundation for Defense and Foreign Policy (ELIAMEP), pp. 55–74.

Brown, James. "Challenges and Uncertainty, NATO's Southern Flank," *Air University Review*, May–June 1980, pp. 3–16.

Coufoudakis, Van. "The Eastern Mediterranean in the Defense of the West—The Case of Greece," *NATO's Sixteen Nations*, October 1986, pp. 34–39.

———. "The Essential Link—Greece In NATO," *Yearbook '88*, ELIAMEP, pp. 19–25.

Coufoudakis, Van and Yannis Valinakis. "The Evolution of Greece's Defense Strategy," *The International Spectator*, Vol. XXII, No. 1, January–March 1987.

Couloumbis, Theodore. "Greece and the European Challenge in the Balkans," *Yearbook '91*, ELIAMEP, pp. 75–88.

Frinking, Ton. "Draft Interim Report of the Sub-Committee on the Southern Region," *North Atlantic Assembly*, November 1984.

Harvard's Center For Science and International Affairs European Security Working Group, "Instability and Change on NATO's Southern Flank," *International Security*, Winter 1978/1979, pp. 150–177.

Ioakimidis, Panayotis. "Greece, the EC and the Eastern European Countries: An Overview," *Yearbook '91*, ELIAMEP, pp. 179–187.

Karaosmanoglou, Ali. "NATO's South-Eastern Region Between Central Europe and the Middle East," *International Defense Review*, 1985/10, pp. 1,569–1,576.

Kazakos, Panos. "Griechenland und die Zukunftsentwürfe für die EG," *Yearbook '90,* ELIAMEP, pp. 171–192.

Kikiras, Fotis. "Europe's Contribution to the Defense of the Western Alliance: An Ongoing Discussion," *Yearbook '88,* ELIAMEP, pp. 27–30.

Kohlhase, Norbert. "Der griechisch-türkische Konflikt in der Sicht des Europäischen Gemeinschaft," *Europa-Archiv,* 1981/6, pp. 161–170.

Kourvetaris, Yorgos. "The Southern Flank of NATO: Political Dimensions of the Greco-Turkish Conflict Since 1974," *East European Quarterly,* 21 (4), January 1988, pp. 431–446.

Lesser, Ian. "The United States and the Mediterranean after the Cold War," *Yearbook '90,* ELIAMEP, pp. 223–236.

Mashin, Veniamin. "For Stability in the Mediterranean," *International Affairs,* June 1987, pp. 90–95.

Meinardus, Ronald. "Griechenlands gestörtes Verhältnis zur NATO," *Europa Archiv, 1982/4,* pp. 105–114.

Noyon, Jennifer. "Bridge over Troubled Regions," *The Washington Quarterly,* Summer 1984.

Paparella, Ivo. "Les Balkans et al défense du flanc sud de l' OTAN," *Défense Nationale,* October 1983, pp. 105–120.

"Perspectives on NATO's Southern Flank," a Report to the Committee on Foreign Relations, *United States Senate,* 96th Congress, 2nd Session, Washington, D.C., April 13, 1980.

Phocion. "Papandreou Moves for Strategic Crisis in NATO's Vital Southern Flank," *Executive Intelligence Review,* October 1985, pp. 42–43.

Platias, A.G. "Small States and the Procurement of Arms Supplies: Problems, Options and Strategies," *Yearbook '88,* ELIAMEP, pp. 41–57.

Roubatis, Yannis. "The US and the Operational Responsibilities of the Greek Armed Forces, 1947–1987," *Journal of the Hellenic Diaspora,* Vol. VI, No. 1, Spring 1979, pp. 39–57.

Spiroiu, Nikulae Constantin. "The Balkans and European Security," *Yearbook '91,* ELIAMEP, pp. 125–131.

Stefanou, Constantine. "The Impact of the Cyprus Question on EEC-Turkish Relations," *Yearbook '88,* ELIAMEP, pp. 153–161.

Tsakaloyannis, Panos. "The European Community and the Greek-Turkish Dispute," *Journal of Common Market Studies,* September 1980, pp. 35–54.

Tsoukalis, Loukas. "The Shaping of European Economy," *Yearbook '88,* ELIAMEP, pp. 163–165.

"Turkey, Greece and NATO: The Strained Alliance," *A Staff Report to the Committee on Foreign Relations, United States Senate,* 96th Congress, 2nd Session, Washington, D.C., March 1980.

"US Security Assistance to NATO's Southern Flank," *A Report to the Committee on Foreign Relations, United States Senate,* 98th Congress, 1st Session, Washington, D.C., April 1983.

Valinakis, Yannis. "Balkan Security: Recent Developments and Prospects for the Future," *Balkan Studies 1986,* Thessaloniki, 1988, pp. 81–89.

———. "The Strategic Importance of Greece," *Yearbook '88,* ELIAMEP, pp. 59–69.

Veremis, Thanos. "The Future of European Security: The South East" in Armand Clesse and Lothar Ruehl, *Searching for a New Security Structure in Europe,* Baden-Baden: Nomos Verlagsgesellschaft, 1990, pp. 342–350.

————. "Greece and NATO," *Yearbook '88,* ELIAMEP, pp. 71–81.

————. "An Overview of Greek Security Concerns in the Eastern Mediterranean and the Balkans," *Lo Spettatore Internazionale,* Rome, IAI, Vol. 4, No. 4, October–December 1982, pp. 339–345.

Vernant, Jacques. "M. Papandreou, le peuple grec et les bases," *Défense Nationale,* October 1983, pp. 137–144.

Yakemtchouk, Romain. "La Méditerranée orientale dans la politique des puissances—Détroits—Chypre. Enjeux greco-turcs dans la Mer Egée. Connexions européennes," *Studia Diplomatica,* 40 (3–5), 1987, pp. 449–613.

Zoppo, Ciro. "Political and Military Cooperation and Security in NATO's Southern Flank," *The International Spectator,* Vol. XXII, No. 1, January–March 1987.

3. GREEK-TURKISH RELATIONS

Alexandris, Alexis. "Imbros and Tenedos: A Study in Turkish Attitudes Towards two Ethnic Greek Island Communities Since 1923," *Journal of the Hellenic Diaspora,* Vol. VII, No. 1, Spring 1980, pp. 5–31.

Angelopoulos, Angelos. "Une réduction des dépenses militaires entre la Grèce et al Turquie est-elle possible?" *Revue des Deux Mondes,* April 1986.

Bohle, Hermann. "Griechen und Türken: Endlich Dialog der feindlichen NATO-Brüder," *Loyal,* March 1988, pp. 6–9.

Brown, James. "From Military to Civilian Rule: A Comparative Study of Greece and Turkey," *Defense Analysis,* 2 (3), September 86, pp. 175–189.

Camp, Glen, "Greek-Turkish Conflict over Cyprus," *Political Science Quarterly,* Spring 1980, pp. 43–70.

Coufoudakis, Van. "Greco-Turkish Relations and the Greek Socialists: Ideology, Nationalism and Pragmatism," *Journal of Modern Greek Studies,* October 1983, pp. 373–392.

————. "Greek-Turkish Relations, 1973–1983: The View from Athens," *International Security,* Spring 1985, pp. 185–217.

Drakidis, Phil. "La démilitarisation du Dodécanèse," *Défense Nationale,* April 1983, pp. 123–136.

————. "Le Statut de démilitarisation de certaines Iles grècques," *Défense Nationale,* August–September 1984, pp. 73–82.

Economides, Constantin. "La prétendue obligation de démilitarisation de l'île de Lemnos," *Revue Hellénique de Droit International,* 1981, Nos. 1–4, pp. 7–14.

————. "Nouveaux éléments concernant l'île de Lemnos: Un Problème totalement artificiel." *Revue Hellénique de Droit International,* 1984, pp. 4–10.

————. "Lemnos and the Alleged Obligation for its Demilitarisation," *Yearbook '88,* Hellenic Foundation for Defense and Foreign Policy (ELIAMEP), pp. 85–92.

Hallerbach, Ralf. "Die Insel Lemnos: Stein des Anstosses in der Ägäis," *Europäische Wehrkunde,* February 1985, pp. 30–33.

Ioannou, Kroteros, M. "The Judicial Factor in Greek-Turkish Relations," *Yearbook '88,* ELIAMEP, pp. 169–175.

Kartalis, Yannis. "The 'Davos Spirit': Recent Developments," *Yearbook '88,* ELIAMEP, pp. 183–185.

Kramer, Heinz. "Der türkische EG-Beitrittsantrag und der 'griechische Faktor,'" *Europa Archiv,* 42, No. 21, 10, Nov. 1987, pp. 605–614.

Kuniholm, Bruce. "Greece and Turkey in NATO," *SAIS Review,* Winter–Spring 1986, Vol. 6, No. 1, pp. 137–157.

Laipson, Ellen. "The Seven-Ten Ratio in Military Aid to Greece and Turkey: A Congressional Tradition," *Congressional Research Service Report,* No. 85–89, Washington, D.C., April 10, 1985.

Lazarides, Nikolaos. "A War-Time Scenario in the Aegean," *Yearbook '88,* ELIAMEP, pp. 31–40.

Leighton, Kirsch M. "Greco-Turkish Friction: Changing Balance in the Eastern Meditarranean," *Conflict Studies,* No. 109, Institute for the Study of Conflict, London, July 1979.

Luciani, Giacomo. "Economic Cooperation Between Greece, Italy and Turkey," *The International Spectator,* Vol. XXII, No. 1, January–March 1987, pp. 24–29.

Mango, Andrew. "Greece and Turkey: Unfriendly Allies," *The World Today,* August/September 1987, pp. 144–147.

Maurer, Dieter Horst. "Sperrung der Ägäis," *Marine-Forum,* April 1985, pp. 102–104.

Meinardus, Ronald. "Die griechisch-türkischen Beziehungen in den achtziger Jahren," *Beiträge zur Konfliktforschung,* 18. Jahrgang, Heft 2/1988, pp. 83–98.

———. "Der griechisch-türkische Konflikt über den militärischen Status der ostägäischen Inseln," *Europa Archiv,* 1985/2, pp. 41–48.

————. "Die griechisch-türkische Minderheitsfrage." *Orient,* 26. Jahrgang, No. 1 March 1985, pp. 48–61.

Papacosmas, Victor. "Legacy of Strife: Greece, Turkey and the Aegean," *Studio Diplomatica,* 1984, pp. 295–319.

Pazarci, Huesein. "Has the Demilitarized Status of the Aegean Islands as Determined by the Lausanne and Paris Treaties Changed?," *Turkish Review Quarterly Digest,* Winter 1985, pp. 24–45.

Rozakis, Christos. "An Analysis of the Legal Problems in Greek-Turkish Relations," *Yearbook '89,* ELIAMEP, pp. 193–251.

Silvestri, Stefano. "Political Factors Affecting Cooperation Between Italy, Greece and Turkey," *The International Spectator,* Vol. XXII, No. 1, January–March 1987, pp. 20–23.

Snyder, Jed. "Threats to Southern Flank Security: The Soviet Buildup and the Greek-Turkish Dispute," Hearing on the FY 1986 Security Assistance Budget. Prepared for Delivery to the Subcommittee on Foreign Operations, Committee on Appropriations, U.S. Senate, March 27, 1985.

Umr, Semir S. "An Analysis of the Aegean Crisis," *Contemporary Review,* September 1982, pp. 142–147.

Vaner, Semih. "Die Türkei, Griechenland und die Grossmächte. Jeder gegen jeden, drei gegen einen oder jeder für Sich?," *Europäische Rundschau,* (14.4), 1986, pp. 59–74.

Veremis, Thanos. "Greece and Turkey: In Search for Autonomous Security Policies," *Revue Hellénique de Droit International,* 1982–1983, pp. 111–116.

————. "Greek-Turkish Relations and the Balkans," *Yearbook '91,* ELIAMEP, pp. 237–242.

4. CYPRUS

Bruce, Leigh H. "Cyprus: A Last Chance," *Foreign Policy,* Spring 1985, pp. 115–132.

Calligas, C. "The Cyprus Problem: The Key to Greek-Turkish Relations," *Yearbook '88*, Hellenic Foundation for Defense and Foreign Policy, ELIAMEP, pp. 177–181.

Coufoudakis, Van. "Cyprus and the European Convention on Human Rights: The Law and Politics of Cyprus v. Turkey, Applications 6780/75, and 6959/75," *Human Rights Quarterly*, Fall 1982, pp. 450–473.

———. "The Cyprus Question and the Issue of the Implementation of the United Nations Resolutions on Cyprus in the Aftermath of the Gulf War," *Yearbook '91*, ELIAMEP, pp. 135–143.

Da Costa, Hélène. "Le nationalisme chypriote turc entre dissidence et fédération," *L'Afrique et l'Asie Modernes*, 148, Spring 1986, pp. 56–64.

Karaosmanoglu, Ali, "Cyprus: What Kind of a Federal Solution?," *Journal of South Asian and Middle Eastern Studies*, Spring 1980, pp. 33–46.

Meinardus, Ronald. "Eine Neue Phase im Zypern-Konflikt," *Europa Archiv*, 1984/10, pp. 297–306.

Norton, Augustus Richard. "Post-Election Flexibility. New Hope for Unity in Cyprus," *The New Leader*, March 7, 1988, pp. 7–9.

Prakesh, Sanjiv. "Divided Cyprus." *Defense & Foreign Affairs*, Vol. XV, No. 4, April 1987, pp. 47–49.

Reddaway, John. "A Cyprus Settlement-Revelations in a Crystal Ball," *International Relations* (London), 9 (1), May 1987, pp. 23–30.

Theodoropoulos, Byron. "Elections in Greece and Turkey and their Implications for Cyprus," *Yearbook '89*, ELIAMEP, pp. 273–280.

Vaner, Semih. "Chypre petites îles, Grandes puissances," *Politique Etrangère,* 1985/1, pp. 157–172.

Woodhouse, C.M. "The Problem of Cyprus," *The Indiana Social Studies Quarterly,* Vol. XXXII, No. 1, Spring 1979, pp. 11–12.

5. INTERNAL AFFAIRS

Arvanitopoulos, Constantine. "The Rise and Fall of the Greek Military Regime: 1967–1974," *Journal of Modern Hellenism,* No. 8, Winter 1991, pp. 97–116.

Catsiapis, Jean. "Les dix ans de la constitution grècque du juin 1975," *Revue du Droit Public et de la Science Politique,* (2), March–April 1987, pp. 399–418.

Clogg, Richard. "The Constitutional Crisis in Greece," *Journal of Modern Hellenism,* No. 2, October 1985, pp. 103–112.

————. "PASOK in Power: Rendezvous with History or Reality?," *World Today,* November 1983, pp. 436–442.

Couloumbis, Theodore A. "Karamanlis and Papandreou: Style and Substance of Leadership," *Yearbook '88,* Hellenic Foundation for Defense and Foreign Policy, ELIAMEP, pp. 129–149.

Couloumbis, Theodore A. and P.M. Yannas. "The Stability Quotient of Greece's Post-1974 Democratic Institutions," *Journal of Modern Greek Studies,* October 1983, pp. 359–372.

Diamandouros, Nikiforos. "Transition and Consolidation of Democratic Politics in Greece 1974–1983: A Tentative Assessment," *West European Politics,* April 1984, pp. 50–71.

Dimitras, Panayotes Elias. "Greece," *Electoral Studies,* 1984, 3:3, pp. 285–289.

Dobratz, Betty. "A Discriminant Analysis," *European Journal of Political Research,* 14 (4), 1986, pp. 441–463.

Economou, Nikos, and Thanos Veremis. "Parties of the Liberal Center in the Greek Elections of 1981," *Journal of the Hellenic Diaspora,* Vol. XI, No. 4, Winter 1984, pp. 33–44.

Evriviades, Marios. "Greece After Dictatorship," *World Affairs, Monthly,* November 1979, pp. 162–166.

Featherstone, Kevin. "The Greek Socialists in Power," *West European Politics,* July 1983, pp. 237–250.

Frangoudakis, Anna (ed.). "Education in Greece Today: A Symposium," *Journal of the Hellenic Diaspora,* Vol. VIII, Nos. 1–2, Spring–Summer 1981.

Kitroeff, Alexandros. "Greek Wartime Attitudes Towards the Jews in Athens," *Forum on the Jewish People, Zionism and Israel,* Issue No. 60, Summer 1987, pp. 41–51.

Lyrintzis, Christos. "Political Parties in Post-Junta Greece: A Case Of Bureaucratic Clientelism?," *West European Politics,* April 1984, pp. 99–118.

———. "The Rise of PASOK: The Greek Elections of 1981," *West European Politics,* July 1982, pp. 322–327.

Mcdonald, Robert. "Greece After PASOK's Victory," *The World Today,* July 1985, pp. 133–136.

———. "Prospects for the Greek Economy," *Yearbook '90,* ELIAMEP, pp. 237–252.

———. "Prospects for the Greek Economy," *Yearbook '91,* ELIAMEP, pp. 89–106.

Minard, Lawrence. "Greece Goes Left," *Forbes,* 28 September 1981, pp. 34–37.

Mouzelis, Nikos. "On the Analysis of Social Stratification in Greece," *Journal of the Hellenic Diaspora,* Vol. XI, No. 4, Winter 1984, pp. 69–78.

Petras, James. "Greek Socialism: Walking the Tightrope," *Journal of the Hellenic Diaspora,* Vol. IX, No. 1, Spring 1982, pp. 7–15.

————. "A Greek Tragedy (Papandreou Sets the Stage for a Right-wing Revival)," *In These Times,* Vol. 10, No. 10, January 28–February 4, 1986, pp. 16–17 and 22.

Pollis, Adamantia. "Notes on Nationalism and Human Rights in Greece," *Journal of Modern Hellenism,* No. 4, Autumn 1987, pp. 147–160.

Robinson, Robert. "Drama and Polemic in Greece: The 1985 General Election," *Political Quarterly,* Vol. 57, No. 1, January–March 1986, pp. 88–94.

Rousseas, Stephen. "Greece: Twisting the Elephant's Tail," *World View,* November 1982.

Schlegel, Dietrich. "Papandreou—A Gain in Predictability," *Assenpolitik,* 1982/4, pp. 391–407.

Skouras, Thanos. "Rentier Capital, Industrial Development and the Growth of the Greek Economy in the Postwar Period," *Journal of the Hellenic Diaspora,* Vol. XII, No. 1, Spring 1985, pp. 5–15.

Smith, Ole. "The Impact of Gorbachev on the Greek Communists," *Yearbook '91,* ELIAMEP, pp. 225–235.

Spourdalakis, Michalis. "The Greek Experience," *Socialist Register 1985–1986,* pp. 249–267.

Vatikiotis, P.J. "Greece: The Triumph of Socialism?," *Survey,* Spring 1982, pp. 50–65.

Xenos, Nicholas. "The Greek Change," *Democracy,* Spring 1983, pp. 78–86.

Yannakakis, Ilios. "Phénomène communiste et cultures politiques en Grèce," *Communisme,* 11–12, 1986, pp. 53–68.

APPENDIX A

KINGS OF GREECE (1833–1973)

Otto (Wittelsbach)	1833–62
George I (Glucksburg)	1863–1913
Constantine I	1913–17
Alexander	1917–20
Constantine I	1921–22
George II	1922–3, 1935–47
Paul	1947–64
Constantine II	1964–73

APPENDIX B

PRESIDENTS OF GREECE

Ioannis Kapodistrias	1828–31
Admiral Pavlos Koundouriotis	1924–26
(General Theodoros Pangalos)	1926
Admiral Pavlos Koundouriotis	1926–29
Alexandros Zaimis	1929–35
(Colonel Georgios Papadopoulos)	1973
(General Phaidon Gizikis)	1973–74
Mikhail Stasinopoulos	1974–75
Konstantinos Tsatsos	1975–80
Konstantinos Karamanlis	1980–85
Christos Sartzetakis	1985–90
Konstantinos Karamanlis	1990–

(Parentheses indicate dictatorial rule)

APPENDIX C

PRIME MINISTERS OF GREECE

Spyridon Trikoupis	January 1833–October 1833
Alexandros Mavrokordatos	October 1833–May 1834
Count Armansberg	May 1835–February 1837
Knight Rundhart	February 1837–December 1837
Presidency of King Otto	December 1837–June 1841
Alexandros Mavrokordatos	June 1841–October 1841
Presidency of King Otto	October 1841–September 1843
Andreas Metaxas	September 1843–March 1844
Alexandros Mavrokordatos	March 1844–August 1844
Ioannis Kolettis	August 1844–September 1847
Kitsos Tzavelas	September 1847–March 1848
Georgios Koundouriotis	March 1848–October 1848
Constantinos Kanaris	October 1848–December 1849
Antonios Kriezis	December 1849–May 1854
Alexandros Mavrokordatos	May 1854–September 1855
Dimitrios Voulgaris	September 1855–November 1857
Athanasios Miaoulis	November 1857–May 1862
Gennaios Kolokotronis	May 1862–October 1862
Dimitrios Voulgaris	October 1862–February 1863
Zinon Valvis	February 1863–March 1863
Diomidis Kiriakou	March 1863–April 1863
Benizelos Roufos	April 1863–October 1863
Dimitrios Voulgaris	October 1863–March 1864
Constantinos Kanaris	March 1864–April 1864
Zinon Valvis	April 1864–July 1864
Constantinos Kanaris	July 1864–March 1865
Alexandros Koumoundouros	March 1865–October 1865
Epaminondas Deligeorgis	October 1865–November 1865
Dimitrios Voulgaris	November 1865–November 1865
Alexandros Koumoundouros	November 1865–November 1865
Epaminondas Deligeoris	November 1865–November 1865
Benizelos Roufos	November 1865–June 1866
Dimitrios Voulgaris	June 1866–December 1866
Alexandros Koumoundouros	December 1866–December 1867

Aristotelis Moraitnis	December 1867–January 1868
Dimitrios Voulgaris	January 1868–January 1869
Thrasivoulos Zaimis	January 1869–July 1870
Epaminondas Deligeorgis	July 1870–December 1870
Alexandros Koumoundouros	December 1870–October 1871
Thrasivoulos Zaimis	October 1871–December 1871
Dimitrios Voulgaris	December 1871–August 1872
Epaminondas Deligeorgis	August 1872–February 1874
Dimitrios Voulgaris	February 1874–April 1875
Charilaos Trikoupis	April 1875–October 1875
Alexandros Koumoundouros	October 1875–November 1876
Epamindondas Deligeorgis	November 1876–December 1876
Alexandros Koumoundouros	December 1876–February 1877
Epaminondas Deligeorgis	February 1877–May 1877
Alexandros Koumoundouros	May 1877–May 1877
Constantinos Kanaris	May 1877–January 1878
Alexandros Koumoundouros	January 1878–October 1878
Charilaos Trikoupis	October 1878–October 1878
Alexandros Koumoundouros	October 1878–March 1880
Charilaos Trikoupis	March 1880–October 1880
Alexandros Koumoundouros	October 1880–March 1882
Harilaos Trikoupis	March 1882–April 1885
Theodoros Diligiannis	April 1885–April 1886
Dimitrios Valvis	April 1886–May 1886
Harilaos Trikoupis	March 1886–October 1890
Theodoros Diligiannis	October 1890–February 1892
Constantinos Konstantopolous	February 1892–June 1892
Harilaos Trikoupis	June 1892–May 1893
Sotirios Sotiropoulos	March 1893–October 1893
Harilaos Trikoupis	October 1893–January 1895
Nikolaos Diligiannis	January 1895–May 1895
Theodoros Diligiannis	May 1895–April 1897
Dimitrios Rallis	April 1897–September 1897
Alexandros Zaimis	September 1897–April 1899
Georgios Theotokis	April 1899–November 1901
Alexandros Zaimis	November 1901–November 1902
Theodoros Diligiannis	November 1902–June 1903
Georgios Theotokis	June 1903–June 1903
Dimitrios Rallis	June 1903–December 1903

Georgios Theotokis	December 1903–December 1904
Theodoros Diligiannis	December 1904–June 1905
Dimitrios Rallis	June 1905–December 1905
Georgios Theotokis	December 1905–July 1909
Dimitrios Rallis	July 1909–August 1909
Kyriakoulis Mavromichalis	August 1909–January 1910
Stefanos Dragoumis	January 1910–October 1910
Eleftherios Venizelos	October 1910–February 1915
Dimitrios Gounaris	February 1915–August 1915
Eleftherios Venizelos	August 1915–September 1915
Alexandros Zaimis	August 1915–October 1915
Stefanos Skouloudis	October 1915–June 1916
Alexandros Zaimis	June 1916–September 1916
Nikolaos Kalogeropoulos	September 1916–September 1916
Spyridon Lambros	September 1916–April 1917
Alexandros Zaimis	April 1917–June 1917
Eleftherios Venizelos	June 1917–November 1920
Dimitrios Rallis	November 1920–January 1921
Nikolaos Kalogeropoulos	January 1921–March 1921
Dimitrios Gounaris	March 1921–March 1922
Dimitrios Gounaris	March 1922–May 1922
Nikolaos Stratos	May 1922–May 1922
Petros Protopapadakis	May 1922–August 1922
Nikolaos Triantafillakos	August 1922–September 1922
Anastasios Charalabis	September 1922–September 1922
Sotirios Krokidas	September 1922–November 1922
Stylanios Gonatas	November 1922–January 1924
Eleftherios Venizelos	January 1924–February 1924
Georgios Kafantaris	February 1924–March 1924
Alexandros Papanastasiou	March 1924–July 1924
Themistoklis Sofoulis	July 1924–October 1924
Andreas Michalakopoulos	October 1924–June 1925
Theodoros Pangalos	June 1925–July 1926
Athanasios Eftaxias	July 1926–August 1926
Georgios Kondilis	August 1926–December 1926
Alexandros Zaimis	December 1926–August 1927
Alexandros Zaimis	August 1927–February 1928
Alexandros Zaimis	February 1928–July 1928
Eleftherios Venizelos	July 1928–June 1929

Eleftherios Venizelos	June 1929–December 1929
Eleftherios Venizelos	December 1929–May 1932
Alexandros Papanastasiou	May 1932–June 1932
Eleftherios Venizelos	June 1932–November 1932
Panaghis Tsaldaris	November 1932–January 1933
Eleftherios Venizelos	January 1933–March 1933
Alexandros Othonaios	March 1933–March 1933
Panaghis Tsaldaris	March 1935–October 1935
Georgios Kondilis	October 1935–November 1935
Constantinos Demertzis	November 1935–May 1936
Ioannis Metaxas	May 1936–January 1941
Alexandros Korizis	January 1941–April 1941
Emmanouel Tsouderos	April 1941–April 1944
Sofoklis Sophocles	April 1944–April 1944
Georgios Papandreou	April 1944–May 1944
Georgios Papandreou	May 1944–January 1945
Nicolaos Plastiras	January 1945–April 1945
Petros Voulgaris	April 1945–August 1945
Petros Voulgaris	August 1945–October 1945
Archbishop-Regent Damaskinos	October 1945–November 1945
Panagiotis Kanellopoulos	November 1945–November 1945
Themistoklis Sophoulis	November 1945–April 1946
Panagiotis Poulitsas	April 1946–April 1946
Constantinos Tsaldaris	April 1946–October 1946
Constantinos Tsaldaris	October 1946–January 1947
Dimitrios Maximos	January 1947–August 1947
Constantinos Tsaldaris	August 1947–September 1947
Themistoklis Sophoulis	September 1947–November 1948
Themistoklis Sophoulis	November 1948–January 1949
Themistoklis Sophoulis	January 1949–April 1949
Themistoklis Sophoulis	April 1949–June 1949
Alexandros Diomidis	June 1949–January 1950
Ioannis Theotokis	January 1950–March 1950
Sophocles Venizelos	March 1950–April 1950
Nikolaos Plastiras	April 1950–August 1950
Sophocles Venizelos	August 1950–September 1950
Sophocles Venizelos	September 1950–November 1950
Sophocles Venizelos	November 1950–October 1951

Nikolaos Plastiras	October 1951–October 1952
Dimitrios Kioussopoulos	October 1952–November 1952
Alexandros Papagos	November 1952–October 1955
Constantinos Karamanlis	October 1955–February 1956
Constantinos Karamanlis	February 1956–March 1958
Constantinos Georgakopoulos	March 1958–May 1958
Constantinos Karamanlis	May 1958–September 1961
Constantinos Dovas	September 1961–November 1961
Constantinos Karamanlis	November 1961–June 1963
Panagiotis Pipinelis	June 1963–September 1963
Stylianos Mavromichalis	September 1963–November 1963
Georgios Papandreou	November 1963–December 1963
Ioannis Paraskevopoulos	December 1963–February 1964
Georgios Papandreou	February 1964–July 1965
Georgios Athanasiadis-Novas	July 1965–August 1965
Ilias Tsirimokos	August 1965–September 1965
Stefanos Stefanopoulos	September 1965–December 1966
Ioannis Paraskevopoulos	December 1966–April 1967
Panagiotis Kanellopoulos	April 1967–April 1967

[DICTATORSHIP PERIOD (1967–1974)]

Constantinos Karamanlis	July 1974–November 1974
Constantinos Karamanlis	November 1974–November 1977
Constantinos Karamanlis	November 1977–May 1980
Georgios Rallis	May 1980–September 1981
Georgios Rallis	September 1981–October 1981
Andreas Papandreou	October 1981–June 1985
Andreas Papandreou	June 1985–July 1989
Tzannis Tzannetakis	July 1989–October 1989
Ioannis Grivas	October 1989–November 1989
Xenophon Zolotas	November 1989–April 1990
Constantinos Mitsotakis	April 1990–September 1993

PRIME MINISTERS APPOINTED BY THE JUNTA

Constantinos Kollias	April 1967–December 1967
Georgios Papadopoulos	December 1967–October 1973
Spyridon Markezinis	October 1973–November 1973
Adamantios Androutsopoulos	November 1973–July 1974

Appendix D

BASIC DATA ON GREECE

Name: Greece—Hellas—Hellenic Republic

Total area: 131,957 km; land area: 130,800 km
Land boundaries: 1,210 km total; Albania 282 km, Bulgaria 494 km, Turkey 206 km, FYROM 228 km
Coastline: 15,021 km
Climate: temperate; mild winters; hot, dry summers
Terrain: Mountainous with ranges extending into sea as peninsulas
Natural resources: bauxite, lignite, magnesite, crude oil, marble
Land use: arable land 23%; permanent crops 8%; meadows and pastures 40%; forest and woodland 20%; other 9%; includes irrigated 7%
Environment: archipelago of 2,000 islands dominating the Aegean Sea (including islets and rock islands, 9,841)
Population: 10,200,000 (1991 census), growth rate 1.10% (1991)
Infant mortality rate: 9 deaths/1,000 live births (1991)
Life expectancy at birth: 75 years male, 81 years female (1991)
Military Personnel: (Professional and conscripts) 214,000
Ethnic divisions: Greek 98%, other 2%
Religion: Greek Orthodox 97.6%, Muslim 1.3%, Roman Catholic 0.4%, other 0.3%
Literacy: 93% (male 98%, female 89%) age 15 and over can read and write (1990 est.)
Labor force: 3,657,000; services 44%, agriculture 27%, manufacturing and mining 20%, construction 6% (1988)
Organized labor: 10–15% of total labor force, 20–25% of urban labor force

Government

Type: presidential parliamentary government: monarchy rejected by referendum 8 December 1974
Capital: Athens

Administrative divisions: 52 departments (*nomoi*): Achaia, Aitolia kai Akarnania, Argolis, Arkadia, Arta, Attiki, Dhodhekanisos, Dhrama, Evritania, Evros, Evvoia, Florina, Fokis, Fthiotis, Grevena, Ilia, Imathia, Ioannia, Iraklion, Kardhitsa, Kastoria, Kavala, Kefallinia, Kerkira, Khalkidhiki, Khania, Khios, Kikladhes, Kilkis, Korinthia, Kozani, Lakonia, Larisa, Lasithi, Lesvos, Lefkas, Magnisia, Messinia, Pella, Pieria, Piraeus, Preveza, Rethimno, Rodhopi, Samos, Serrai, Thesprotia, Thessloniki, Trikala, Voiotia, Xanthi, Zakinthos, autonomous region: Agion Oros (Mt. Athos)

Independence: 1829 (from Ottoman Empire)

Constitution: 11 June 1975

Legal system: based on codified Roman law: judiciary divided into civil, criminal, and administrative courts

National holidays: Independence Day (proclamation of the War of Independence), 25 March (1821); Day of Resistance against Axis Forces—"Ochi day," 28 October (1940)

Executive branch: President, Prime Minister, Cabinet

Legislative branch: unicameral Chamber of Deputies (Vouli ton Ellinon)

Judicial branch: Supreme Court

Leaders: *Chief of State*—President Konstantinos KARAMANLIS *Head of Government*—Prime Minister Andreas PAPANDREOU

Political parties and leaders: New Democracy (ND), Miltiades EVERT; Panhellenic Socialist Movement (PASOK), Andreas PAPANDREOU; Left Alliance, Nikos CONSTANTOPOULOS; Communist Party (KKE), Aleka PAPARIGA

Suffrage: universal and compulsory at age 18

Elections:

President—last held 4 May 1990 (next to be held May 1995); results—Konstantinos KARAMANLIS; elected by Parliament

The following are the results of the October 10 elections, 1993

Registered voters: 8,940,342
Ballots cast: 6,995,023
Valid: 6,875,961
Invalid: 88,779
Blank: 30,283
Participation: 78.24 percent

Votes received and seats earned:

Party	Votes	Percentage	Seats
New Democracy	2,701,535	39.29	111
PASOK	3,224,128	46.89	170
Coalition of the Left and Progress	202,155	2.94	—
KKE	312,068	4.54	9
Political Spring	335,125	4.87	10

Flag: nine equal horizontal stripes of blue alternating with white; there is a blue square in the upper hoist-side corner bearing a white cross; the cross symbolizes Greek Orthodoxy, the established religion of the country

Economy

Overview: Greece has a mixed economy with a dominant entrepreneurial system. Tourism is a major industry, and agriculture—although handicapped by geographic limitations and fragmented—is self-sufficient except for meat, dairy products, and animal feedstuffs. In early 1991, the government secured a $2.5 billion assistance package from the EC under the strictest terms yet imposed on a member country. Over the next three years, Athens was obligated to bring inflation to 7%, cut the current account deficit and central government borrowing as a percentage of GDP, slash public-sector employment of 10%, curb public-sector pay raises, and broaden the tax base. It did not.

GDP: purchasing power equivalent—$77.6 billion; per capita $7.730; real growth rate 1.8% (1991), 1.5% (1992)

Inflation rate (consumer prices): 18% (1991), 14.5% (1992)

Unemployment rate: 8.3% (1992)

Budget: revenues $24.0 billion, expenditures $33.0 billion, including capital expenditures of $3.3 billion (1991)

Exports: $8.1 billion (f.o.b., 1990);

commodities—manufactured goods 48%, food and beverages 22%, fuels and lubricants 6%.

partners—Germany 22%, Italy 17%, France 10%, UK 7%, US 6%

Imports: $19.8 billion (c.i.f., 1990);
commodities—consumer goods 33%, machinery 17%, foodstuffs 12%, fuels and lubricants 8%.
partners—Germany 21%, Italy 15%, Netherlands 11%, France 8%, UK 5%.
External debt: $25.5 billion (1990)
Industrial production: growth rate—2.4% (1990); accounts for 22% of GDP
Electricity: 10,500,000 kW capacity: 36,420 million kWh produced, 3,630 kWh per capita (1991)
Industries: food and tobacco processing, textiles, chemicals, metal products, tourism, mining, petroleum
Agriculture: including fishing and forestry, accounts for 17% of GDP and 27% of labor force; principal products—wheat, corn, barley, sugar beets, olives, tomatoes, wine, tobacco, potatoes; self-sufficient in food except meat, dairy products, and animal feedstuffs; fish catch of 115,000 metric tons in 1988
Currency: drachma
Exchange rates: (Dr) per US$—230 (1994)

Communications

Railroads: 2,479 km total; 1,565 km 1.425-meter standard gauge, of which 36 km electrified and 100 km double track, 892 km 1,000-meter gauge; 22km 0.750-meter narrow gauge; all government owned
Highways: 38,938 km total; 16,090 km paved, 13,676 km crushed stone and gravel, 5,632 km improved earth, 3,540 km unimproved earth
Inland waterways: 80 km; system consists of three coastal canals and three unconnected rivers
Pipelines: crude oil 26 km; petroleum products 547 km
Merchant marine: 977 ships (1,000 GRT or over) totaling 23,450,910 GRT/42,934,863 DWT; includes 15 passenger, 66 shortsea passenger, 2 passenger-cargo, 136 cargo, 24 container, 15 roll-on/roll-off cargo, 18 refrigerated cargo, 1 vehicle carrier, 196 petroleum tanker, 18 chemical tanker, 9 liquefied gas, 37 combination ore/oil, 3 specialized tanker, 417 bulk, 19 combination bulk, 1 livestock carrier; note—ethnic Greeks also

own large numbers of ships under the registry of Liberia,
Panama, Cyprus, Malta and The Bahamas

Civil air: 39 major transport aircraft—Olympic Airways

Airports: 77 total, 77 usable; 77 with permanent surface runways;
none with runways over 3,659 m; 19 with runways 2,440–3,659
m; 23 with runways 1,220–2,439 m

Telecommunications: networks reach all areas; 4,080,000 tele-
phones; microwave carries most traffic; extensive open-wire
network; submarine cables to offshore islands; broadcast stations—29 AM, 17 (repeaters) FM, 361 TV; tropospheric links,
8 submarine cables; 1 satellite earth station operating in
INTELSAT (1 Atlantic Ocean and 1 Indian Ocean antenna),
and EUTELSAT systems

Member of: AG, BIS, CCC, CE, CERN, COCOM, CSCE,
EBRD, EC, ECE, EIB, FAO, GATT, IAEA, IBRD, ICAO, ICC,
IDA, IEA, IFAD, IFC, ILO, IMF, IMO, INTELSAT, INTER-
POL, IOC, ITU, NACC, NAM (guest), NATO, NEA, OAS
(observer), OECD, UN, UNCTAD, UNESCO, UNHCR,
UNIDO, UPU, WEU, WHO, WIPO, WMO, WTO.

SOURCES

Military Balance 1992–93, London: International Institute for
Strategic Studies, 1993.

The World Factbook 1992, Washington, DC: Central Intelligence
Agency, 1993.

A Fresh Look at Greece. The Country and the People, Athens:
General Secretariat for Press and Information, 1988.

ABOUT THE AUTHORS

THANOS M. VEREMIS, born in Athens, 1943, (B.A., Boston University, D. Phil. Trinity College, Oxford) is Professor of Political History at the Political Science Faculty of Athens University and Director of the Hellenic Foundation for European and Foreign Policy (ELIAMEP). He has been Research Associate at the International Institute for Strategic Studies, London (1978–79), a Visiting Scholar at the Center for European Studies of Harvard (1983), Visiting Professor at the Woodrow Wilson School of Princeton University (1987), and Visiting Fellow at St. Antony's College, Oxford. He is a member of the Advisory Board of the *European History Quarterly* and the author of many books on Greece and the Balkans. His most recent publication is a comparative study of Greek and Western European history from the First World War to the Cold War.

MARK DRAGOUMIS, a Greek writer and government official, was born in Athens in November 1926. He studied Medicine at the universities of Geneva and Athens but soon became involved in politics and journalism. While in London, in the late sixties, he became active in the movement against the colonel's regime in Greece. Upon the junta's collapse in July 1974, he was appointed head of the Press Office at the Greek Embassy in London, where he served until March 1982. He was subsequently posted as Press Counselor to Warsaw, Poland. In the course of his service, he had the opportunity to put to good use his knowledge of languages (English, French, and German) as well as domestic and foreign issues concerning Greece—including information on Greek history, geography, and culture.

In 1984 he left the Press and Information Service temporarily and became Director of the Greek Translation Department of the European Parliament in Luxembourg. In 1991 he published *The Course Towards Liberalism,* in Greece. In 1992 he returned to

Athens and to the Press and Information Service, having been appointed director in charge of Press Offices around the world. A number of publications in English and French dealing with Greek affairs have been issued under his guidance.

He is the author of numerous articles of political, economic, and academic interest and has on many occasions represented Greece in International Forums and Conferences speaking on issues of foreign policy.